·THE NEW·
CAJUN-CREOLE
COOKBOOK

TERRY THOMPSON

HPBooks

Contents

Update on Cajun-Creole Cooking 3

Introduction 6

Appetizers 17

Soups, Gumbos, Bisques & Breads 28

Salads & Salad Dressings 44

Poultry & Meat 55

Fish & Shellfish 70

Vegetables & Rice 96

Desserts 108

Cajun Country 123

Creole-Italian 137

Brunch 151

Beverages 165

Index 173

Mail-Order Sources 176

HPBooks
are published by
The Berkley Publishing Group
200 Madison Avenue
New York, NY 10016
Copyright © 1986 by Price Stern Sloan, Inc.,
revised edition copyright © 1994 by HPBooks,
a member of The Berkley Publishing Group
Printed in the United States of America
10 9 8 7 6 5 4 3 2 1

Food Stylist: Carol Peterson
Photography: deGennaro Associates

Library of Congress Cataloging-in-Publication Data

Thompson, Terry,
    The new Cajun-Creole cookbook / Terry Thomp-
son.—Rev. and updated.
        p.   cm.
    Rev. ed. of: Cajun-Creole cooking. 1986.
    Includes index.
    ISBN 1-55788-186-3
    1. Cookery, American—Louisiana style.   2. Cookery,
Cajun.   3. Cookery, Creole.   I. Thompson, Terry,
1946– Cajun-Creole cooking.   II. Title.
TX715.2.L68T49   1994
641.59763—dc20   94-17319
                                                         CIP

NOTICE: The information in this book is true and complete to the best of our knowledge. All recommendations are made without guarantees on the part of the author or publisher. The author and publisher disclaim all liability in connection with the use of this information.

Cover Photo: Clockwise from top: Boiled Blue Crabs, page 71; boiled potatoes and corn; Mustard Sauce, page 72; Boiled Shrimp, page 71; Boiled Crawfish, page 72

On the following pages a Mardi Gras Pre-Parade Party, starting clockwise from bottom left: Paula's Dill Dip with crudités, page 26; Jezebel Sauce with cream cheese, page 22; baked Cajun Meat Pies, page 21; Cajun Glazed Mushrooms, page 22; Cayenne Toasts, page 20; cucumber slices; Cajun Mimosas, page 167; Shrimp in Mustard Sauce, page 18; Patty Shells with Oyster Filling, pages 24 and 25.

Update on Cajun-Creole Cooking

Back in 1985, right after the manuscript for this book had been safely mailed off to my editor, I was asked to speak to a very august group of culinary professionals in San Francisco. I was given the topic "Cajun-Creole, What's All the Rage About?" Now I naturally thought that it was going to be a real piece of bread pudding to write that speech, but the more I thought about it, the more complex it got. The first thing I had to reckon with was the word *rage*. Was the Cajun-Creole cuisine a rage? I asked myself. The answer was a resounding no, and that no became the basis for my speech. Nothing that has been simmering along in thousands of carefully tended pots and cast-iron skillets, developing subtle new sub-flavors with each ethnic hand that settled in to stir it over a period of 250 years or so, could be called a "rage." I said back then that I thought Cajun-Creole was here to stay. I still think so today.

My book was published, then Paul Prudhomme's book came out, then about a hundred other Cajun-Creole books came out. A multitude of brands of Cajun-Creole seasoning concoctions flooded the market. Major food product manufacturers were scrambling to package jambalaya and etouffee and red beans and rice mixes. Restaurants all over the country were hiring anybody from Louisiana to teach them how to cook Cajun-Creole. Blackening redfish almost decimated the redfish population. "Blackening" became an everyday culinary term for a new cooking method. Whew! What a time it was for anything from Louisiana.

Upon reflection, I believe that America was looking for something back then. And they found a part of it in the simple, honest taste of Cajun-Creole foods. The country was in the throes of one of the greatest eras of materialism in history. The label on your pants, or the name printed all over your purse, or the scent you wore, or the restaurants in which you were seen, were the things that mattered. Even food had become caught up in the frenzy. One had to know what color peppercorns and what flavor of vinegar were "in" before planning a dinner party. It was scary. I mean, what would've happened if you used a mushroom that was not on the current list of "Who's Who in the Mushroom Kingdom"?

Then along came Paul Prudhomme and K-Paul's Louisiana Kitchen in New Orleans. It was a homely little place with not much room and a hodgepodge of rickety, mismatched tables and chairs. Didn't even take reservations. But the tourists fleeing to New Orleans, that city where you can let go of all the pretenses around which you generally operate, began to discover Paul's little place and the word spread. What they discovered there was food that wasn't trendy at all. It was made out of common stuff like onions, bell peppers and celery with bits of fresh meats, poultry, fish and shellfish thrown in, and lots of decidedly untrendy vegetables like greens, eggplant, mirlitons and humble yellow squash. It was simple food with simple, bold seasonings. It felt good. Like that old flannel nightgown that kept you warm and cozy when you were a kid. So Cajun-Creole food started making America feel good. Everybody could relax. You could have a dinner party with a big pot of white rice and a few scraps of meat and aromatic vegetables. You simply stirred in some salt, pepper and cayenne, added broth, and called it "jambalaya." The country was hooked.

During those past ten years, the cuisine has continued to evolve, and the evolution has been bolstered by the dozens of talented young chefs who have been drawn to Louisiana to help it grow. There was a great deal of concern about the amount of fat used in the cuisine. The evolution has responded to that concern by compromising on the amount of animal fat used. Where a recipe might have originally called for 1/2 cup of bacon drippings or lard, the recipe would now read 1/4 cup vegetable oil and 1 tablespoon bacon drippings, leaving just enough of the animal fat to preserve the magic flavor it gives the food. Greens are being stir-fried in olive oil, as opposed to being cooked for four hours with slabs of smoked pork jowl. Mind you, I still like them both ways. Stir-fried greens make me feel invigorated and health smart, but...on a cold, dreary day, nothing beats a big bowl of long, slow-cooked greens with seasoning meat and a hunk of butter-laden cornbread for restoring the spirits! My personal philosophy on dealing with the issue of dietary fat has undergone some changes. On a day-to-day basis I have reduced the amount of fat that I eat and use in food preparation, substituting unsaturated vegetable oils in lieu of animal fats. *However*, when I go out to eat, or prepare a special meal, or just want to reward myself, then fat content be damned.

Now elements of even newer ethnic and regional foods are slipping into the gumbo and eggplant dressing. Roasted red bell peppers and poblano chilies can be seen peeking out from the etouffee, and the pungent aroma of fresh ginger wafts from Louisiana's salad bowls and seafood platters. Sun-dried tomatoes step in when fresh Creole tomatoes take their seasonal bow and head south for the winter. This revised edition of *Cajun-Creole Cooking* presents a look at this "New Cajun-Creole Cuisine."

Whatever name we may call it in the future, the Cajun-Creole cuisine will never fade away. That's what rages do. They just burn out. Cajun-Creole Cooking, just like that pot of catfish courtbouillon from 250 years ago, will simply get better with the passing of time and the loving tending of the pot.

Introduction

Ensconced among the moss-draped oaks and cool, still bayous of South Louisiana, the Cajuns and Creoles live—noted for their traditions of fine dining and slow, easy living. Here it is believed that in the savoring of exquisite food among good friends and close families, life seems a little fuller.

With the same fervor or *joie de vivre* for which they are famous, the Cajuns and Creoles resist change. Perhaps that is why South Louisiana retains its old-world flavor and why its cuisine has been largely sheltered from the ravages of changing food trends.

The area's history, both political and otherwise, has been nothing shy of tempestuous—often marked by bloodshed, revolt, chicanery and general foolishness.

The city of New Orleans began as what may have been the world's first "worthless swamp-land swindle." Early attempts to populate and develop the entire Louisiana territory were hindered by charter holders whose only concern for the struggling colony was how many francs they could extract from its lagging economy.

History cannot explain exactly how or why these determined people stayed and dredged up one of the world's most interesting cities from an Indian clearing on an island between the Mississippi River and Lake Ponchartrain. Nor can we say what took the Cajuns into the primeval, mosquito- and alligator-infested marshlands and bayous to establish a way of life unlike that found anywhere else upon the earth.

If you have an *envie,* as the Cajuns would say, or yearning or covetous desire to cook and eat Cajun-Creole foods, come with me and explore these unique people and their foods.

The first European to reach what is now New Orleans was the French explorer LaSalle in 1682. He erected a cross and claimed the land for France. Various plans were tried to develop the land into a thriving colony; most failed.

Thousands of unsuspecting German farmers, mainly from poverty-stricken Alsace-Lorraine, were lured to the colony with the promise of free land, transportation, and tools to farm the soil. Within 10 years, 8,000 German settlers were brought to Louisiana, voluntarily or otherwise. It is estimated that half of them perished as the swampy settlement hovered at the brink of extinction. Their settlement became known as the Cote des Allemands or "the German Coast." They gave a German influence to the culture and the cuisine.

New Orleans managed to survive the weather, financial ruin and the devastating epidemics of yellow fever, cholera, typhus and smallpox, each one claiming sizeable chunks of the population.

In 1763, Louis XV gave the Louisiana territory to Spain. The colony had been deemed more trouble than profit. Lawlessness abounded despite attempts at bringing order, and the population was simply not increasing.

Through the years, the Spanish tried desperately to populate the colony. In 1785 they imported 1600 Acadians from France. These Acadians were originally citizens of French Nova Scotia forced from their homeland by the conquering British. Devoutly Catholic, they had refused to worship in the Anglican church. The English scattered them in small groups over the British colonies. Having heard about the French territory of Louisiana, many were drawn to that area by the hope that they would be welcome in a French colony. But even though the colony was comprised mostly of Frenchmen, it was now ruled by Spain. When these Acadians got together with the large group that the Spaniards had imported from France, they decided to leave New Orleans and establish their own settlement. They journeyed to the bayou country and established early settlements in the areas of Lafayette, Breaux Bridge and St. Martinville. These Acadians came to be known as "Cajuns" by the Indians, who could not pronounce the word properly.

At the same time, a title had been bestowed on the residents of New Orleans. The Spanish word "Criollo" was given to all residents of European descent and their direct heirs. The name soon became "Creole."

Adversity struck the city of New Orleans once again on Good Friday of 1788. A candle ignited an altar cloth in a house on Chartres Street. The usual practice for fires was to ring the huge bells of the St. Louis Cathedral to summon volunteers to man the bucket brigades. This being a holy day, however, the priests would not allow the bells to be rung. The ensuing holocaust burned down four-fifths of the town. Six years later, a second fire destroyed many of the shops and warehouses spared in the first great fire!

After the fact, the fires were seen as a blessing for the Vieux Carre, which was subsequently rebuilt under Spanish rule. It was rebuilt using the European-style architecture still standing in the French Quarter today. Two-story, brick-walled houses with wide galleries edged with wrought-iron railings overlooking the streets replaced the one-story wooden structures. These intricate works of art came to be known as iron lace. The interior courtyard was also incorporated into houses during this rebuilding.

The Spanish now adopted a general policy of open immigration and welcomed virtually anyone who would come: British fleeing the American Revolution, Canary Islanders who settled downriver from New Orleans in what is now St. Bernard Parish, 500 Malagans who settled along the Bayou Teche in what is now New Iberia—and many other ethnic groups.

In the 1790s, the city's culture was further broadened by the arrival of thousands of French refugees who fled the slave uprisings of Santo Domingo (now Haiti). The Santo Domingans brought blacks and mulattoes, who introduced voodoo to Louisiana.

Meanwhile in France, Napoleon now in power, decided that Spain must return Louisiana to France. Napoleon deduced that he was bound to lose the colony to either England or America. He moved quickly to turn this possession into cash before fate could intervene.

Once again, Louisiana and her residents were traded off. In 1803 the Louisiana Purchase was completed. The United States bought the entire territory from France for 11.25 million dollars and the cancellation of a 3.75 million-dollar debt.

The Americanization of Louisiana began under its first governor, William Charles Cole Claiborne. Businessmen from the East came in droves and settled in the new Faubourg St. Mary District, across Canal Street from the Vieux Carre. This area, and eventually St. Charles Avenue, became known as the American Sector. The Creoles stayed rigidly within the old quarter, guarding their dignified European society against the vulgarity of the Americans. Louisiana began to grow by leaps and bounds, spurred perhaps by the promise of commerce or the success of the cotton and sugar plantations. Maybe it was the lure of the West Indian atmosphere, the European elegance or its strong reputation for vice.

In 1812 Louisiana became the 18th State, and in 1815 it was forced to defend itself against the British. In the years after the War of 1812, Louisiana prospered. With the invention of the steamboat, a new way of life on the Mississippi emerged. New Orleans became a major world port and a leading world supplier of cotton, sugar and indigo. Gambling flourished in the city, with casinos open 24 hours a day. Bourré, a win-or-lose-it-all card game, ruled lives in the Cajun country.

During the great potato famine in Ireland, some 25,000 Irish settled in New Orleans. They were clannish people and kept to themselves, forming their own sector of the city. The "Irish Channel" still exists today, a neighborhood inhabited by the descendants of these hardworking, fun-loving people.

Dark days began in 1861 when Louisiana seceded from the union. In February of 1862, Union troops laid siege for over a month, crippling New Orleans and its commerce. New Orleans, the Confederacy's largest city, fell. Many historians believe the South was doomed by the loss of this vital port and center of commerce.

Occupation of the city, under Major General Benjamin Butler, brought hard times for the city and the entire state. Occupation continued for 15 years, extending into the Reconstruction Era after the war.

The last two decades of the 19th century saw a rapidly booming economy for the State. Carpetbaggers from the North

---

---

came in droves to set up businesses, lured by the plight of the broken land owners. Industry flourished, and traffic on the Mississippi almost choked the port of New Orleans. The era came to be known as the "Gilded Age."

In the late 1800s, large numbers of immigrants from Sicily began to settle mainly in New Orleans and in the town of Independence, about 50 miles upriver. The Sicilians quickly became involved in the food enterprises of the city. They added an entirely new and exciting dimension to the city's culture and to its cuisine.

The early part of the 20th century saw political turmoil in Louisiana and poverty in many of its rural areas. However after World War II, Louisiana became a leader in the petrochemical industry, and many poor Cajun farmers became millionaires overnight with the discovery of oil and gas on their lands. Many, sadly, were duped into selling for peanuts.

New Orleans has meant many different things to many people. Exotic, captivating and exciting are but a few of the words often used to describe her. New Orleans has always been an entity unto herself—in, but not entirely of, the South, or for that matter, the state or the nation! She is a little bit of each ethnic

group which formed her.

But she always maintains her dignity, even during the Carnival Season. Called "the greatest free show on earth," Mardi Gras begins each year on Twelfth Night, January 6th. The season is marked by a succession of elaborate private balls and by the lavish street parades which begin about two weeks before *Fat Tuesday*. With the dawning of *Ash Wednesday*, a period of religious fasting begins, and the city reflects the somber mood of the Lenten Season.

New Orleans has always been a unique city of neighborhoods, beginning with the original division between the Creoles of the Old City and the Americans of the Faubourg St. Mary District. As other ethnic groups arrived, they too formed their own neighborhoods.

The neighborhood gave birth to two of New Orleans' best assets, the neighborhood grocery and meat market and the neighborhood restaurant and bar. Many remain today, selling and serving true Creole food in its own element.

When one goes to the food store to shop in New Orleans, it is referred to as "making groceries" and is a truly unique experience. At the small markets, such as Langenstein's, Puglia's and Meme's, there are real, old-fashioned meat counters with meats cut to order and sausages made by hand. These markets have honest-to-goodness butchers who have spent their lives selling fine meats to generations of New Orleanians. These are markets where smiling Creoles lean over the counter to ask: "Wotcha' need today, dawlin?" And if you don't know, they can make suggestions, tell you how much you need to buy for the number of people you want to feed, how to cook and season it and what to serve with it. A dying art!

For the most mind-boggling shopping trip, quite comparable to a hallucinogenic experience, Schwegmann Brothers Giant Supermarket is your destination. There are several of the markets, all independently owned by the Schwegmanns. The largest Schwegmann's is in the Gentilly area of eastern New Orleans. Under its roof you will find literally everything from appliances to cleanser—with dry cleaning, watch repair, tax preparation and veterinary services thrown in. It takes an hour just to walk, gape-mouthed, through the place, much less think about "making groceries." The mere massiveness of the place is intimidating; choosing groceries from the myriad selections and facing the 30-basket-deep checkout lanes looms as an insurmountable task. But not to worry, brother John Schwegmann has taken your fears into consideration. Just past the place where you fight for a shopping cart stands one of the biggest bars in New Orleans. You can sip Bloody Marys as you wind your merry way through the maze!

Grocery shopping in Cajun country is also unique, but in a very different respect. Small grocery stores and meat markets are plentiful. The common thread in these markets is that everybody—butchers, checkers and customers alike—speaks Cajun-French patois. If you don't happen to speak it yourself, just wave your hands and look forlorn. They'll understand right away that you probably don't speak their language. The bad news is that you probably won't be able to understand their English either!

With such a rich and mixed historical background in mind, it is possible to

unravel the mysteries that together make up Cajun-Creole cuisine. It was formed with French roots, livened with Spanish spices, inspired by African vegetables and general magic, "Caribbeanized" by West Indian hands, laced with black pepper and pork by the Germans, infiltrated with potatoes by the Irish, blasted with garlic and tomatoes by the Italians, and even touched in some small ways by the Swiss, Dutch, Malagans and Malaysians. Small wonder that what emerged was a complex taste!

The question most often asked of South Louisiana residents is *"What is the difference between Cajun and Creole food?"* The answer, quite simply, is that Cajun food is the "rough-around-the-edges," robust food of country people. It is most often characterized by a very dark roux and very spicy flavor with a lot of animal fat thrown in. Creole food is a

more refined "city" food with greater emphasis on the use of cream and butter. Some say that the Creoles use more tomatoes than the Cajuns, but that point is debatable from Cajun to Cajun.

As a matter of fact, many of the differences between the cuisines are often hot-

ly debated. Cajuns and Creoles love to argue about food.

Any cookbook attempting to teach Cajun-Creole cookery, food that will bring people begging back to your table, must first explain *la bouche Creole,* or "the Creole mouth." It is a complex matter, but basically it is a sense of taste that is developed by a deep-seated love for the cuisine, a definitive palate, an inherent affinity for seasoning foods and lots and lots of tasting. Thankfully, the Creole mouth may be attained by diligent dedication to eating and cooking things Cajun and Creole.

If you have visited South Louisiana and have fallen in love with the food, then concentrate with all your might on one particular dish you enjoyed. Can you bring the taste back to your "mind's tongue" so sharply that your mouth begins to water? If so, get out your pots and pans and start cooking!

A few important pointers are in order before you start "cookin' Cajun," or "preparing Creole." Cajuns and Creoles take their food and its preparation very seriously. It is said that they don't just like to eat; they really like to cook as well!

Many of the Cajun-Creole dishes require tedious, time-consuming steps in their preparation. Shortcuts will result in a loss of flavor. Complex tastes are being developed and coaxed out of the foods by the long-cooking methods. Before attempting to prepare ANY recipe, read it through to be certain that you understand the various procedures. Then prepare all of your ingredients before you begin cooking. Chop the meats and vegetables as instructed. Gather spices, herbs and seasonings. Sift flours, grease pans, set ovens, heat fat and assemble all pots, pans and utensils that you will

need. It becomes critically important to "get it together first" when dealing with complex recipes containing many ingredients.

South Louisianians do a lot of frying. There is a definite art to successful frying, and the subject demands a few pointers in this book. Although it may seem that slipping a piece of food into hot fat and cooking it would be one of the simpler culinary operations, I find that cooks in many parts of the country know absolutely nothing about proper frying procedures. Their efforts, more often than not, produce limp, soggy and grease-laden products—hardly a tribute to the crispy, golden-brown fried foods of South Louisiana. However, if foods are fried properly, there will be a minimum amount of fat absorption. For more information on frying, see box on page 15.

Building Blocks of the Cuisine

Every regional or ethnic food has certain rules that make it unique and set it apart from other styles of cooking in ways that are sometimes vast, sometimes very subtle. Each major cuisine seems to have its own pastries and breads, its own particular seasonings, flavors, and, certainly, its own character.

Cajun-Creole food is no exception. The building blocks of Cajun-Creole cuisine are simple to master and yet are very important to the success of "cookin' Cajun."

Indeed, we have a standard reply in South Louisiana when asked "What is your recipe?" for this or that dish. We say, "Well, cher, first you make a roux...." Classically, the roux is the basis for the oldest and most authentic of the Cajun-Creole dishes, gumbos, etouffées, stews, courtbouillons and sauce piquants. If you start with a weak and underdeveloped roux, you will produce a very ho-hum dish. If you start, on the other hand, with a burned or scorched roux, you will create a dish with an overpowering bitter taste.

I am adamantly classic about roux! An actual revolution of thought has occurred within the Cajun-Creole cuisine in favor of the fast, high-heat method of roux-making. Well, I say, that method is okay, but it's not the best. And it doesn't taste the same! It is my no-longer-secret theory that the love and dedication given to that slowly cooked pot of roux are somehow magically transferred into the taste. Often we seem to be so intent upon finding shortcuts that we sacrifice a most essential thing—perfection of taste.

Once you have mastered the roux—and you'll probably burn two or three batches before you get the hang of it, then turn your attention to the stocks. In all likelihood, the stocks used in most Cajun-Creole foods are very different from those you have worked with. They are quite dark and have an assertive taste.

The Seafood Stock bears no resemblance to the delicate French fish fumet which is cooked 20 minutes and is almost clear with a faint essence of seafood and white wine. The Cajun-Creole variety of Seafood Stock contains many bold-flavored creatures and is cooked three hours! The stock is almost black in color, and the aroma and taste are indescribable.

Ingredients

Food experts who sample South Louisiana cuisine may try with all their culinary might to identify the various elements of the taste, but they invariably encounter a great deal of difficulty. Many Cajun-Creole dishes have lengthy ingredient lists. The unique cooking methods result in tastes not found outside of the Cajun-Creole kitchen. To really understand some of the ingredients used in this cuisine, it is necessary to understand the people.

Both Cajuns and Creoles are thrifty people who feel that it is an abomination to waste food. Even seemingly useless scraps are put to delicious use in the South Louisiana household. Leftover rice and French bread are treasures. From the rice will come tomorrow morning's Rice Calas; from the bread scraps, crisp and tasty bread crumbs or, eventually, a bread pudding. Meat and vegetable scraps will find their way into the next day's soup, gumbo or jambalaya. Bones and carcasses are saved for stocks, as are shrimp and crawfish heads and shells. Onion, green onion, celery and carrots scraps are saved for the stock pot.

The most controversial ingredient in the cuisine is animal fat, and we use a lot of it in the form of lard, butter or beef suet. It is possible to substitute cholesterol-free, polyunsaturated vegetable oils and margarine in the recipes, but you will do them irreparable damage. It has often been said that when you remove the animal fat and the time-consuming stocks from the Cajun-Creole cuisine, you have removed much of its magic. I heartily agree. Since you will probably not be preparing Cajun-Creole dishes on a regular basis, save up your cholesterol allotment to splurge on a South Louisiana feast.

Cajun-Creole foods are steadfastly un-trendy. The adherents of the cuisine

could care less what color peppercorns are "in" this year, or what obscure fruit has been discovered on a remote South Pacific island to command five dollars apiece in New York markets. And now for the big jolt to the world of haughty—or haute—cuisine. It doesn't even matter if you use canned artichoke bottoms or garlic powder or premixed Cajun-Creole seasonings. *The taste of the completed dish is the final judge*. If it tastes wonderful, isn't that what it's all about?

When shopping for ingredients, let freshness, rather than rigid compliance to recipes, be your guide. If the recipe calls for "ripe, fresh tomatoes," but the only ones available at the market are the cardboard-skinned, pale pink hothouse variety, then by all means, use canned tomatoes! Fresh does not always mean unfrozen either. If you live in a part of the country where the supplies of fresh fish and shellfish are questionable at best, use frozen fish and shellfish from a reputable source.

On the subject of freshness—you will note throughout this book that the recipes call for unsalted butter, and I am fairly adamant on the subject. Unsalted butter is the freshest butter available. It contains no additives and therefore has fewer liquids, a fact to consider when preparing delicate pastries. When you purchase unsalted butter, keep all but the portion currently in use in the freezer to prevent spoilage. It will remain fresh indefinitely. Cajuns and Creoles, Cajuns especially, rarely, if ever, clarify butter before using. Actually, the taste of the browned bits of milk solids forms an important aspect of the taste in many classic dishes. Cajuns rarely seed their tomatoes, either.

The five most important vegetables in Cajun-Creole cookery are onions, celery, bell peppers (known as the holy trinity), green onions and parsley, preferably the flat-leaf variety.

After a lengthy cooking process, many Cajun-Creole dishes are finished off with chopped green onions and parsley. The green onions lend a subtle onion taste and a bit of crunch to the dish. Here's a bit of trivia. Many of the junior league, church and service organization-published cookbooks in South Louisiana call for *shallots* in their recipes. That's not what they really mean, however. Cajuns and Creoles rarely, if ever, use real shallots. What these recipes really mean is green onions. To confuse matters even more, if you talk to a Cajun housewife, she might refer to green onions simply as *onion tops,* but what she really means is green onions—tops, bottoms and all!

Parsley is another serious subject in South Louisiana. Parsley is in, or on top of, literally every dish except breakfast cereal and desserts. This common herb is an important flavor enhancer.

If possible, use the flat-leaf variety, often called "Italian parsley." It has more flavor than the curly variety, which is generally used for garnishing. Do not use "Chinese parsley" or cilantro. Use only fresh parsley, never dried parsley flakes.

What cuisine that was strongly influenced by both the Spanish and the Italians would not be a garlic-laden one? When using garlic, mince the cloves almost to a pulp. Never brown or scorch it, lest you develop a bitter taste that will overpower the entire dish. It is for this reason that garlic powder, never garlic salt or garlic flakes, is often used in Cajun-Creole food. Often there are instances when you wish a batter to contain a hint of garlic. If you were to use fresh minced garlic, it would burn during the process of frying and impart a bitter taste.

1. Catfish, **2.** Speckled trout, **3.** Red snapper, **4.** Redfish fillet, **5.** Shrimp, **6.** Frog legs, **7.** Cooked crawfish, **8.** Oysters on the half shell, **9.** Blue crab

FISH & SHELLFISH

Blue Crab—Crab is available in many forms. You can buy whole live crabs to boil and pick yourself. You can buy boiled crabs, or you can buy the picked meat by the pound. When preparing dishes using a lot of crabmeat, the time saved can significantly offset the purchase price. It takes from 12 to 16 crabs to produce 1 pound of crabmeat!

Crabmeat is usually available in four categories—claw meat, plain white crabmeat, lump crabmeat and backfin lump crabmeat. The backfin lump meat is the most expensive because there are only two backfin lumps per crab. They are attached to the small "flippers" on the back part of the crab.

When you purchase live crabs, place the crabs in a cooler; cover with ice. Let sit for an hour or so. They will be stunned from the cold and will be very inactive!

Many people think that softshells are a separate species of crab doomed to live their entire lives with paper-thin shells and no protection from predators. This is not the case. As crabs mature, they simply outgrow their shells, so they shed the whole thing and grow a new one! The entire process of shedding the old shell and hardening the new one takes only a few hours and is one of nature's true miracles. It is during this brief period that the softshell crab is harvested.

To prepare softshell crabs for cooking, using kitchen shears, remove the small "feelers" in the front and the eyes and eye stalks. Lift the top shell from each side using the points as handles. Remove the gills or "dead man's fingers" which will be right under the shell. Pat the shell back into place and your crab is ready to cook. And yes, you do eat the whole thing!

Crawfish—Crayfish or "mudbug" as it is affectionately known in South Louisiana. Crawfish are freshwater crustaceans that thrive in almost every area of the world. Louisiana, however, is the only place in the world where crawfish are revered.

The crawfish season runs from about the end of November to the first part of June. With sophisticated processing and freezing techniques, peeled crawfish tails are generally available the entire year.

Crawfish may be purchased in three forms: Live, boiled in the shell or peeled tails. The peeled tails are sold in 1-pound packages and have the vitally important fat from the head of the crawfish spread over the meat. The fat is the golden-colored substance; don't waste a drop. Squeeze every bit of it out of the bag. Peeled tails may seem expensive when compared to live crawfish. But consider that you must peel about 8 pounds of whole crawfish to get 1 pound of tails. The price for peeled tails suddenly becomes rather insignificant. When purchasing live crawfish, discard any that are dead before you boil them. When serving boiled crawfish as a meal, allow 3 to 5 pounds per person, depending upon appetite.

To eat boiled crawfish, first put on your jeans and T-shirts, because it is a messy affair! Hold the head with one hand; separate it from the rest of the crawfish. Gently squeeze the tail section between your thumb and forefinger to crack the shell. Then turn over and pull the shell in half. Remove the meat; pull out the dark vein on the outside curve. To sample the tasty fat, place your little finger inside the body. Gently pull out the golden fat to enjoy a Cajun treasure.

Oysters—Oysters purchased in the shell should be alive, indicated by a tightly closed shell. Discard any opened shells. If purchased by the jar, the oysters should be plump and creamy in color with viscous, clear—not cloudy—liquid. They should have a pleasant odor with no hint of sourness. If you buy oysters by the jar, pick them over carefully with your fingertips to remove any small bits of shell.

Store oysters in the shell at about 39F (5C), not directly on ice. They must be kept dry. Store shucked oysters at the same temperature, covered by their own "liquor" as it is called in Louisiana. If bought *FRESH,* shucked oysters may be kept up to 5 days.

When shucking oysters save all of the oyster liquor from the shells. It is worth its weight in gold to flavor sauces, soups, gumbos or gravies. It freezes very well.

Oysters are available year around, but during the warm months, they become very fat. This makes them difficult to fry, but dry them thoroughly on paper towels before breading and you will increase the odds for success.

Shrimp—When purchasing shrimp, purchase "heads-on" shrimp whenever possible. The tomalley of the shrimp is contained in the head and is an important taste ingredient both in boiled shrimp and in seafood stock. Fresh shrimp should have a translucent appearance. The flesh should never appear dry and opaque. Fresh shrimp should not have a strong odor. Shrimp are sold by graded categories known as count. Shrimp labeled *15 to 20 count* will yield 15 to 20 shrimp per pound. Medium shrimp, the size most often available, are usually 26 to 35 count.

When serving boiled, heads-on shrimp for a meal, allow 2 to 2-1/2 pounds per person. Two pounds of heads-on shrimp makes 1 pound of peeled shrimp.

Catfish—Fried catfish with hush puppies is a staple meal in southern Louisiana and Mississippi. And the demand is spreading. Fast-food fried-catfish restaurants are popping up all over the country. Catfish are so popular that to meet the demand, they are commercially raised on large catfish farms.

The two varieties of catfish normally cooked are the blue catfish and the channel catfish. They are both white-fleshed, medium-oily fish and are excellent cooked in any manner, either whole or filleted. The head and skin must be removed. If served whole, they are usually fried. Large catfish can be cut through the backbone into steaks.

Flounder—The Gulf Coast flounder is actually a member of the fluke family, a strange-looking group of flatfish. Most whole flounder found in markets weigh from 12 ounces to 3 pounds. Flounder, either fresh or frozen, is available in most areas of the country.

Flounder is one of the most delicate tasting of all Gulf fish. Its flesh is pure white with a very fine texture. It lends itself to any method of preparation, either whole or filleted. It is often served whole, stuffed with a crabmeat dressing and baked, a worthy dish by anyone's standards!

Pompano—Pompano is one of the most regal, and certainly one of the most expensive, fish used in Creole cookery. Gourmets the world over acclaim the taste of the pompano.

While it lives in both the Atlantic and the Caribbean, more pompano is consumed in New Orleans than in any other place in the world. In the market, pompano is usually from 1 to 3 pounds. It is an oily fish and does not fry well. But it lends itself to any other type of preparation, including charcoal grilling, a cooking method which really makes its flavor shine.

Pompano has a one-of-a-kind taste. However, if it's not available, substitute your favorite fish in the elegant *en papillote* dish. I often use flounder fillets. While the flavor, of course, is not the same, the dish is still impressive.

Redfish—A cousin to speckled trout and a member of the drum family, found on the Atlantic and the Gulf coasts. On the Eastern seaboard, it is called the red drum. Redfish is easily identifiable by the large black spot or spots on its tail.

Like its relative, speckled trout, redfish is a white-fleshed fish with a delicate taste and low-fat content. An individual redfish can weigh as much as 25 to 30 pounds, but smaller fish are more desirable for home cooking. Speckled trout works well in most redfish recipes, or you may substitute grouper, tilefish, drum or croaker.

Red Snapper—One of the most distinctive-appearing fish in the Gulf of Mexico. Its bright red body is familiar throughout the country. It is the most widely available Gulf fish. Red snapper is a tasty fish with a low fat content. It is often baked whole, but lends itself equally well to cooking as fillets. As a substitute for red snapper, use grouper, tilefish or redfish.

Shark—Shark meat is delicious and is becoming more widely available. Shark meat is available either as steaks or fillets. The meat is white and has a very mild flavor similar to that of redfish. The flesh is firm textured, much like swordfish or dolphin, and is delicious charcoal grilled.

The most commonly processed shark is the relatively small, about 40 pound, bull shark. Several varieties of shark are very poor in quality and high in uric acid, which gives the meat a strong and unacceptable taste. Use your nose to select, or reject, shark meat. If the meat has a strong and unpleasant ammonia odor, it is not likely to improve with cooking.

Speckled Trout—Or "spec" as it is called by Gulf fishermen, is the most sought-after fish in South Louisiana. It is a member of the weakfish family, which also includes croakers, drum and redfish. Its flesh is firm, white, delicate in taste and non-oily. The speckled trout is available year around. Its average size of about 1-1/2 pounds makes its fillets just the right size for single servings.

Speckled trout can be prepared using any cooking method. Because it has a very delicate flavor, it has a natural affinity for a wide variety of herbs and all types of shellfish. As a substitute for speckled trout, use any white, firm-fleshed, non-oily fish, either salt or freshwater. Rainbow trout is an excellent substitute.

Cajun Roux

Over the years I have resisted many attempts by colleagues who have tried to convince me to make microwave roux, or who have shown me short-cut, fast roux methods. To me, the way the gumbo tastes is the measure of a roux, and I've never tasted a quick roux gumbo yet that would hold a candle to one made the right way! So I advise students, apprentices and readers to get a nice glass of wine and pull a comfortable stool up to the stove. Making a proper roux is just going to take some time. There's a flavor development going on in that long, slow cooking process that can't be created any other way.

1 cup vegetable shortening or vegetable oil   1 cup all-purpose flour

Melt shortening or vegetable oil in a heavy, preferably cast-iron, Dutch oven or 12-inch skillet over medium heat. When fat is hot, add flour all at once; stir or whisk quickly to blend flour and fat. If necessary, use the back of a spoon to smooth out any lumps of flour. Reduce heat to medium-low. Cook, STIRRING OR WHISKING CONSTANTLY, until roux is desired color. The darker the color, the more intense the flavor of the roux. This process should not be rushed. If small black or dark brown flecks appear in the roux, it has been burned and must be discarded. A burned roux will impart a bitter and scorched taste to any dish in which it is used. Use extreme caution not to splash any of the roux onto your skin. It is lethally hot and can cause a serious burn. To stop the cooking process, either add the vegetables called for in the individual recipe or immediately transfer the finished roux to a heavy metal bowl. Continue to whisk the roux for about 15 minutes to prevent separation. May be refrigerated for up to a week, or frozen for up to 6 months. Makes 1 cup.

How to Make Cajun Roux

1/Peanut-butter-colored roux.

2/Mahogany-colored roux.

❧ *Making Roux* ❧

- When stirring and handling the roux, be extremely careful not to splash any of it onto your skin. Roux sticks to the skin and can cause a very serious burn.
- If you are preparing a larger quantity of roux, use a pan large enough to hold all of the fat and flour and allow enough room for stirring or whisking without splash-overs.
- The choice of a stirring implement is a personal one. I find that a long-handled metal whisk covers more of the pan surface. If you are more comfortable with spoons, then use a wooden spoon. Metal spoons become extremely hot during the long cooking process.
- Even after the roux has been removed from the pan to a metal bowl, you must still be very careful with it. Do not set the bowl on a polyethylene or plastic cutting board or on your plastic laminate counter top. These materials will melt and burn. Remember that you are dealing with a substance that is in excess of 500F (260C)!

❧ *Preparing Stocks* ❧

- It is important to give as much time and thought to the preparation of your stocks as you do to each finished dish in which you will use them. If you start with a mediocre or bad stock, things generally go downhill from that point!
- Never use internal organs such as livers, hearts, gizzards or kidneys in making stock. They contain blood which gives stock a very strong and unpleasant taste.
- Chicken fat will smoke during browning. The kitchen will smell like fried chicken about a day. Do not make stock on a day when you plan to have guests.
- Stock is **never** salted until it is used in its final product, such as a sauce or soup. Otherwise, the saltiness would increase as the stock is reduced during cooking.
- Bring stock to a full boil and skim the surface **before** adding your seasonings or herbs so that you don't skim them all away!
- Cooling stock quickly is very important. Improperly cooled stock will spoil rapidly. To cool a large amount of stock, strain first. Place in smaller containers. Place containers in a sink of cold water, changing water as it becomes warm. Do not put hot stock directly in the refrigerator.
- Remove all traces of fat after stock is chilled and fat has solidified on surface of stock. Stock stored with fat remaining in it will have a fatty, oily taste. Fat becomes rancid rapidly, affecting the taste of the stock.
- To avoid the risk of bacterial growth, do not leave prepared stock in the refrigerator longer than two days. Freeze for longer storage. Do not freeze stocks longer than six months. After that length of time the poultry and veal stocks begin to lose their flavor, and fish stocks get very *fishy*.
- When preparing fish stock, it is important to remove the heads of any fish carcasses and to rinse the entire bony carcass under running water to remove every last trace of blood from the bones, lest your stock be a bit too "aromatic."
- When straining stocks for use or storage, be sure to press firmly on the bones and vegetables to release the flavor.
- If you use fresh herbs, save all of your herb stems—even parsley—in a bag in the freezer. Use the stems for making stocks. They contain even more flavor than the leaves, and you get a smug feeling of being economical.

Louisiana Brown-Poultry Stock

The secret to the greatness of this stock is the use of as many types of poultry bones as possible. And be sure that you have duck bones in there—they add a wonderful flavor.

10 to 12 lbs. uncooked mixed poultry bones
    and carcasses, such as chicken, duck,
    game hen, quail, dove and turkey
2 carrots, coarsely chopped
2 large onions, unpeeled, coarsely chopped
1 large leek, coarsely chopped

1 celery stalk with leafy top,
    coarsely chopped
6 parsley sprigs
6 thyme sprigs or 2 teaspoons dried
    leaf thyme
1 bay leaf

Preheat oven to 425F (220C). Place all bones and carcasses in large roasting pans. Brown bones and carcasses in preheated oven until very dark, but not burned, turning often. This takes about 2 hours. Do not burn the bones, or the stock will have a very bitter taste. Place browned bones in a 20-quart stockpot. Leaving a *thin* film of fat in 1 pan, pour off and discard fat from pans. Place carrots, onions and leek in pan with thin film of fat, spreading evenly. Cook in preheated oven, stirring frequently, until well browned. Add browned vegetables to stockpot. Pour off all remaining fat from pan; place pan over high heat. Add 1 cup water to pan to deglaze, scraping up all browned bits from pan bottom. Repeat with remaining pan. Add browned mixture to stockpot. Add enough water to stockpot to completely cover bones and vegetables by about 2 inches. Bring to a boil; skim grey foam from surface often. Boil until no more foam forms. Reduce heat; add seasonings. Simmer 8 hours. Skim fat from surface occasionally. Cool slightly. Strain stock 3 times through a fine strainer or cheesecloth; discard bones and vegetables. Pour into shallow pans; cool in sink of cold water to room temperature. Refrigerate until chilled. Remove all fat from surface. Pour into quart containers; seal tightly. Refrigerate up to 2 days or freeze up to 6 months. Makes 8 to 10 quarts.

Seafood Stock

There is no completely acceptable substitute for handmade seafood stock. However, if time simply does not allow for making your own stocks, then either bottled clam juice or stock made from Knorr fish bouillon cubes is your best bet. In larger cities, especially in coastal areas, there seems to be a trend toward upscale fish markets/gourmet food shops selling handmade stocks. Check to see if you might happen to be lucky enough to be in proximity of such a treat. To make your own, use any non-oily (inland or coastal), white-fleshed fish bones (no heads). Include whole crabs, shrimp heads and shells, lobster carcasses, crawfish heads and shells whenever possible.

10 lbs. mixed shellfish shells or
    fish carcasses and bones
5 onions, unpeeled, quartered
1 tablespoon whole cloves
2 celery stalks, coarsely chopped

5 garlic cloves, unpeeled, smashed
1 large lemon, sliced
1 (3-oz.) box shrimp and crab boil
1 tablespoon peppercorns

Place all ingredients in a 15- to 20-quart stockpot. Add enough water to cover by 4 to 5 inches. Bring to a full boil over high heat. Skim gray foam from surface. Continue to skim until no more foam appears. Reduce heat and simmer stock for 3 hours. Cool slightly. Strain 3 times through a fine strainer or cheesecloth, pressing down hard on the bones, shells and vegetables to extract all of the stock. Discard bones, shells and vegetables. Pour stock into shallow bowls; cool in sink of ice water to room temperature. Refrigerate until chilled. Remove any fat from surface of stock. Pour into quart containers; seal. Refrigerate up to 2 days or freeze up to 6 months. Makes 8 to 10 quarts.

Brown Veal & Pork Stock

The use of pork bones in a veal stock may seem a very radical thing to non-Southerners, but the flavor derived from them is marvelous and is right at home in the hearty dishes of South Louisiana. If you cannot find pigs' feet, substitute 4 pounds pork neck bones.

8 lbs. veal bones and knuckles, cut in half
4 lbs. veal shoulder and shanks
5 pigs' feet, cut in half
6 onions, coarsely chopped
3 carrots, coarsely chopped
3 celery stalks, coarsely chopped

6 thyme sprigs or 2 teaspoons dried
  leaf thyme
2 bay leaves
Parsley stems
1 tablespoon peppercorns
1 (6-oz.) can tomato paste

Preheat oven to 425F (220C). Place all bones, meat and pigs' feet in large roasting pans. Brown in preheated oven until very dark, but not burned, turning often. This takes about 2 hours. Melting fat will create a lot of smoke in the oven. If too much melted fat collects in the pan during cooking, skim it off using a non-plastic bulb-baster. Do not let it overflow into the oven, because it could cause a fire. Place browned bones in a 15- to 20-quart stockpot. Leaving a *thin* film of fat in 1 pan, pour off and discard fat from pans. Place onions, carrots and celery in pan with thin film of fat, spreading evenly. Cook in preheated oven, stirring frequently, until well browned. Add browned vegetables and tomato paste to stockpot. Pour off all remaining fat from pan; place pan over high heat. Add 1 cup water to pan to deglaze, scraping up all browned bits from pan bottom. Repeat with remaining pan. Add browned mixture to stockpot. Add enough water to stockpot to completely cover bones and vegetables by about 2 inches. Bring to a full boil, skimming grey foam from surface often. Continue boiling until no more foam forms. Reduce heat. Add seasonings; simmer 10 hours. Cool slightly. Strain 3 times through a fine strainer or cheesecloth. Pour into shallow pans; cool in sink of cold water to room temperature. Refrigerate until chilled. Remove all fat from surface. Pour into quart containers; seal. Refrigerate up to 2 days or freeze up to 6 months. Makes 8 to 10 quarts.

 # Frying

    The two methods of cooking foods in fat in the Cajun-Creole cuisine are sautéeing, which is also known as pan-frying or paneéing, and deep-frying. Sautéeing involves cooking food in a small amount of hot fat in a heavy skillet. The fat should be hot and the food dry.

    But if the vegetables to be sautéed are soggy, they will lie in a pool of fat diluted with, and cooled by, their own liquid. They will be steaming or boiling rather than sautéeing. The taste is not the same and the texture will lack the crunch of a sautéed food. Vegetables which are chopped in the food processor become very watery; they simply will not sauté properly. The sauté is of extreme importance in Cajun-Creole cooking, and if not done properly, the final taste is altered. In those many instances in which the vegetables will be sautéed in a roux, it becomes downright dangerous to toss soggy vegies into a pan of hot fat which registers in excess of 500F (260C). So get out your chef's knife, please, and hand chop vegetables for a sauté.

    To fry means to immerse completely in deep fat heated to a high temperature. The object of deep frying is to quickly sear the outside of the food in order to seal it with a crisp crust. Then the oil cannot seep in to make the food soggy and greasy. The juices of the food cannot seep out to make the food tasteless.

    Any type of food to be sautéed or deep-fried must be free of surface moisture. If the meat or vegetables to be sautéed or fried are not coated, then they must be patted very dry with paper towels. If the vegetable or fruit to be fried or sautéed has a high liquid content, such as strawberries, eggplant or zucchini, you must batter it or coat with an egg wash and flour or bread crumbs before frying or sautéeing.

UNUSUAL INGREDIENTS

1. Creole cream cheese—A special cream cheese with a texture that is similar to sour cream but more tart. Used as a topping or for Frozen Creole Cream Cheese.

2. Crab and shrimp boil—A special blend of spices used for boiling seafood.

3. Coffee with chicory—A blend of coffee and the ground, dried root of the chicory plant. Chicory adds a slight bitterness.

4. Satsumas—Mandarian oranges that are grown in South Louisiana and other areas.

5. Lard—Rendered pork fat used to make Cajun Roux and for frying.

6. Herbsaint—An anise-flavored liqueur developed in New Orleans.

7. Picante sauce—A spicy tomato-and-chili sauce. Use the Tabasco brand if it's available. If not, substitute a thick local brand.

8. Red (cayenne) pepper—Ground, dried cayenne peppers.

9. Pickled okra—Pickled okra pods. Available in regular or hot flavors.

10. Yellow cornmeal—Ground yellow corn. Used in hush puppies, corn bread and spoon bread.

11. Red beans—An essential ingredient in Red Beans & Rice.

12. Corn flour or unseasoned fish fry—A fine corn flour used for coating ingredients for frying.

13. Filé powder—A woody seasoning ground from the dried leaves of the sassafras tree. It was originally used by the Indian tribes living in the bayou country. It is readily available in specialty markets.

14. Creole mustard—A stone-ground mustard. Use Zatarain's, if it's available.

15. Hot-pepper sauces—Both red and green hot-pepper sauces are used extensively in Cajun-Creole cooking and at the table.

16. Peychaud Bitters—Alcoholic liquor containing a blend of herbs developed by A. A. Peychaud, a New Orleans' pharmacist. Used in making Sazeracs.

17. Tasso—A smoked pork or beef seasoning meat made from poor quality cuts which are coated with a very spicy seasoning mixture and smoked until hard and flavorful. You may substitute smoked ham.

18. Andouille sausage—A spicy smoked pork sausage. Available in some meat markets and by mail order.

Appetizers

Having been raised in a part of the country where you didn't "go visiting" without a proper invitation, I was totally unprepared for life in Cajun country.

When I first moved to Louisiana many years ago, I lived in Lafayette—right in the heart of Acadia. I remember the day the moving van arrived with our belongings. Within 30 minutes, every neighbor on the block had been through the house to meet us and say "Welcome." They came with thermos jugs of rich black coffee and boxes of croissants and goodies from Poupart's Bakery.

Late that afternoon, when the movers had gone and we were tired and dirty and hungry, they came back. This time each lady had a little plate or bowl containing a shared portion of her family's supper. There was even a small portion of the best carrot cake in the world. My, did we feast that night—and for two days!

As soon as my house was in reasonable order, I planned a Friday evening party to pay back all the gracious hospitality. I cooked and cooked, preparing my best party foods. I garnished the platters and used mountains of greens and parsley. At the appointed hour, the guests began to arrive—each one carrying a platter of his

Mardi Gras Pre-Parade Party

Blue-Crab-Stuffed Mushrooms
Shrimp in Mustard Sauce
Patty Shells with
Mushroom & Oyster Fillings
Jezebel Sauce over Cream Cheese
Cajun Glazed Mushrooms
Paula's Dill Dip with
Vegetable Crudités
Cayenne Toasts
Cajun Mimosas, page 167

or her very best party food! We had enough food that night for a army.

Well, it never changed, thank goodness. In South Louisiana you never need an excuse to get together with friends and neighbors. And through the years I have learned the element common to all Cajun and Creole get-togethers. The occasion or location may vary, the conversation and activities may change with the times, but there is always lots of food. An entire reputation can be based on one's collection of party-food recipes! When I moved to New Orleans, it took a week to return all the platters, plates and bowls from various events and to collect all of mine.

Party food need not be fancy, expensive or require hours of preparation time. It should be food that can be eaten with one hand, and ideally, should not require the use of silverware. It should be one or two bites in size and not oily, sticky or drippy. Foods that are not totally edible, such as strawberries with tops, require plates for leftover bits or wooden picks.

There are two standard party foods in Cajun country—pepper jelly and Jezebel Sauce. As long as you have a jar of pepper jelly on hand and a block of cream cheese to pour it over, you can have a party. My personal standby is Jezebel Sauce over cream cheese. Your favorite cracker goes well with both.

This chapter provides a wide range of party foods, from plain to fancy, easy to complex, delicate to spicy; but there's something for every occasion and every budget.

Cleaning Oyster Shells

Most raw-oyster bars or seafood markets will be happy to save oyster shells for you. Get more than you actually need because you will want to sort through them, discarding the flat top shells or the grossly large ones. Place shells in the sink under running water. Scrub vigorously, inside and out, using a stiff brush. Next fill the sink with water; add enough bleach to make a strong solution. Soak the shells in the bleach solution overnight. Drain and place them in the top rack of the dishwasher. Run them through a full cycle. Each time you use the shells, merely scrape out the bits of food, and put them in the dishwasher!

Blue-Crab-Stuffed Mushrooms

Visitors to South Louisiana fall in love with the delicate, sweet flavor of the Louisiana blue crab. Just boiled with spices is one of our favorite ways to eat it. The succulent meat from the crab is also used to create a bevy of delicious and elegant dishes. This popular appetizer is one of the best!

30 medium to large mushrooms, stems removed	6 green onions, thinly sliced, including green tops
1 cup unsalted butter, melted and blended with 1 tablespoon fresh lemon juice	1/4 cup minced flat-leaf parsley
	1/2 teaspoon salt
1 lb. backfin lump crabmeat or other crabmeat	1/2 teaspoon red (cayenne) pepper
	1-1/2 cups (6 oz.) shredded Monterey Jack cheese
3/4 cup dry bread crumbs	About 10 toast points

Preheat oven to 350F (175C). Wipe mushrooms clean using a damp paper towel. Dredge the mushroom caps in the butter and lemon mixture, reserving leftover butter. Place the mushroom caps, stem side up, on a heavy baking sheet; set aside. Carefully pick through crabmeat to remove any bits of shell or cartilage. Combine all remaining ingredients except toast points and then pour in reserved butter and lemon. Toss to blend well and moisten all ingredients. Fill each mushroom cap with a portion of the crabmeat mixture, packing it tightly into the cap and mounding the top. Bake in preheated oven 10 minutes, or just until the tops are lightly browned and cheese has begun to melt. Arrange the mushrooms on toast points and drizzle the buttery drippings from the pan over the top. Serve hot. Makes 30 stuffed mushrooms.

Shrimp in Mustard Sauce   *Photo on pages 4-5.*

This is a great make-ahead recipe. At the last minute, you need only garnish, serve and reap the compliments.

1/4 cup tarragon-flavored vinegar	1/4 cup minced parsley, preferably flat-leaf
1/4 cup red-wine vinegar	6 green onions, chopped
1 teaspoon freshly ground black pepper	2-1/2 lbs. uncooked medium shrimp, peeled, deveined
1/4 cup dry mustard	
2 teaspoons hot red-pepper flakes	1 (3-oz.) pkg. crab and shrimp boil
2 teaspoons salt	Cucumber slices
1/2 cup vegetable oil	Crackers

In a 3-quart bowl, whisk together vinegars, black pepper, mustard, pepper flakes and salt. While whisking, slowly pour in oil until slightly thickened. Stir in parsley and green onions. Set sauce aside. To cook shrimp, fill a 6-quart pot half full of water; add crab and shrimp boil. Bring mixture to a boil; boil 3 to 4 minutes. Add shrimp to boiling water; cook just until pink, 2 to 3 minutes. Quickly pour shrimp into a colander; shake to remove excess water. Immediately stir drained shrimp into reserved sauce. Cover and refrigerate overnight or up to 2 days. To serve, spoon into a glass serving bowl. Place bowl in center of a platter. Serve with cucumber slices and crackers. Serve with wooden picks or cocktail forks. Makes 8 to 10 appetizer servings.

How to Make Fried Fish Tails

1/Holding fin portion of tails, dip meaty sections into batter.

2/Serve fried fish tails hot.

Fried Fish Tails

This unique party appetizer may become a house favorite. The tails, which are about 2 inches long, contain one of the most flavorful chunks of meat on the fish. And to think that they are usually discarded when the fish are filleted. They are a bonus for the fisherman, or ask your fish market to save them for you.

1-3/4 cups all-purpose flour
2 eggs
1-1/2 teaspoons salt
1-1/2 teaspoons baking powder
2 tablespoons vegetable oil
3/4 cup beer
1 teaspoon red (cayenne) pepper
1-1/2 tablespoons ketchup

2 tablespoons prepared horseradish
1-1/2 teaspoons fresh lemon juice
2 teaspoons Worcestershire sauce
3 tablespoons minced green onions
Peanut oil
36 fish tails with meaty portion above fin
Tartar Sauce, page 83, or Red Cocktail Sauce, page 72, for dipping.

In a medium bowl, combine all ingredients except oil and fish tails to form a batter. In a heavy 12-inch skillet over medium heat, heat 3 inches peanut oil to 350F (175C) or until a 1-inch bread cube turns golden brown in 65 seconds. Holding fin portion of tails, dip meaty sections into batter, swirling to coat entire surface. Leave fin free of batter to use as a handle. Carefully slide battered tails into hot oil. Do not crowd tails in skillet. Fry to a rich golden brown on both sides, about 4 minutes, turning once. Remove fried fish tails from oil with a slotted spoon. Drain on paper towels. Keep warm while frying remaining fish tails. Makes 36 appetizers.

Cajun Party Spareriblets

Your party guests will never forget you for these incredible, falling-off-the-bone tender treats. They evoke a response similar to potato chips—nobody can eat just one.

2 lbs. pork baby back ribs
1 tablespoon peppercorns
1 large onion, coarsely chopped

Marinade, see below
2-1/2 cups peanut oil

Marinade:
1/2 cup honey
1/2 cup soy sauce
1/2 cup dry sherry
1/2 cup red-wine vinegar
2 large garlic cloves, minced

2-1/2 teaspoons grated gingerroot
4 green onions, minced
1-1/2 teaspoons Tabasco sauce
Pinch of salt

Cut spareribs into individual ribs. Place ribs, peppercorns and onion into a 6-quart pot. Cover with cold water; bring to a boil over medium heat. Reduce heat to simmer; cook 45 minutes. Drain ribs well. Place drained ribs in a 13" x 9" baking pan; set aside. Prepare Marinade. Pour marinade over ribs in baking pan; cover and refrigerate at least 4 hours or up to 8 hours. Drain ribs, reserving marinade. Place reserved marinade in a 2-quart saucepan; cook over high heat until reduced by 1/2, about 8 minutes. Heat a wok or deep 12-inch skillet until hot. Add oil; heat until oil is almost smoking. Add drained ribs to hot oil in batches; stir about 3 minutes or until slightly crisp and mahogany colored. Remove with a slotted spoon; drain on paper towels. Arrange on a serving platter; drizzle reduced marinade over top. Serve hot. Makes 8 to 10 servings.

To prepare marinade, combine all marinade ingredients in a heavy 2-quart saucepan over medium heat; bring to a boil. Reduce heat to low; simmer 15 minutes.

Cayenne Toasts   *Photo on pages 4-5.*

Watch out! These party crackers are addictive. They are an excellent use for leftover French bread. I have students all over the country who couldn't live without these spicy little toasts. For best results, do not prepare toasts more than a day or two before serving.

3 French-bread loaves

Topping, see below

Topping:
1 cup olive oil
2 teaspoons red (cayenne) pepper
1-1/2 teaspoons salt
1-1/2 teaspoons sugar

1/2 teaspoon finely ground black pepper
1 teaspoon paprika
1-1/2 teaspoons garlic powder
1-1/2 teaspoons onion powder

Preheat oven to 200F (95C). Prepare topping; set aside. Using a serrated bread knife or electric knife, cut French bread into slices about 1/4 inch thick. Lay slices in single layers on ungreased baking sheets. Using a pastry brush, lightly coat 1 side of each bread slice with topping. Whisk mixture often while using so that seasonings do not settle to bottom of the bowl. Dry in preheated oven until very crisp, about 1 hour. The texture should be similar to Melba toast. Remove from baking sheets; cool on wire racks. When completely cool, store in airtight containers until served or up to 2 days. Cooled toasts can be packed in freezer containers and frozen up to 2 months. Recrisp frozen toasts in preheated 350F (175C) oven 5 to 7 minutes. Serve with a salad or soup. Makes 12 to 18 servings.

To prepare Topping, in a 2-quart bowl, whisk all topping ingredients until blended.

Baked Cajun Meat Pies   *Photo on pages 4-5.*

Meat pies are a staple item in Louisiana. One of the state's nicest little towns has its reputation built entirely around meat pies! So if you're ever passing through Natchitoches (pronounced NAK-o-tish), you owe it to yourself to stop and sample the best. Meat pies, like many Cajun dishes, can be made from whatever you have on hand, or whatever suits your fancy. They can be baked or fried.

Pastry, see below
Pork Filling, see below

Pastry:
2-1/2 cups all-purpose flour
1 teaspoon sugar
1 teaspoon salt

Pork Filling:
1/4 cup olive oil
1/2 lb. lean ground pork
1/4 cup all-purpose flour
1/2 medium onion, finely chopped
4 green onions, finely chopped
1-1/2 teaspoons rubbed sage or
  1-1/2 tablespoons chopped fresh sage
2 tablespoons minced parsley,
  preferably flat-leaf

1 egg, well beaten
  with 2 tablespoons milk

1/2 cup unsalted butter or margarine, frozen
1/2 cup milk

12 shucked oysters with their liquor (1 pint),
  finely chopped, liquor reserved
3/4 cup Brown Veal & Pork Stock, page 15,
  or canned beef broth
1/2 teaspoon red (cayenne) pepper
Salt to taste
Freshly ground black pepper

To prepare pastry, in a food processor fitted with the steel blade, process flour, sugar and salt until blended. Cut butter or margarine into 1-inch chunks; add to flour mixture. Process just until butter or margarine has been broken into pea-sized bits. Then, with motor running, pour milk through feed tube, processing just until dough begins to come together. Place dough on a lightly floured surface; shape into 2 flat pieces. Wrap in plastic wrap; refrigerate until chilled or up to 24 hours.

To prepare filling, heat bacon drippings or lard in a heavy 10-inch skillet. When fat is hot, add pork. Cook, stirring, until all traces of pink are gone, 6 to 7 minutes. With a slotted spoon, place cooked pork into a medium bowl; set aside. Return skillet containing fat to medium heat. Add flour all at once; stir to blend. Cook, stirring constantly, until roux is a light peanut-butter color, about 15 minutes. Add onion, green onions, sage and parsley to browned roux; cook until vegetables are slightly wilted, about 15 minutes. Stir in reserved oyster liquor and stock. Cook over medium heat until mixture has thickened, about 5 minutes. Add oysters; cook 2 minutes. Stir in reserved pork and seasonings. Spoon mixture into bowl. Refrigerate until chilled.

To complete pies, preheat oven to 375F (190C). Spray 2 baking sheets with nonstick vegetable spray. On a lightly floured surface, roll out the pastry pieces into thin circles. Using a 5-inch-round cutter, cut 6 circles from each disc. Place a portion of the filling in the center of each circle. Using a pastry brush, paint a 1/2-inch border of egg wash around edge of each circle; fold dough in half, encasing the filling. Seal edge with the tines of a fork. Turn pie over and seal on opposite edge. Place pies on prepared baking sheets. Gather up dough scraps, gently press together and re-roll. Cut and fill as before. Bake pies in preheated oven 15 minutes. Turn and bake until golden brown on both sides, about 10 more minutes. Serve hot. Makes about 12 meat pies.

Sun-Dried Tomato Pesto

This is a sinfully delicious party food. Serve with garlic bagel chips, or best of all, Cayenne Toasts (see recipe, page 20).

1 (8 to 12-oz.) jar sun-dried tomatoes in olive oil
4 medium garlic cloves, peeled
2 whole flat-leaf parsley sprigs
10 fresh basil leaves
8 jumbo pitted ripe olives
1 teaspoon pepper

1/2 teaspoon salt
1/2 teaspoon sugar
2 green onions, roughly chopped
1/3 cup grated Parmesan cheese
2 (4-oz.) goat cheese rounds
Cayenne Toasts, page 20, or garlic bagel chips

Combine all ingredients except goat cheese and Cayenne Toasts in a food processor fitted with steel blade. Process, using on-off pulses, to make a slightly chunky pesto. Add additional olive oil if needed for a loose consistency. Pour over goat cheese rounds to serve and place small knives for spreading nearby. Makes 8 to 10 servings.

Cajun Glazed Mushrooms   *Photo on pages 4-5.*

These mushrooms are one of my favorite foods. They may be served with wooden picks as appetizers during the cocktail hour. Or serve two or three with each entree or first course. They can be habit-forming with steaks. Beware—these mushrooms are on the spicy side!

1-1/2 lbs. small button mushrooms
1 cup unsalted butter or margarine
1 (5-oz.) bottle Worcestershire sauce

1/4 cup finely ground pepper
1/2 teaspoon salt
5 to 6 drops Tabasco sauce

Trim any woody ends from mushroom stems. Wipe trimmed mushrooms with a damp towel. Melt butter or margarine in a heavy saucepan over medium heat. Add mushrooms; toss to coat with butter or margarine. Stir in Worcestershire sauce, pepper, salt and Tabasco sauce. Increase heat to medium high. Cover pan; cook mushrooms, stirring frequently. Do not let mushrooms stick to pan. Mushrooms are done when butter or margarine separates from Worcestershire sauce and mushrooms are glazed with a heavy, dark caramel-colored sauce, about 20 minutes. Remove with a slotted spoon, discarding any sauce. Serve hot. Makes about 8 servings.

Jezebel Sauce   *Photo on pages 4-5.*

This sauce is an institution in South Louisiana. No respectable home would be without a supply in the refrigerator for unexpected guests. Serve over cream cheese to be spread on crackers.

1 (10-oz.) jar pineapple preserves (1 cup)
1 (10-oz.) jar apple jelly (1 cup)
1/4 cup dry mustard

1/3 cup prepared horseradish
1-1/2 teaspoons finely ground pepper

In a food processor fitted with the steel blade, process all ingredients until blended. Spoon into jars. Cover and refrigerate until needed, up to 2 weeks. Makes about 2-1/2 cups.

Baked Cheese with Andouille & Mushrooms

Andouille is a deliciously spicy Cajun sausage. The combination of tastes in this fun party food is very exciting. Serve with a variety of breads for spreading: corn and flour tortillas, pita breads, French bread and Indian bread.

1/2 lb. andouille sausage, or substitute Polish kielbasa
1/4 cup olive oil
1 small onion, chopped
3 medium garlic cloves, minced
1/2 lb. sliced mushrooms
1/2 teaspoon salt
1/2 teaspoon freshly ground pepper
1/4 cup hot or medium picante sauce, according to taste
8 green onions, chopped, including green tops
1 cup (4 oz.) shredded Monterey Jack cheese
1 cup (4 oz.) shredded mozzarella cheese

Preheat oven to 350F (175C). Slice the sausage into thin diagonal slices; arrange slices on a baking sheet and bake 20 minutes in preheated oven. Drain slices on paper towels; set aside. Heat olive oil in a heavy 12-inch skillet over medium heat. Add onion, garlic, mushrooms, salt and pepper. Cook, stirring often, until mushrooms are wilted and liquid has evaporated, about 8 minutes. Drain fat from skillet and return to heat. Add picante sauce and green onions. Stir to blend well; set aside to cool. Preheat broiler and position oven rack 6 inches below heat source. Combine the cheeses, tossing to blend well. Fold the mushroom mixture into the cheese, blending well. Turn the mixture out into a shallow baking dish and arrange the sausage slices over the top. Place dish under preheated broiler and cook just to melt the cheese, 2 or 3 minutes. Serve hot with a variety of breads for spreading. Makes about 6 servings.

Patty Shells

In South Louisiana a hostess is judged by the patty shells she serves! Patty shells filled with various things are required at a good party. This recipe is worth the price of the book! It is shamefully simple, but you certainly do not have to share your secret with your guests. Just accept their compliments on your wonderful pastry.

**1/4 cup unsalted butter or
  margarine, melted**

24 soft white-sandwich-bread slices

Preheat oven to 400F (205C). Using a pastry brush, coat inside of 24 miniature (2-inch diameter) muffin cups with melted butter or margarine. Set aside. Using a 2-1/2-inch round cutter, cut a round from each slice of bread. Save scraps from bread to dry for bread crumbs. Push each round gently into buttered muffin cups, pressing snugly against bottom and sides. If bread tears, patch with a small piece of bread from scraps; pat patches in firmly. Bake shells in preheated oven until lightly browned, 10 minutes. Remove from muffin pans; cool on wire racks. When completely cooled, shells may be packed in plastic freezer bags and frozen up to 3 months. Or fill for immediate use. Makes 24 shells.

Home-Smoked Sausage

This complex and peppery-tasting sausage is probably stored, at this moment, in half of the freezers in South Louisiana! It is so simple to prepare that it is almost magic. It cures overnight and needs no sausage casings. The secret is the special salt, a fairly common item in large grocery stores.

2 lbs. lean ground beef
1 cup water
1 teaspoon freshly ground black pepper
1 tablespoon peppercorns
1 tablespoon garlic powder

1 tablespoon liquid smoke
1 tablespoon onion powder
2 tablespoons Morton's Tender Quick Salt
2 teaspoons Tabasco sauce
Horseradish Sauce, see below

Horseradish Sauce:
**1 (8-oz.) pkg. cream cheese,
  room temperature**
1 tablespoon powdered sugar
1 tablespoon lemon juice

1 tablespoon Worcestershire sauce
3 tablespoons prepared horseradish
**1/2 cup whipping cream,
  whipped to stiff peaks**

In a 6-quart bowl, combine all sausage ingredients with a wooden spoon. Do not use your hands; curing salt is very irritating to any nicks or scratches you may have. Divide meat mixture into 4 equal portions; set aside. Cut 4 (15-inch-long) plastic-wrap pieces. Place 1 plastic-wrap piece on work surface; place 1 meat portion about 3 inches from long side. Fold over edge nearest sausage; use it to form sausage, packing it well to be sure there are no air pockets left within the mixture. Roll completed sausage tightly in plastic wrap; place on baking sheet. Repeat procedure with remaining sausage. Refrigerate sausages 36 hours. Preheat oven to 300F (150C). Carefully remove plastic wrap from refrigerated sausages. Place unwrapped sausages on a wire rack in a large ungreased baking pan. Bake in preheated oven 1 hour, turning after 30 minutes. Cool completely. Refrigerate until chilled or up to 2 days. To freeze sausage, bake before freezing. Refrigerate until chilled. Wrap first in plastic wrap, then in foil. Thaw frozen sausage in refrigerator before slicing and serving. To serve, prepare sauce. Slice sausage into rounds; serve with sauce. Makes 4 (8-ounce) sausages. **To prepare Horseradish Sauce,** in a food processor fitted with the steel blade, process all ingredients except whipped cream until smooth. Using a rubber spatula, scrape mixture into a 2-quart bowl. Fold in whipped cream. Cover and refrigerate until needed or up to 2 days.

Oyster-Filled Patty Shells
Photo on pages 4-5.

Oyster lovers will rave about these bite-sized treats.

1/4 cup unsalted butter or margarine
4 green onions, finely minced
1 small celery stalk, minced
1/2 small green or red bell pepper, minced
1 small onion, minced
1/4 cup all-purpose flour
12 shucked oysters with their liquor
   (1 pint), finely chopped,
   liquor reserved

1 bay leaf, minced
1/4 cup finely minced parsley,
   preferably flat-leaf
1/4 teaspoon red (cayenne) pepper
1/4 teaspoon freshly ground black pepper
Salt
24 baked Patty Shells, opposite
Thyme sprigs
Bell-pepper strips

Melt butter or margarine in a heavy 10-inch skillet over medium heat. Add green onions, celery, bell pepper and minced onion. Sauté until vegetables wilt, about 5 minutes. Stir in flour. Cook, stirring, over medium heat 2 to 3 minutes. Stir in oysters, oyster liquor and remaining ingredients except patty shells, combining well. Bring mixture to a boil, stirring. Reduce heat. Simmer until thickened, 3 to 4 minutes. If mixture is too thick, thin with a small amount of cream or milk. Preheat oven to 350F (175C). Place patty shells on an ungreased baking sheet; fill each patty shell with filling. Bake in preheated oven until filling bubbles, about 10 minutes. Decorate with thyme and bell-pepper strips. Serve at once. Makes 24 appetizers.

Mushroom-Cream-Filled Patty Shells

Rich and creamy, these are sure to be a hit!

1/4 cup unsalted butter or margarine
4 green onions, finely chopped
2 tablespoons minced parsley,
   preferably flat-leaf
2 tablespoons finely minced chives
1/2 lb. mushrooms, finely chopped
3 tablespoons all-purpose flour
3/4 cup whipping cream
1/4 teaspoon dried leaf thyme or
   3/4 teaspoon chopped fresh thyme

1/4 teaspoon red (cayenne) pepper
1-1/2 teaspoons freshly ground black pepper
Salt
1 tablespoon fresh lemon juice
24 baked Patty Shells, opposite
Grated Parmesan cheese
2 tablespoons plus 2 teaspoons unsalted
   butter or margarine, room temperature

Melt 1/4 cup butter or margarine in a heavy 10-inch skillet over medium heat. Add green onions, parsley and chives; cook over medium heat until vegetables are wilted, about 3 minutes. Stir in mushrooms. Cook 10 minutes or until liquid evaporates. Sprinkle flour over mixture; stir until blended. Cook 2 minutes, stirring. Mixture will be very dry. Stir in cream, thyme, cayenne, black pepper, salt and lemon juice, stirring to blend in all of flour. Reduce heat to low; cook 5 minutes or until thickened. Preheat oven to 350F (175C). Place patty shells on an ungreased baking sheet; fill each with mushroom filling. Top with a little Parmesan cheese and 1/4 teaspoon butter or margarine. Bake in preheated oven until filling is bubbly, 10 minutes. Serve hot. Makes 24 appetizers.

Crawfish or Shrimp Savory Beignets

One of the more trendy dishes developed from a traditional old recipe by New Orleans' innovative young chefs, this one, I believe, deserves immortality.

3/4 cup water
1 teaspoon sugar
1/2 cup evaporated milk
1 (1/4-oz.) pkg. active dry yeast
   (about 1 tablespoon)
3 to 3-1/2 cups soft, southern wheat flour,
   page 164, or all-purpose flour
1 egg
2 tablespoons canola oil

3 medium garlic cloves
1/2 small green bell pepper, coarsely chopped
5 green onions, coarsely chopped
1 teaspoon salt
1/4 teaspoon freshly ground black pepper
1/4 teaspoon red (cayenne) pepper
1 teaspoon Creole mustard or other
   stone-ground mustard
1/2 lb. peeled boiled crawfish tails or 1/2 lb. peeled
   boiled shrimp

In a medium saucepan over low heat, combine water, sugar and evaporated milk. Heat to 110F (45C). Pour hot mixture into a 2-cup measure. Stir in yeast until blended. Let stand 5 to 10 minutes or until foamy. Lightly oil a 6-quart bowl. In a food processor fitted with the steel blade, combine 3 cups flour and all remaining ingredients except oil and yeast mixture. Process until ingredients are chopped and blended. Add yeast mixture all at once. Process until blended. Dough should be smooth and nonsticky. If additional flour is needed, add 1 tablespoon at a time; process until blended after each addition. Process 15 seconds to knead dough. Oil a large bowl. Place dough in oiled bowl, turning to coat all surfaces of dough. Cover with plastic wrap. Let rise until doubled in bulk, about 1-1/2 hours. Punch down dough. Turn out onto a lightly floured surface. Roll out dough into a rectangle about 1/2 inch thick. Working at a diagonal to rectangle, with a sharp knife, cut dough into 2-inch-wide strips, moving from left to right. Starting at top left and moving toward bottom of rectangle, cut dough diagonally into 2-inch-wide strips to form diamond shapes. See photos. Carefully place all completed diamonds 1/2 inch apart on ungreased baking sheets. Cover loosely with plastic wrap. Gather up remaining dough scraps; knead together. Cover loosely with plastic wrap; let rest 15 minutes to relax dough. Roll out and cut as before. Repeat until all dough has been used. Let rise 45 minutes. Do not double in bulk. Heat about 3 inches oil in a large saucepan to 350F (175C) or until a 1-inch bread cube turns golden brown in 65 seconds. Carefully slide raised beignets into oil, 3 or 4 at a time; do not crowd. Fry until puffy and golden brown on both sides, 2 to 3 minutes per side, turning once with tongs. Remove beignets with a slotted spoon; drain on paper towels. Serve hot. Makes about 36.

Paula's Dill Dip   *Photo on pages 4-5.*

I first discovered this very tasty and easy-to-prepare dip many years ago, when Paula Fisher, my assistant at my cooking school in Lafayette, Louisiana, whipped it up for us one day in the kitchen. Paula became a lifelong friend and soul mate and we never got tired of making this great dip.

2/3 cup mayonnaise
2/3 cup dairy sour cream
1 (1/4-inch-thick) medium onion slice
4 parsley sprigs without stems

1 tablespoon dried dill weed or
   3 tablespoons chopped fresh dill
1 teaspoon Beau Monde seasoning

In a blender or food processor fitted with the steel blade, process all ingredients until pureed. Place puree in a small bowl; cover and refrigerate until chilled or up to 2 days. Makes about 1-1/2 cups.

How to Make Crawfish or Shrimp Savory Beignets

1/After processing, dough should be smooth and nonsticky.

2/For second cuts, start at top left and move toward bottom of rectangle; cut dough diagonally into 2-inch wide strips to form diamonds.

3/Fry until puffy and golden brown on both sides, 2 to 3 minutes per side.

4/Serve hot as part of an appetizer selection.

Soups, Gumbos, Bisques & Breads

If I were asked to name one dish that epitomizes Cajun or Creole food—worldwide—it would have to be gumbo. A simmering pot of gumbo embodies all of the rich and mysterious, complex and spicy tastes of the cuisine.

Gumbo, like so many of our wonderful dishes, can be created from whatever is available. This can vary from the most meager combination of greens, possibly with a tiny piece of pork; to tough and otherwise unusable cuts of beef; to the richest seafood-laden concoction affordable.

Gumbo is sublime. Indeed, one of my favorite meals is a spinach salad, a steaming bowl of gumbo, French bread and a glass of red wine. But we have much more than gumbo to offer for the soup course.

Turtle soup belongs in a class by itself. It is special. I have tasted turtle soup all over the country, but I have never tasted one that came even close to matching the complex taste of New Orleans-produced, roux-based turtle soup. The magic may be in the slightly soupy green bayou water in which our turtles live. But I really believe that the secret lies in the unique seasonings. As you read through the recipe you may think that you are going to make a pumpkin pie rather than a soup! But try it before you dismiss it. I guarantee you'll never again question anything that tastes that good!

The word bisque, in Cajun-Creole cookery, can refer to two entirely different dishes or variations of them. There are fine and delicate bisques derived from the cuisine's French heritage—cream-laden and pureed to velvet smoothness, finished perhaps,

Supper for a Card Game

Green Salad with Garlic-Cream Dressing, page 53
Baked Cajun Meat Pies, page 21
Chicken & Andouille-Sausage Gumbo
New Orleans French Loaves
Praline Cheesecake, page 122

with a hint of liqueur. Many bisques are variations of this classic dish, with whole pieces or chunks of whole crab legs or lump crabmeat, chopped or whole shrimp or whole kernel corn added at the end and

heated just to cook through. Or, as in Crawfish Bisque, it can be a smoky tasting, dark-roux-and-stock-based mixture served over rice and spicy enough to clear your sinus troubles.

Eating onion soup in South Louisiana is an experience not to be missed. It is one of those refreshing dishes composed of what I call honest tastes. That kind of flavor makes no pretenses. It simply says, "I'm good just like I come." New Orleans onion soup takes three of these tastes, onions,

stock and cheese, and combines them in one soul-satisfying bowl of soup.

In short, we take the soup course very seriously. Sometimes we make it the whole meal.

A few words of advice before you tackle the recipes. Good stocks are the basis for soups. If you start with a weak stock, you will have a weak soup. Of course, a bad stock will produce nothing good. Master the three stocks, pages 14 to 15, and your soups, gumbos and bisques will have great foundations. Use canned stocks only if you must. Taste your soups carefully before salting, especially those made from canned stocks. Remember that the only way to duplicate the complex depth of taste so characteristic of Cajun-Creole soups, gumbos and bisques is to use good homemade stocks.

Okra and filé powder are added to gumbo both for their taste and for their inherent thickening qualities. Both, however, break down with excessive cooking, resulting in a pot of stringy, viscous gumbo. Add sliced okra to the gumbo about 20 minutes before serving; cook just until tender. When reheating an okra gumbo, cook just to heat all of the ingredients thoroughly.

Filé powder should be added to the individual serving bowl, 1/4 to 1/2 teaspoon each, depending on personal preference and bowl size. If you add it to the whole pot of gumbo, do not reboil.

So now you're ready to haul out the big pots and simmer away. But don't be surprised if the neighbors show up for supper, having been lured by the aromas wafting from your kitchen!

Chicken & Andouille-Sausage Gumbo

Gumbo may be fashioned from almost any ingredient on hand as evidenced by this popular chicken and andouille combination. Andouille is a hearty Cajun sausage somewhat on the spicy side.

1 lb. andouille sausage, cut into bite-size rounds
2 cups dark-cooked Cajun Roux, page 12
2 medium onions, chopped
2 medium green bell peppers, chopped
4 large celery stalks, chopped
4 medium garlic cloves, minced
2 tablespoons gumbo filé powder
1 tablespoon minced fresh thyme
 or 1 teaspoon dried leaf thyme
1 teaspoon dried leaf oregano

3 qts. Louisiana Brown-Poultry Stock, page 14, or canned chicken broth
3 cups cooked chicken meat, cut into bite-size pieces
1 (10-oz.) pkg. frozen sliced okra, thawed, or 2 cups sliced fresh okra
Salt, freshly ground black pepper and red (cayenne) pepper to taste
Cooked white rice
Sliced green onions and minced flat-leaf parsley for garnish

Preheat oven to 350F (175C). Spread the andouille on a baking sheet and bake in preheated oven about 25 minutes, to render much of the fat. Drain sausage on paper towels. In a heavy, preferably cast-iron, 12-inch skillet over medium heat, combine the roux, onions, bell pepper, celery, garlic, filé powder, thyme and oregano. Cook, stirring often, until vegetables are wilted and onion is transparent, about 25 minutes. Meanwhile, bring the stock to a full boil in a heavy 10-quart soup pot. When the vegetables are cooked, empty the roux into the boiling stock and stir rapidly to blend well. Add the sausage, chicken meat and okra, stirring to blend well. Season to taste and cook 1 hour. Taste and adjust seasoning, if needed. Serve in soup plates over rice. Garnish with a sprinkling of green onions and parsley. Makes 8 to 10 servings.

Gumbo Z'Herbes

Gumbo Z'Herbes is often referred to as *the king of gumbos* in New Orleans. In predominantly Catholic South Louisiana, it was traditionally served on Good Friday. The logic was that, after so many days of Lenten abstinence and fasting, the body needed the sort of revitalization provided by a combination of greens. The old Creole women would rise early in the morning on Good Friday and head for the Vieux Carre's French Market to buy their greens for the day's Gumbo Z'Herbes. The vendors would have their bright, crisp greens temptingly arrayed. Stalls would be filled with the cries of "Get your twelve greens, lady," or "Get your seven greens, madame." Legend had it—and it is still nice to believe—that for every green added to the Gumbo Z'Herbes on this day, a new friend would be made during the following year!

1 bunch fresh mustard greens
1 bunch fresh collard greens
1 bunch fresh turnip greens
1 bunch fresh green kale
1 bunch fresh dandelion greens
1/2 medium green cabbage, shredded
1/2 cup minced flat-leaf parsley
1 large onion, halved lengthwise, then sliced
4 large celery stalks, chopped, including
   leafy tops
4 large garlic cloves, minced
2 bay leaves, minced

1-1/2 teaspoons pepper
1/2 cup hot or medium picante sauce, to taste
1 tablespoon sugar
1 lb. smoked pork jowl or 1 lb. smoked ham, such
   as Hormel Cure-81, cut into tiny dice
4 qts. Louisiana Brown-Poultry Stock, page 14, or
   canned chicken broth
Salt to taste
1 pint shucked oysters and their liquor
Cooked white rice
Chopped green onions as garnish
Gumbo filé powder

Wash all greens thoroughly to remove dirt and sandy residue. Tear into bite-size pieces, discarding stems and tough center veins. Combine the greens, cabbage, parsley, onion, celery, garlic, bay leaves, pepper, picante sauce, sugar and pork jowl or ham in a 12-quart soup pot. Add stock and stir to blend well. Cover and cook about 2 hours, stirring occasionally. Add salt to taste; correct other seasonings, if desired. Stir in the oysters and their liquor. Cook just until oysters curl around the edges. Serve gumbo in soup plates over rice. Garnish with green onions and pass filé powder, stirring in about 1 teaspoon per bowl at the table. Makes 8 to 10 servings.

When purchased, greens are almost always sandy and dirty. It is very important to remove every trace of sandy material before cooking. To wash, fill sink with water; cut off and discard stem ends. Add trimmed greens to water, gently submerging them once or twice. Let stand in water a few minutes. With your hands, lift out washed greens; do not disturb sand that has accumulated in bottom. Place washed greens in a large colander to drain. Before cooking, rinse drained greens under running water two or three times.

New Orleans Seafood Filé Gumbo

Seafood filé gumbo is one of the most often-ordered dishes in New Orleans, by both tourists and locals alike. Gumbo is a staple in the Louisiana home, and now we are happy to share it with the rest of the world. When you make a pot of gumbo, make it a big one. Gumbo is one of those great dishes that gets even better after a day or so!

2 cups medium-dark Cajun Roux, page 12
2 large onions, chopped
2 medium green bell peppers, chopped
1 large red bell pepper, chopped
5 celery stalks, chopped
5 medium garlic cloves, minced
2 tablespoons gumbo filé powder
1 tablespoon minced fresh thyme or
 1 teaspoon dried leaf thyme
4 fresh bay leaves, minced, or 2 dried bay leaves
1 tablespoon minced fresh basil or 1 teaspoon
 dried leaf basil

1/4 cup minced flat-leaf parsley
1-1/2 teaspoons dried leaf oregano
1 teaspoon freshly ground black pepper
4 qts. Seafood Stock, page 14, bottled clam juice or
 stock made from Knorr fish bouillon cubes
Salt and red (cayenne) pepper to taste
2 lbs. peeled and deveined small shrimp
1 lb. claw crabmeat
1 qt. oysters and their liquor
Cooked white rice
Chopped green onions and minced flat-leaf parsley
 for garnish

Combine the roux, onions, bell peppers, celery, garlic, filé powder, herbs and pepper in a heavy, preferably cast-iron, skillet over medium heat. Stir to blend well and cook, stirring often, until vegetables are wilted and onion is transparent, about 25 minutes. Meanwhile, bring stock to a full boil in a 12-quart soup pot. When vegetables are done, add the roux mixture to boiling stock. Stir rapidly to blend well. Add salt and cayenne to taste. Add shrimp and crabmeat, stirring to blend well. Cover, reduce heat to a simmer and cook 1 hour. When ready to serve, add the oysters and their liquor. Cook just until oysters curl around the edges. Taste and adjust seasoning, if needed. Serve gumbo over rice in soup plates. Garnish with green onions and minced parsley. Makes 8 to 10 servings.

Crawfish Bisque

If you visit the home of a Cajun and are served Crawfish Bisque, my friend, you are honored indeed. My opinion is very prejudiced, at best. I truly believe that this bisque, most regal of all bisques, is one of the finest concoctions ever put upon this earth. NOTHING can match the complexity of this smoky, spicy delicacy. Each Cajun household has its own recipe for Crawfish Bisque. A Cajun's Crawfish Bisque is as unique as his signature.

It is always interesting to watch tourists eating real Crawfish Bisque for the first time. They stir it around, peering carefully into the bowl to see what lurks there in the dark liquid. And lo and behold—they scoop up these unidentified *things* from the bottom, down there with the rice. Dilemma number one is, of course, "What in the world are they?" Then the questions arise: "Do you really eat them?" and, if so, *How* in the world do you eat them?" To answer the questions, we say: "Those are the thorax region, or body, of the crawfish shell. It is broken off right behind the beak and eyes, cleaned out and stuffed with a bread-and-crawfish-tail dressing. And good heavens, yes, you eat them. After you finish your bisque, just reach down there and hold onto them with one hand and scoop out the dressing with your spoon. That dressing has soaked up lots of the bisque liquid, and it is the best part of the meal!"

It is a very time-consuming process to make real Crawfish Bisque, but it is delicious to the very last drop you scrape out of the pot. The best way to make bisque is to make it a two-day project. If you are serving it on a weekend to guests, do a little each day during the week. Prepare ingredients for each step. Read directions carefully BEFORE you begin in order to avoid the frustration of leaving out a crucial step or ingredient. Crawfish Bisque is normally served in big soup plates as a full meal. Pass crisp French bread with lots of butter.

Boiled Crawfish, see below
Stuffed Crawfish Heads, see below
1/2 recipe Cajun Roux, page 12
1 large onion, chopped
2 medium garlic cloves, minced
1 medium, green bell pepper, chopped
2 celery stalks, chopped
2 medium tomatoes, peeled, chopped
1/4 cup tomato paste
2 bay leaves, minced
1/2 teaspoon dried leaf thyme or
   1-1/2 teaspoons chopped fresh thyme

1/4 teaspoon red (cayenne) pepper
1/2 teaspoon freshly ground black pepper
Salt to taste
1 tablespoon fresh lemon juice
2 teaspoons Worcestershire sauce
About 5 cups hot cooked rice
About 1 cup minced parsley,
   preferably flat-leaf
About 2 cups chopped green onions

Boiled Crawfish:

2 large onions, coarsely chopped
1 large lemon, sliced
3 garlic cloves, unpeeled, smashed
2 teaspoons red (cayenne) pepper
1 tablespoon freshly ground black pepper

2 tablespoons salt
1 (3-oz.) box crab and shrimp boil
10 lbs. live crawfish

Stuffed Crawfish Heads:

1/4 cup unsalted butter or margarine
1/4 cup vegetable oil
1 medium onion, finely chopped
1/3 cup minced green bell pepper
3 green onions, minced
2 medium garlic cloves, minced
1 tablespoon minced parsley,
   preferably flat-leaf
1/4 teaspoon freshly ground black pepper

1/4 teaspoon red (cayenne) pepper
Salt to taste
1/2 teaspoon dried leaf thyme
1 small bay leaf, minced
2 teaspoons fresh lemon juice
2 day-old bread slices
   soaked in 1/4 cup milk
1 egg

Prepare Boiled Crawfish. Prepare Stuffed Crawfish Heads. In a heavy, deep 10-inch skillet, make roux as directed on page 12, cooking until mahogany colored. Add onion, garlic, bell pepper and celery to hot roux. Cook, stirring, until onion is wilted and transparent, about 5 minutes. Add tomatoes; cook 5 minutes. Add tomato paste, seasonings, remaining 1/2 of crawfish fat and remaining crawfish tails. Cook 5 minutes. Meanwhile, bring reserved 4 quarts stock to a rapid boil in an 8-quart soup pot. Add roux mixture to boiling stock, 1 large spoonful at a time until all has been added. Reduce heat. Add baked stuffed heads; simmer mixture 1 hour. Taste for seasoning; adjust if necessary. Spoon about 1/2 cup rice rice into each soup plate. Nest about 5 or 6 stuffed heads in rice. Ladle in bisque; sprinkle with parsley and green onions. Makes 8 to 10 servings.

To prepare Boiled Crawfish, place all ingredients except crawfish in a 20-quart stockpot; add 4 gallons water. Bring to a full rolling boil. Reduce heat; simmer, uncovered, 20 minutes to develop flavor. Bring back to a boil. Add live crawfish all at once; stir into water. Cook 20 minutes; drain, reserving 4 quarts cooking stock for bisque. Separate bodies from tails of crawfish. Using your little finger, reach into each body and scrape out yellow fat. This fat is a very important part of the taste of the bisque, so be sure to get it all. Set aside. Peel all tails; set aside. Holding body, break off and discard head with eyes and beak. Clean 40 to 50 heads; rinse under running water. Set aside while preparing stuffing.

To prepare Stuffed Crawfish Heads, preheat oven to 350F (175C). Heat butter or margarine and oil in a heavy 12-inch skillet over medium heat. Add onion, bell pepper, green onions, garlic and parsley; sauté until thoroughly wilted and transparent, about 8 minutes. Add 2 cups reserved crawfish tails, seasonings and lemon juice; cook 10 minutes, stirring often. Squeeze milk from bread. Tear bread into pieces. Add bread pieces, 1/2 reserved crawfish fat and egg to skillet. Stir until blended; remove from heat. Let mixture stand until cool enough to handle. Pack cooled mixture into reserved heads. Place on an ungreased baking sheet. Bake in preheated oven until stuffing is firm, about 10 minutes. Cool slightly; cover and refrigerate until needed.

How to Make Crawfish Bisque

1/Pack cooled stuffing mixture into crawfish heads.

2/Spoon rice into soup plate. Top with stuffed heads. Ladle bisque over heads and rice.

Shrimp Bisque

This pureed bisque in classic Creole-French style is elegant enough for the most special occasion.

2 lbs. peeled and deveined shrimp
2 qts. Seafood Stock, page 14, bottled clam
   juice or stock made from Knorr fish
   bouillon cubes
1/4 cup unsalted butter
1/4 cup olive oil
5 green onions, chopped, including
   green tops
1/4 cup minced flat-leaf parsley
1 medium onion, chopped
1 large carrot, peeled and chopped
1/2 lb. mushrooms, sliced

2 fresh bay leaves, minced, or 1 dried bay leaf,
   crumbled
1/2 teaspoon freshly ground black pepper
1 tablespoon minced fresh basil or 1 teaspoon
   dried leaf basil
1 heaping tablespoon tomato paste
1/2 cup all-purpose flour
Salt and red (cayenne) pepper to taste
1-1/2 cups whipping cream
2/3 cup sherry
Snipped chives for garnish

Combine shrimp and Seafood Stock in a heavy 6- to 8-quart soup pot over medium heat and bring to a simmer. In a heavy 14-inch skillet over medium heat, combine the butter and olive oil. When fat is hot, add green onions, parsley, onion, carrot, mushrooms, bay leaves, black pepper and basil. Cook, stirring often, until vegetables are wilted and mushroom liquid has evaporated. Stir in the tomato paste and cook, stirring constantly, 2 or 3 minutes. Add flour all at once and stir to blend well. Cook, stirring constantly, 2 or 3 minutes. Bring the shrimp and stock to a full, rolling boil, then transfer the contents of the skillet to the pot, stirring rapidly to blend well. Reduce heat to a simmer. Season to taste with salt and cayenne. Cover and cook 1 hour. Puree the soup in batches in a blender or food processor. Return to soup pot and add the whipping cream. Cook just to heat through. Taste for seasoning and adjust if needed. Add the sherry and remove from heat. Serve hot, garnished with snipped chives. Makes 8 to 10 servings.

Yellow-Squash Bisque   *Photo on page 37.*

This recipe comes from the heart of Acadiana around Lafayette, Louisiana where both squash and potatoes grow in every rural backyard. It is simple, economical and really delicious.

6 tablespoons butter or margarine
1 large onion, chopped
2 medium baking potatoes, peeled, sliced
2 carrots, sliced
4 cups yellow crookneck squash (1-1/2 lbs.),
   sliced
3 tablespoons all-purpose flour

1-1/2 qts. Louisiana Brown-Poultry Stock,
   page 14, or canned chicken broth
Salt to taste
1/4 teaspoon red (cayenne) pepper
1/2 pint whipping cream (1 cup)
1/4 teaspoon freshly grated nutmeg
About 2-1/2 teaspoons Hungarian paprika

To reduce liquids, put liquid to be reduced into pan in which it will be cooked. Place handle of a wooden spoon on bottom of pan; use a small knife to mark a notch at level of liquid. Remove spoon; make a second notch at level of desired reduction, such as one-half or one-fourth. As liquid is reducing, use spoon handle as your measuring stick! If a recipe instructs you to reduce a liquid to one cup, or other measure, simply place one cup of water in pan in which you will reduce liquid; mark the one-cup level on your wooden spoon. Discard water. Add liquid; use spoon as your guide.

In a 4-quart heavy saucepan, melt butter or margarine. Add onion; sauté until wilted and transparent, about 5 minutes. Add potatoes, carrots and squash; toss to coat with butter or margarine. Add flour all at once; stir to combine. Cook over medium heat 3 to 4 minutes, stirring. Slowly stir in stock or broth. Season to taste with salt and cayenne. Cover; cook until all vegetables are fork tender, about 45 minutes. Puree soup in batches in blender or food processor fitted with a steel blade. When all soup has been pureed, return to soup pot. Stir in cream. Taste for seasoning; adjust if necessary. Heat through; do not boil. Stir in nutmeg; cook 3 to 4 minutes. Sprinkle 1/4 teaspoon paprika into each soup bowl. Ladle hot soup over paprika. Stir soup in bowls; when soup is stirred, paprika will create an attractive marbled pattern. If desired, the soup base may be pureed, cooled and frozen up to 1 month. Thaw base in refrigerator; bring to a boil. Reduce heat; add cream. Makes 8 to 10 servings.

Turtle Soup with Madeira

Turtle Soup, or Terrapin Soup, as it used to be called, is indeed one of the "grand old ladies" of classic Creole cuisine. Recipes for its preparation were closely guarded secrets written down in the "receipt books" of plantation cooks and passed down through the generations. For the finest bowl of turtle soup in New Orleans, maybe the world, head for Commander's Palace.

5 lbs. bone-in turtle meat	2 fresh bay leaves, minced, or 2 dried bay leaves
3 qts. beef broth	2 teaspoons minced fresh thyme or 1 teaspoon
1/2 cup unsalted butter	dried leaf thyme
1/2 cup vegetable oil	1/2 teaspoon ground cloves
1 cup all-purpose flour	1/2 teaspoon ground Allspice
1/2 lb. smoked ham, cut into tiny dice	1/4 teaspoon ground mace
1 large onion, finely chopped	3 qts. hot Brown Veal & Pork Stock, page 15, or
2 celery stalks, finely chopped, including	canned beef stock
leafy tops	1 tablespoon Worcestershire sauce
2 tablespoons minced flat-leaf parsley	3 tablespoons fresh lemon juice
3 large garlic cloves, minced	2/3 cup dry Madeira
1 teaspoon freshly ground black pepper	2 or 3 hard-cooked eggs for garnish, chopped
Dash of red (cayenne) pepper	

Combine turtle meat and beef broth in a heavy 10-quart soup pot over medium heat. Simmer the turtle about 1-1/2 hours, covered, until meat is tender and pulls easily from the bones. Drain meat and cool. Discard cooking stock. Pull turtle meat from the bones and chop finely; set aside. Combine butter and vegetable oil in a heavy 6- to 8-quart soup pot over medium heat. When fat is hot, add flour all at once and stir constantly to make a peanut-butter-colored roux, about 25 minutes. Add the ham and turtle meat, vegetables, herbs and spices. Cook, stirring constantly, until vegetables are very wilted, about 15 minutes. Slowly add the hot stock, stirring to blend well. Stir in Worcestershire sauce and lemon juice. Reduce heat, cover pan, and simmer the soup 1 hour. Just before serving, stir in the Madeira and cook just to heat through. Serve hot, garnished with chopped hard-cooked eggs. Makes 8 to 10 servings.

When pureeing hot soups or sauces in a blender, start machine on low speed with container filled only half full. This prevents a splash-over of hot liquid.

Oyster-Artichoke Bisque

Delicate is the word to describe this classic New Orleans bisque. Even avowed oyster haters love this one because the oysters are pureed! The garnish of smoked oysters is the perfect touch.

3 bacon slices, finely chopped
1/4 cup unsalted butter or margarine
4 green onions, chopped
1 (14-oz.) can artichoke hearts, drained,
  quartered
1 medium onion, chopped
1/2 cup all-purpose flour
18 shucked oysters (1-1/2 pints), drained,
  liquor reserved
1 cup Seafood Stock, page 14, or 1 (8-oz.)
  bottle clam juice
1 cup Louisiana Brown-Poultry Stock,
  page 14, or canned chicken broth

1 bay leaf, minced
1 tablespoon minced parsley,
  preferably flat-leaf
1 teaspoon dried leaf thyme or
  1 tablespoon chopped fresh thyme
1/2 teaspoon freshly ground black pepper
Salt to taste
Red (cayenne) pepper to taste
1 pint whipping cream (2 cups)
1/3 cup dairy sour cream
1 (3-2/3-oz.) can smoked oysters, drained,
  patted dry on paper towels

In a 6-quart heavy soup pot over medium heat, sauté bacon until lightly browned. Add 1/4 cup butter or margarine to bacon. Add green onions, artichoke hearts and onion; cook until onion is wilted and transparent, about 5 minutes. Do not brown. Stir in flour until combined; cook 4 to 5 minutes, stirring. Slowly stir in reserved oyster liquor and stocks or clam juice and broth. Bring to a boil to thicken. Reduce heat; add bay leaf, parsley, thyme, black pepper, salt and cayenne. Add oysters; simmer just until oysters begin to curl at edges. Puree soup in batches in blender or food processor fitted with a steel blade. When all soup has been pureed, return to soup pot over medium heat. Stir in whipping cream until blended. Stir in sour cream; whisk until combined. Heat through, about 6 minutes. Do not boil. Taste for seasoning; adjust if necessary. Stir in smoked oysters; heat through. Remove from heat. Spoon into bowls; place 1 to 2 smoked oysters in each bowl. Makes 8 to 10 servings.

Andouille & Green Onion Bisque

This hearty soup makes half of a great soup-and-sandwich meal.

1/2 cup olive oil
2 bunches green onions, chopped, including
  green tops
4 celery stalks, chopped, including leafy tops
3 large garlic cloves, minced
10 oz. andouille sausage or Polish kielbasa,
  cut into bite-size rounds
3 tablespoons all-purpose flour
3 cups hot Louisiana Brown-Poultry stock,
  page 14, or canned chicken broth

3 cups hot Brown Veal & Pork Stock,
  page 15, or canned beef broth
Salt to taste
1/2 teaspoon freshly ground pepper
3 cups whipping cream
1 teaspoon freshly grated nutmeg
1/2 teaspoon Tabasco sauce
Snipped chives for garnish

Heat olive oil in a 6-quart soup pot over medium heat. When oil is hot, add green onions, celery, garlic and sausage. Cook, stirring often, until vegetables are very wilted, about 10 minutes. Add flour all at once and stir to blend well. Cook, stirring constantly, 2 or 3 minutes. Slowly add the hot stocks, while stirring. Bring to a gentle boil, then reduce heat and simmer 20 minutes. Puree the soup in batches in food processor or blender and return to soup pot over medium heat. Stir in seasonings and whipping cream and cook just to heat through. Stir in nutmeg and Tabasco sauce. Serve hot, garnished with snipped chives. Makes about 6 servings.

Left to right: Crab-Corn Soup, page 38; Yellow-Squash Bisque, page 34; Oyster-Artichoke Bisque

How to Make Creole Onion Soup

1/Cook onion mixture until onions are lightly browned and slightly crisp on edges.

2/After broiling until cheese melts, serve hot.

Crab-Corn Soup   *Photo on page 37.*

Many restaurants in South Louisiana serve their own version of this satisfying soup. To get the very best, you have to journey to the Inn at the Asphodel Plantation outside Jackson, Louisiana.

1/2 cup unsalted butter or margarine
1 medium onion, chopped
1 medium garlic clove, minced
1/4 cup all-purpose flour
2 cups Seafood Stock, page 14, or
  2 (8-oz.) bottles clam juice
2 cups Louisiana Brown-Poultry Stock,
  page 14, or canned chicken broth
1 (17-1/2-oz.) can whole-kernel corn
  (1-1/2 cups), drained

1/4 teaspoon dried leaf thyme or
  3/4 teaspoon chopped fresh thyme
1 teaspoon salt
1/2 teaspoon freshly ground black pepper
1/4 teaspoon red (cayenne) pepper
1 pint whipping cream (2 cups)
1 lb. lump crabmeat
4 green onions, chopped

Melt butter or margarine in a heavy 4- to 6-quart soup pot over medium heat. Add onion and garlic. Sauté until wilted and transparent, about 5 minutes. Add flour all at once; stir until blended. Cook 3 to 4 minutes, stirring. Slowly stir in stocks or clam juice and broth. Bring to a boil to thicken. Stir in corn, thyme, salt, black pepper and cayenne; reduce heat to medium. Cook, uncovered, 25 minutes. Stir in cream; cook 10 minutes. Taste for seasoning; adjust if necessary. Using your fingertips, carefully pick through crabmeat; remove any bits of shell or cartilage. Do not break up lumps of meat. Add crabmeat and green onions to soup; cook over medium heat just to heat through, 5 to 6 minutes. Serve hot. Makes 8 to 10 servings.

Creole Onion Soup

The combination of two stocks added to the lightly caramelized onions creates a wonderful taste. Topped with garlic-bread rounds and lots of cheese, you have a New Orleans classic.

1-1/2 cups unsalted butter or margarine
5 large onions, chopped
2 teaspoons sugar
1/2 cup all-purpose flour
6 cups Brown Veal & Pork Stock, page 15, or canned beef broth

6 cups Louisiana Brown-Poultry Stock, page 14, or canned chicken broth
Salt to taste
1/2 teaspoon freshly ground pepper
Garlic Bread, see below
10 (1/4-inch-thick) Gruyère-cheese slices

Garlic Bread:
10 (1/2-inch-thick) French-bread slices
1/4 cup olive oil

6 large garlic cloves
Salt

Melt butter or margarine in a heavy 5- to 6-quart soup pot over medium heat. Add onions; sauté, stirring often, until very limp and completely transparent, about 20 minutes. Sprinkle sugar over onions; stir to blend. Increase heat to medium-high; cook, stirring, until onions are lightly browned and slightly crisp on edges, 5 to 6 minutes. Reduce heat to medium. Add flour all at once; stir until combined. Cook 3 to 4 minutes, stirring. Slowly stir in stocks or broths. Bring to a boil to thicken slightly. Reduce heat. Season with salt and pepper; simmer 1 hour, stirring occasionally. Taste for seasoning; adjust if necessary. Prepare Garlic Bread. When ready to serve, ladle soup into flameproof bowls. Place a garlic-bread slice on each bowl of soup. Top each bread slice with a cheese slice. Broil under preheated broiler until cheese melts, 1-1/2 to 2 minutes. Serve hot. Makes 6 to 8 servings.
To prepare Garlic Bread, position oven rack 6 inches below heat. Preheat broiler. Using a pastry brush, brush both sides of bread lightly with olive oil. Place on an ungreased cookie sheet. Broil until crisp, turning once. Cool slightly. When toasts are cool enough to handle, rub garlic cloves on 1 side of each piece. Salt lightly; set aside.

Cold Cucumber Soup

In the summer, this soup, with its reduced fat ingredients, is as refreshing as a dip in the pool and easy on the waistline.

2 large cucumbers
1/4 cup minced parsley, preferably flat-leaf
4 green onions, chopped, including green tops
2 cups low-fat buttermilk
1 cup low-fat chicken broth
1 pint (2 cups) light sour cream

1/2 teaspoon freshly ground white pepper
1 teaspoon salt
2 tablespoons fresh lemon juice
2 tablespoons minced fresh dill, or substitute 1-1/2 teaspoons dried dill weed
Red caviar

Cut 6 to 8 thin slices from 1 unpeeled cucumber. Wrap in plastic wrap and refrigerate for use as garnish. Peel, seed and roughly chop remaining cucumbers. In a food processor fitted with steel blade, combine the cucumbers, parsley, green onions, and a small amount of the buttermilk. Process until smooth. Transfer puree to a 5- or 6-quart bowl. Whisk in remainder of the buttermilk and all remaining ingredients, except caviar. Cover with plastic wrap and refrigerate until well chilled, preferably overnight. To serve, taste the chilled soup for seasoning, adding salt if needed. Place caviar in a fine-meshed strainer and rinse under several washings of ice-cold water; drain well. Ladle soup into soup plates. Top each reserved cucumber slice with a teaspoon of the rinsed caviar. Place 1 caviar-topped slice on each serving. Makes 6 to 8 servings.

Duck & Artichoke Gumbo

This rich and hearty gumbo is a must for the duck lover. Served over wild rice, it provides a wonderful marriage of flavors. For a rich, full-bodied taste, prepare the gumbo the day before serving and refrigerate to allow flavors to meld to their peak. Gently reheat to serve.

1/2 cup extra-virgin olive oil
1/4 cup chopped French shallots
1 medium onion, chopped
3 celery stalks, chopped, including leafy tops
2 medium carrots, peeled and chopped
1 medium green bell pepper, chopped
2 (14-oz.) cans artichoke hearts,
  drained and quartered
3 fresh bay leaves, minced, or 2 small dried
  bay leaves, crumbled
2 tablespoons chopped fresh chervil or
  2 teaspoons dried leaf chervil
1/8 teaspoon ground cloves
1 teaspoon freshly ground black pepper

1/4 teaspoon red (cayenne) pepper
1/2 cup all-purpose flour
3 qts. hot Louisiana Brown-Poultry Stock, page 14,
  or canned chicken broth, heated
1-1/2 cups dry vermouth
4 cups chopped duck meat, pulled from 2
  (3- to 4-lb.) domestic ducks, or
  4 wild ducks, poached and cooled in
  cooking liquid until cool enough to handle,
  then skinned
Salt to taste
Cooked wild rice
Minced flat-leaf parsley and chopped green onions
  for garnish

Heat olive oil in an 8-quart soup pot. When oil is hot, add the shallots, onion, celery, carrot, bell pepper, quartered artichoke hearts, bay leaves, chervil, cloves, black pepper and cayenne. Cook, stirring often, until vegetables are very wilted, about 10 minutes. Add flour all at once and stir to blend well. Cook, stirring constantly, 3 or 4 minutes. Add the hot stock or chicken broth and stir rapidly to blend. Bring to a boil to thicken slightly. Add the vermouth and duck meat. Add salt to taste. Reduce heat to a simmer, cover, and cook for one hour. To serve, place about 2/3 cup wild rice in each soup plate and ladle the gumbo over the rice. Garnish with parsley and green onion slices. Makes 8 to 10 servings.

Bread flour, milled especially for baking bread, is higher in gluten (a protein) than all-purpose flours. To determine gluten content of a flour, look at the panel on the side of the bag labeled "Nutritional Information." For bread baking you should use a flour with 14 percent protein. The higher this protein percentage, the greater volume in your bread loaf.

Hearty Country Bread

This rich, tasty bread is a snap to prepare and has a marvelous affinity for the assertive flavors of Cajun-Creole foods. This recipe was Cajunized from a recipe developed by Barbara Brown, baker extraordinaire, from Atlanta, and my mentor at breadmaking.

1-1/4 cups water (110F, 45C)
1 teaspoon sugar
1 tablespoon active dry yeast
3 cups bread flour
1/2 cup wheat germ

1 tablespoon additional sugar
1-1/2 teaspoons salt
2 tablespoons unsalted butter, softened
1/4 teaspoon anise seeds
1/4 teaspoon fennel seeds

In a 2-cup measure, combine water and sugar. Add yeast and stir to blend. Set aside to proof. Let stand until foamy, 5 to 10 minutes. In a food processor fitted with steel blade, combine all remaining ingredients. Pulse machine on/off 3 or 4 times to blend. Add yeast and process to bring the ingredients together. Check consistency of dough and adjust with additional warm water or flour as necessary if dough is too dry or too sticky. Process 25 seconds to knead the dough. Turn dough out onto work surface and knead 2 or 3 times by hand to form a smooth dough ball. Place dough in a lightly oiled bowl, turning to coat well. Cover with plastic wrap and set aside to rise until doubled in bulk, about 1-1/2 hours. When dough has doubled, punch down and remove to work surface. Form the dough into an oval loaf and place on a baking sheet which has been sprayed with nonstick cooking spray. Using a serrated bread knife, make 3 parallel diagonal slashes in the top of the loaf. Cover loosely with plastic wrap and set aside to rise in a warm, draft-free place, until doubled in bulk, about 1 hour. Preheat oven to 425F (220C). When loaf has doubled, bake in preheated oven 10 minutes. Reduce heat to 375F (190C) and continue to bake for an additional 25 minutes, or until golden brown. Transfer to cooling rack and cool before slicing. Makes 1 oval loaf.

New Orleans Luncheon Biscuits

These are the perfect accompaniment to soups and salads. But make plenty—nobody can eat just one…or two…

About 3 cups soft, southern wheat flour,
    page 164, or all-purpose flour
2 teaspoons baking powder
1-1/2 teaspoons salt

1/2 cup plus 1 tablespoon solid vegetable
    shortening
1 to 1-1/4 cups milk
3/4 teaspoon fresh lemon juice

Preheat oven to 400F (205C). Lightly grease 2 baking sheets. In a medium bowl, combine 3 cups flour, baking powder and salt with a fork. Cut shortening into 1-inch cubes; add shortening cubes to flour mixture. Using your fingertips, work shortening into flour mixture until it resembles coarse cornmeal. Add 1 cup milk and lemon juice. Using a wooden spoon, gently stir mixture just until all flour is moist and dough is slightly sticky. If additional milk is necessary, stir in 1 tablespoon at a time. Turn out dough onto a heavily floured surface. Pat out dough into a flat circle about 8 inches in diameter. Flour surface of circle; roll out to a 1/2-inch thick rectangle. Fold pastry in half; line up corners. Reflour surface as necessary. With open edge of your right, roll out pastry and fold as before for a total of 4 times. When 4 folds have been completed, roll out pastry to 1/2 inch thick. Using a 1-1/2-inch biscuit cutter, cut out biscuits. Place biscuits on greased baking sheets. Bake in middle of preheated oven until biscuits have risen and are light golden brown, 10 to 12 minutes. Serve hot. Makes about 36 (1-1/2-inch) biscuits.

New Orleans French Loaves

French Bread—the kind with large, airy holes in the middle and a crispy crust that falls all over the table when you tear off a nice, big piece—can be created in the home kitchen. In fact, it is simple to prepare and bake. You don't need misters, steam, clay bricks or the complicated procedures often recommended in recipes for French bread. The following recipe was developed for the food processor. The loaves require no intricate rolling and measuring to shape them.

1-1/2 cups warm water (110F, 45C)	1 teaspoon apple-cider vinegar or other
1-1/2 teaspoons sugar	mild fruit-flavored vinegar
1 (1/4-oz.) pkg. active dry yeast	1/4 cup vegetable oil
(About 1 tablespoon)	1/4 cup unsalted butter or margarine,
About 3 cups bread flour	melted with 1/2 teaspoon salt
1-1/2 teaspoons salt	

In a 2-cup liquid measuring cup, combine water and sugar. Sprinkle in yeast; stir until blended. Let stand until foamy, 5 to 10 minutes. In a food processor fitted with the steel blade, blend 3 cups flour, salt and vinegar. Add dissolved yeast mixture to flour mixture all at once. Process 3 to 4 seconds to combine. Stop machine to check consistency of dough. The dough should be wet and sticky with a slight degree of body. If it is too soupy, add additional bread flour, ONE TABLESPOON AT A TIME, processing to blend between each addition, until a wet, sticky dough is formed. Process no more than 15 seconds to knead dough. Pour vegetable oil into a large bowl; oil hands and fingers well. Remove blade from processor, placing any dough which clings to it in bowl. Remove rest of dough to oiled bowl, forming dough into a loose ball. Turn dough over several times to coat completely with oil. Cover bowl with plastic wrap; let rise in a warm place, free from drafts, until doubled in bulk, about 1-1/2 hours. When dough has doubled in bulk, stir down dough, removing all air from first rising. Position oven rack in center of oven. Preheat oven to 400F (205C). Lightly grease 1 double-trough French-bread pan, or a triple baguette pan, using some of oil remaining in bottom of bowl. Thoroughly grease hands with some oil from bowl. To make 2 French loaves, pinch dough in half; lift out of bowl, 1 piece at a time. To make baguettes, divide dough into thirds. Lay dough in 1 trough of bread pan; repeat procedure with remaining dough. Because of its very wet and loose consistency, dough will shape itself. Brush dough surface thoroughly with some butter-and-salt mixture. Loosely cover loaves with plastic wrap. Let rise until double in bulk, about 1 hour. Reserve remaining butter-and-salt mixture. When loaves have doubled in bulk, carefully remove plastic wrap; brush loaves with remaining butter-salt mixture. Use very light pressure when applying butter mixture, taking care not to deflate loaves. Bake in center of preheated oven until golden brown on top, 25 minutes. Carefully turn loaves over in pan; bake about 10 minutes more to brown bottoms. Cool completely on cooling racks. To slice, cut at a 45-degree angle using a serrated bread knife. Makes 2 French loaves or 3 baguette-size loaves.

A scientific discovery made by my good friend, Shirley Corriher, led to the addition of flavored vinegar to the French bread recipe. When testing breads prepared according to the age-old, long, slow-rising French method, it was discovered that the dough became acidic during extended and numerous risings. Her conclusion was simply to add acid at the beginning of the bread-making process. The resulting loaves had both the aroma and taste of the slightly soured and yeasty breads of Europe, without the long rising! Try this method with your favorite bread recipe, using as your guide one teaspoon of fruit-flavored vinegar for every three cups of flour. Don't be tempted to add more vinegar; excess acid can destroy the gluten in the flour.

How to Make New Orleans French Loaves

1/After processing, dough should be wet and sticky.

2/Let dough rise until double in bulk.

3/Lay dough in trough of bread pan. Dough will shape itself.

4/To slice, cut at a 45-degree angle using a serrated bread knife.

Salads & Salad Dressings

South Louisiana has a bounty of "salad makings." We were making gigantic salads from offbeat combinations of greens like roquette (rocket), dandelion and chicory long before they became trendy. But our salads are not limited to green things alone!

Often in the hot summer months it is too hot and humid, even in an air-conditioned kitchen, to get excited about any food that requires the use of heat in its preparation. So we put together a big bowl of seafood or vegetable

salad, put some relishes on a plate and pass a loaf of crusty French bread or luncheon biscuits. Ah, just what the doctor ordered to satisfy the hunger, the temperament, and, most importantly, the cook!

Molded salads are very popular in South Louisiana. I've had some that were really inspired dishes. The two very best places to find the greatest salads in Cajun country are a big family reunion with a buffet supper and a church-sponsored covered-dish supper. There you'll find dozens and dozens of imaginative and delicious salads of all varieties that will send you scrambling for your paper and pencil to get the recipe. Now that's what regional food is all about!

Fresh and cold are the key words to salad success. When you shop for salad greens, look for freshness. If the romaine looks as though it had been backed over by the truck that delivered it, but the lowly iceberg lettuce looks picture perfect, then by all means, select the iceberg. If the large tomatoes are pink at best and hard as rocks, check out the cherry tomatoes. If they too

---

Bridge-Club Luncheon

Minted Brandy Ices, page 167
Crabmeat & Vegetable Salad
New Orleans Luncheon Biscuits,
page 41
Creamy Chocolate & Bourbon Pie, page 116

---

are unacceptable, throw in some sliced red bell pepper for sharp color contrast. Let freshness guide your selections. All salad ingredients should be well chilled.

Texture and color are important in the composition of a salad. In each salad you should have a variety of textures. Combine several varieties of greens for contrasts in texture and color, with the bonus of an exciting flavor combination. Garnishes are the cook's opportunity to shine in salad making. With a little imagination in garnishing, you can create world-class salads.

Salad greens should be squeaky clean, but they must also be bone dry. Damp greens will absolutely ruin your finest homemade dressing.

Wash your greens thoroughly under running water to remove dirt, grit and—

yes, they can be there— critters. Then either run them through a marvelous gadget called a *salad spinner* or pat each leaf dry on paper towels. If you would like a little exercise, put the greens in an open mesh bag, step outside and swing them in wide circles 3 or 4 minutes!

Store salad greens dry. The fabric salad bags sold in gourmet shops are very good. Or wrap the greens loosely in paper towels; store in plastic bags in the vegetable crisper.

Suggested Salad Garnishes
Tiny broccoli flowerets; cauliflowerets; grated or paper-thin sliced carrots; shredded red cabbage; alfalfa sprouts or mung-bean sprouts; bite-sized chunks of feta cheese, blue cheeses or Cheddar cheese; grated Parmesan or Romano cheese; whole anchovy fillets; sardines; chopped green olives with pimentos; chopped ripe olives; whole calamata or oil-cured black olives; sliced roasted red bell peppers; zucchini, yellow-squash or cucumber rounds; sliced green onions; thinly sliced purple onions; chopped hard-cooked egg; nuts and seeds, such as sliced almonds, sunflower seeds, toasted pine nuts; thinly sliced water chestnuts; canned crispy chow mein noodles; pepperoni or salami rounds; shredded prosciutto; REAL crumbled, crisp-cooked

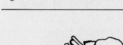

bacon; thinly sliced celery; tomato wedges; cherry-tomato halves; marinated artichoke hearts; canned hearts of palm; pickled baby eggplant; cocktail onions; croutons, especially if homemade.

Basil & Tomato Salad

In summer when big, scrumptious Creole tomatoes are in season and fresh basil is waist-high, this salad becomes a familiar item on my dinner table. It also makes a great buffet salad. Use the ripest home-grown tomatoes available in your area.

5 large, very ripe tomatoes, sliced
1 medium red onion, halved lengthwise,
   then thinly sliced
Dressing, see below

Crumbled hard ricotta cheese or feta cheese
Minced parsley, preferably flat-leaf
Parsley or basil sprigs for garnish, if desired

Dressing:
1/4 cup tomato sauce
1/3 cup balsamic vinegar
1 tablespoon sugar
1/2 teaspoon salt
1/4 cup minced fresh basil or 2 teaspoons dried
   leaf basil
1 teaspoon Worcestershire sauce

1 teaspoon Creole mustard or any whole-grain
   mustard
1/4 teaspoon freshly ground pepper
1/2 teaspoon Tabasco sauce
2 large garlic cloves, peeled
1 cup extra-virgin olive oil

Arrange tomato slices slightly overlapping on a large platter, or on individual salad plates. Scatter red onion slices over top. Cover and refrigerate until ready to serve. Prepare the dressing. To serve, pour dressing over the salad, or over the individual salads. Scatter some of the crumbled cheese and minced parsley over the top and garnish with parsley or basil sprigs, if desired. Makes 6 to 8 servings.
To prepare Dressing, in a food processor fitted with steel blade combine all ingredients except garlic and olive oil. Process until smooth. With machine running, add the peeled garlic cloves through the feed tube. Next add the olive oil through the feed tube in a slow, steady stream. When all has been added, process 10 seconds to form a smooth dressing. Refrigerate until ready to use. Stir or shake well before using.

Spinach Salad Vermillion

This tasty salad with a cooked dressing is elegant enough to serve at the finest dinner party. Serve on clear or smoked glass plates and get ready for the compliments.

1-1/4 lbs. spinach
1/2 lb. medium mushrooms, sliced
3 hard-cooked eggs, finely chopped
1/2 cup grated Parmesan cheese (1-1/2 oz.)
6 bacon slices
2 teaspoons Dijon-style mustard

1 tablespoon sugar
1/2 cup sherry vinegar
1/2 teaspoon salt
1/2 teaspoon freshly ground pepper
1/2 cup olive oil
6 green onions, chopped

Remove large stems from spinach leaves; tear leaves into bite-sized pieces. Place in a large heatproof salad bowl. Add mushrooms, eggs, and cheese; set aside. In a heavy 10-inch skillet, cook bacon slices until crisp. Drain bacon on paper towels, reserving drippings in skillet. Crumble bacon when cool enough to handle; place crumbled bacon in bowl with spinach. Heat drippings over medium heat; whisk in mustard and sugar. Pour in vinegar; whisk until sugar dissolves. Add salt and pepper. Add olive oil in a slow, steady stream, whisking constantly. Stir in green onions; immediately invert skillet over salad bowl. Leave in place 1 minute to slightly wilt greens. Remove skillet; toss salad well. Serve immediately. Makes 6 to 8 servings.

Spinach, Orange & Onion Salad with Poppy-Seed Dressing

This is a refreshing salad with beautiful color contrasts and a sublime taste. Serve with soup for lunch or a light supper.

10 oz. fresh spinach
1 (11-oz.) can mandarin-orange sections, drained
1/2 small red onion, halved crosswise, thinly sliced

2 tablespoons roasted sunflower kernels
Poppy-Seed Dressing, see below

Poppy-Seed Dressing:
3/4 cup sugar
1 teaspoon dry mustard
1 teaspoon salt
1/3 cup raspberry-flavored vinegar

1 tablespoon grated onion
1 cup vegetable oil
1-1/2 teaspoons poppy seeds

Remove large stems from spinach leaves; tear leaves into bite-sized pieces. Place in a large salad bowl; add orange sections, onion and sunflower kernels. Toss gently to combine. Cover and refrigerate until ready to serve. Prepare dressing. Remove salad from refrigerator; drizzle desired amount of dressing over top and toss well. Makes 6 to 8 servings.

To prepare Poppy-Seed Dressing, place all dressing ingredients except oil and poppy seeds in a food processor fitted with the steel blade. Process until combined, about 15 seconds. With motor running, add oil through feed tube in a slow, steady stream. Add poppy seeds; turn on and off 2 to 3 times. Makes 1-1/2 cups.

Marinated Cole Slaw   *Photo on page 48.*

Perfect for picnics, barbecues or do-ahead summer buffets, this cool and crisp salad actually improves if made two or three days ahead.

1 medium cabbage, cored, coarsely shredded
1 cup coarsely shredded red cabbage
6 green onions, chopped
3 medium carrots, shredded

2 medium, green bell peppers, quartered lengthwise, thinly sliced
Dressing, see below

Dressing:
1 cup red-wine vinegar
1/2 cup mayonnaise
1/4 cup grated onion
1 teaspoon Tabasco sauce
2 teaspoons prepared horseradish

1-1/2 tablespoons sugar
1 teaspoon freshly ground pepper
1-1/2 teaspoons salt
1 cup vegetable oil

Toss all vegetables in a large bowl. Set aside. Prepare dressing. Pour dressing over vegetables; stir until coated well. Cover and refrigerate at least 24 hours or up to 3 days. Toss often. To serve, transfer slaw to a serving bowl with a slotted spoon; discard any excess dressing. Makes 6 to 8 servings.

To prepare Dressing, in a medium bowl, whisk all ingredients except oil until combined. Add oil in a slow, steady stream, whisking until combined.

Caribbean Cheese & Vegetable Salad

Caribbean cuisine had a great influence on the evolution of the Creole cuisine and vice versa. Ingredients and tastes were exchanged between large sugar and indigo plantations of the islands and the major port of New Orleans. This very satisfying salad reflects the cool, crunchy and subtly spicy taste that is a blend of these two cultures.

3 large, ripe tomatoes, chopped
1 medium cucumber, chopped
1 small green bell pepper, chopped
1 large red bell pepper, roasted, peeled
  and chopped
3/4 cup chopped canned hearts of palm

1 small red onion, finely chopped
1 cup (4 oz.) shredded provolone cheese
Dressing, see below
Red-tipped lettuce leaves
Minced flat-leaf parsley

Dressing:
2 tablespoons fresh lemon juice
1 tablespoon balsamic vinegar
1 teaspoon minced fresh marjoram or
  1/2 teaspoon dried leaf marjoram
1/2 teaspoon sugar

1/2 teaspoon salt
1/4 teaspoon freshly ground pepper
1/2 teaspoon Tabasco sauce
1/2 cup extra-virgin olive oil

In a 4-quart bowl, combine tomatoes, cucumber, bell peppers, hearts of palm, onion and cheese. Cover and refrigerate until ready to serve. Prepare dressing. Gently toss dressing and vegetable mixture. Line 4 to 6 individual salad plates with lettuce leaves. Spoon salad over lettuce. Garnish with minced parsley. Makes 4 to 6 servings.

To prepare Dressing, combine all ingredients except olive oil in a food processor fitted with steel blade; process until smooth. With machine running, add olive oil in a slow, steady stream through the feed tube. When all has been added, process 10 seconds to form a smooth dressing. Refrigerate until ready to use.

Cajun Deviled Eggs

Everybody loves deviled eggs, and these have a nice Cajun touch. I discovered them at a community supper in Meaux (pronounced Moe), Louisiana and have loved them ever since.

24 eggs
1 (4-1/2-oz.) can deviled ham
2-1/2 tablespoons sweet pickle relish
2 tablespoons cider vinegar
2 tablespoons sugar
2 tablespoons prepared yellow mustard

1/2 teaspoon Tabasco sauce
1/2 teaspoon freshly ground pepper
1/2 teaspoon salt
Paprika
Pimento-stuffed olives, sliced

Place eggs in a 10- to 12-quart Dutch oven. Add enough cold water to completely cover eggs. Bring to a full boil over high heat; immediately set a kitchen timer for 12 minutes. Reduce heat to maintain a low boil. Partially fill a large bowl with water and ice cubes. When timer sounds, drain eggs at once; place into iced water. Peel eggs as soon as they are cool enough to handle. Slice peeled eggs in half lengthwise; carefully scoop yolks into a 2-quart bowl. Place whites on a serving platter; set aside. Add all remaining ingredients except paprika and olives to yolks. Using back of a fork, mash yolks until blended. Using a spoon, fill each white with a portion of filling, rounding off top. Or, for a more elegant presentation, spoon filling into a pastry bag fitted with a 1/2-inch star tip. Pipe filling into whites. Sprinkle stuffed eggs with paprika; place an olive slice in center of each. Makes 48 stuffed egg halves.

Cajun Corn Salad

Vegetable salads are very popular in most of the South. It's probably because they meet so many requirements. They are simple, nutritious, filling, economical, tasty and attractive. The ingredients are also readily available, if not in the backyard, then certainly at a neighborhood market.

2 (17-1/2-oz.) cans whole-kernel corn,
   well drained (3 cups)
1 large green bell pepper, chopped
1 cup hot pickled okra,
   sliced into thin rounds

6 green onions, sliced
1/2 cup minced parsley,
   preferably flat-leaf
1 cup cherry-tomato halves
Dressing, see below

Dressing:
1 teaspoon sugar
1/4 cup herb-flavored white-wine vinegar
1 teaspoon Creole mustard or
   other stone-ground mustard
1 tablespoon dried leaf basil or
   3 tablespoons minced fresh basil

2 tablespoons mayonnaise
1/2 teaspoon freshly ground pepper
1/2 teaspoon Tabasco sauce
1/2 teaspoon salt
1/2 cup olive oil

Toss all salad ingredients together in a serving bowl; set aside. Prepare dressing. Pour dressing over salad; toss gently to coat all ingredients. Cover and refrigerate overnight or up to 3 days before serving. Makes 6 to 8 servings.

To prepare Dressing, in a 2-quart bowl, whisk all dressing ingredients except olive oil until combined. Add olive oil in a slow, steady stream, whisking until slightly thickened.

Marinated Carrot Salad

This colorful and delicious vegetable salad is an old standby in Cajun country. Every lady has her own favorite seasonings. So the salad always tastes different in the many places that it shows up for dinner!

2 tablespoons sugar
1 tablespoon salt
2 lbs. carrots, sliced into thin rounds
1-1/2 cups tomato juice
3/4 cup tarragon-flavored
   white-wine vinegar
3/4 cup sugar
1 tablespoon prepared yellow mustard

1 teaspoon salt
1 teaspoon freshly ground pepper
2 teaspoons dried leaf tarragon or
   2 tablespoons chopped fresh tarragon
3/4 cup vegetable oil
2 medium, green bell peppers,
   sliced into thin strips
2 medium, red onions, halved lengthwise,
   thinly sliced

In a heavy 8-quart stockpot, combine 4 quarts water, 2 tablespoons sugar and 1 tablespoon salt. Bring to a rolling boil; add carrots. Cook until crisp-tender, about 10 minutes. Partially fill a large bowl with ice cubes and water. Drain carrots. Place into iced water; stir until cooled. Drain; set aside. In a 2-quart bowl, whisk tomato juice, vinegar, 3/4 cup sugar, mustard, 1 teaspoon salt, pepper and tarragon until combined. Add oil in a slow, steady stream, whisking until combined. Toss drained carrots, bell peppers and onions in a 13'' x 9'' baking dish; pour dressing over vegetables. Toss gently to coat with dressing. Cover and refrigerate 24 hours or up to 3 days before serving. Makes 8 to 10 servings.

Clockwise from left: Marinated Cole Slaw, page 46; Marinated Carrot Salad; Cajun Corn Salad

Crabmeat & Vegetable Salad

This is an attractive, pleasing, nutritious and positively delicious meal for summer lunches or dinners. Serve with French bread and a well-chilled white wine.

Boston-lettuce leaves
1 lb. lump crabmeat
1 avocado, sliced lengthwise into
   thin slices
12 large mushrooms, sliced
1 large ripe tomato, cut into wedges
1 (6-oz.) jar marinated artichoke hearts,
   drained, quartered
2 carrots, boiled until crisp-tender,
   cut into 2-inch-long julienne strips

6 small turnips, peeled, boiled until
   tender, sliced
3 hard-cooked eggs, halved
Salt to taste
Freshly ground pepper
Avocado Mayonnaise, see below
Paprika
Curly-parsley sprigs

Avocado Mayonnaise:
2 small, dark-skinned avocados, peeled,
   coarsely chopped
1/2 of a small onion, coarsely chopped
1 tablespoon capers, drained
1 tablespoon minced parsley,
   preferably flat-leaf
1 egg
2 teaspoons Creole mustard or
   other stone-ground mustard

1 teaspoon fresh lemon juice
2 teaspoons red-wine vinegar
1/2 teaspoon freshly ground pepper
1/2 teaspoon Tabasco sauce
1-1/2 cups olive oil
Salt to taste

Place lettuce leaves on 4 to 6 individual serving plates. Using your fingertips, carefully pick through crabmeat; remove any bits of shell or cartilage. Arrange equal portions of crabmeat in center of each lettuce-lined plate; arrange vegetables around crabmeat. Season with salt and pepper. Cover and refrigerate until served. Prepare mayonnaise. To serve, top salads with mayonnaise. Garnish plates with a dash of paprika and parsley. Makes 4 to 6 servings.

To prepare Avocado Mayonnaise, place all ingredients except olive oil and salt in a food processor fitted with the steel blade. Process until smooth and thick, stopping once or twice to scrape down side of bowl. With motor running, add olive oil through feed tube in a slow, steady stream. Season with salt.

Garlic Croutons

These crispy croutons will add a subtle hint of garlic to your favorite salad. For the garlic lover, they make great snacks for nibbling.

6 white-sandwich-bread slices
1/4 cup olive oil combined with
   1/4 teaspoon salt

6 medium garlic cloves

Preheat oven to 375F (190C). Trim off crusts from bread; reserve for another use, if desired. Using a pastry brush, lightly brush both sides of bread with salted oil. Place on an ungreased baking sheet. Bake in preheated oven until golden brown and very crisp, about 15 minutes, turning once. Rub ends of garlic on 1 side of each browned bread slice. Cut browned slices into 1/2-inch cubes. Use at once or cool to room temperature on wire racks. Makes about 2 cups.

How to Make Crabmeat & Vegetable Salad

1/To prepare Avocado Mayonnaise, add olive oil to pureed avocado mixture in a slow, steady stream.

2/Spoon Avocado Mayonnaise over crabmeat and vegetables.

Creole Roquefort Dressing

Even if you are not a fan of blue cheeses, this could well be one of your favorite dressings. Decidedly Italian in nature, it is perfect for a lettuce-and-tomato salad.

1 small garlic clove
1/4 cup white-wine vinegar
1 tablespoon fresh lemon juice
4 anchovy fillets, drained
1 teaspoon dried leaf oregano or
** 2-1/2 teaspoons minced fresh oregano**
1 teaspoon celery salt

1/4 teaspoon salt
1 egg
1/4 cup coarsely crumbled Roquefort cheese
** or other blue cheese (1 oz.)**
1/2 teaspoon Dijon-style mustard
1/2 teaspoon sugar
3/4 cup olive oil

In a food processor fitted with the steel blade and with motor running, drop garlic through feed tube to mince. Add all ingredients except olive oil. Process until blended, about 5 seconds. Stop machine; scrape down side of bowl. With motor running, pour oil through feed tube in a slow, steady stream. Process until combined. Pour into a bowl; cover and refrigerate until chilled or up to 3 days before serving. Whisk briefly if dressing separates. Makes about 1 cup.

Tomato Aspic with Cheese Centers

Tomato aspic is a dish born of the South and reminiscent of grand meals in elegant plantation dining rooms. Making GOOD tomato aspic is an art. Thankfully, there are a few restaurants keeping the tradition and fine old recipes alive. If you find yourself in Natchez, Mississippi, have lunch or dinner at the Carriage House and enjoy true southern tomato aspic as your salad course.

4 (1/4-oz.) envelopes unflavored gelatin
   (about 3-1/4 tablespoons)
2/3 cup dry white wine
5 cups tomato juice
2 medium onions, coarsely chopped
1 jalapeño pepper, coarsely chopped
6 green onions, chopped
3 celery stalks, coarsely chopped
2/3 cup Brown Veal & Pork Stock, page 15,
   or canned beef broth

2 tablespoons Worcestershire sauce
Juice of 2 lemons
2 bay leaves
1-1/2 teaspoons celery salt
8 chopped basil leaves or
   1/2 teaspoon dried leaf basil
Cheese Centers, see below
Boston-lettuce leaves
Mayonnaise
Curly-parsley sprigs

Cheese Centers:
2 (3-oz.) pkgs. cream cheese,
   room temperature
1 tablespoon grated onion
1 tablespoon prepared horseradish

2 tablespoons mayonnaise
1 tablespoon chili sauce
1/4 teaspoon Tabasco sauce
2 teaspoons powdered sugar

In a small bowl, combine gelatin and wine. Stir well; let stand 5 minutes. Meanwhile, combine tomato juice, green onions, jalapeño pepper, green onions, celery, stock or broth, Worcestershire sauce, lemon juice, bay leaves, celery salt and basil in a heavy 4-quart saucepan. Bring to a boil over high heat. Reduce heat. Cover; simmer 30 minutes. Stir gelatin-wine mixture into hot mixture; heat until gelatin dissolves, stirring often. Strain mixture through a fine strainer, pressing down on vegetables to extract all liquid. Lightly oil 8 (3/4-cup) molds. Pour aspic liquid into oiled molds. Cover and refrigerate. Prepare Cheese Centers. When aspics have thickened slightly, but are not set, drop 1 cheese ball into center of each aspic. Refrigerate until set, about 6 hours. Line 8 individual plates with lettuce leaves. Run tip of a knife around each aspic to loosen. Dip each mold into warm water a few seconds. Immediately invert on lettuce-lined plates. Remove molds. Top each aspic with a dollop of mayonnaise; garnish with parsley. Makes 8 servings.
To prepare Cheese Centers, place all ingredients in a food processor fitted with the steel blade. Process until smooth, stopping once to scrape side of bowl. Form mixture into 8 balls.

Blueberry-Cream Dressing

This tasty dressing does justice to the noble blueberry. Blueberry-flavored vinegar may be purchased at specialty food stores, or in the gourmet section of many grocery stores. You may substitute another fruit vinegar, if desired.

1/2 pint (1 cup) dairy sour cream
1/4 cup whipping cream
1/2 teaspoon salt
1 tablespoon powdered sugar
1/4 cup blueberry-flavored vinegar or
   another fruit-flavored vinegar

1/4 cup canola oil
1/2 cup fresh blueberries or
   another fruit, according to the flavor of
   vinegar used

In a 2-quart bowl, whisk all ingredients except berries and oil. Whisk until well blended. While whisking, add the oil in a slow, steady stream. When all has been added, whisk 8 or 10 times to form a smooth dressing. Stir in berries. Refrigerate until ready to serve. Serve dressing over a salad of fresh spinach leaves and sliced cucumber, or fresh fruit. Makes about 2 cups.

Cajun Caesar Dressing

Over the years this recipe has come to be a favorite with family, friends and restaurant patrons. It is marvelous on a hearty tossed salad, served with a steaming bowl of gumbo.

**3 egg yolks, heated in a double boiler
   (see page 62)**
2/3 cup red-wine vinegar
**1 tablespoon Creole mustard, or substitute
   any whole-grain mustard**
1 tablespoon plus 1 teaspoon sugar
1 teaspoon salt
1 teaspoon freshly ground black pepper
12 anchovy fillets, roughly chopped

1/2 cup loosely packed flat-leaf parsley leaves
1 tablespoon minced fresh basil
1 teaspoon dried leaf oregano
1/4 cup sour cream
1/4 cup mayonnaise
1/2 cup whipping cream
1 teaspoon Tabasco sauce
5 medium garlic cloves, peeled
1 cup extra-virgin olive oil

Place egg yolks in work bowl of food processor fitted with steel blade. Process for 2 minutes, or until yolks are thickened and light lemon-yellow in color. Add remaining ingredients, except garlic and olive oil; process until smooth. With machine running, add the garlic cloves through the feed tube, then add the olive oil in a slow, steady stream. When all has been added, process for 10 seconds to form a smooth emulsion. Refrigerate until ready to serve. Stir or shake well before using. Makes 1 quart.

Garlic-Cream Dressing

South Louisianians take their garlic very seriously. Many house dressings found in restaurants are quite redolent of this not-so-delicate member of the lily family. This creamy dressing is my house version. Serve over a mixed green salad.

3 large garlic cloves
**1/3 teaspoon dried leaf basil or
   1 teaspoon minced fresh basil**
1/2 teaspoon salt
1/4 teaspoon freshly ground pepper

6 tablespoons red-wine vinegar
6 tablespoons whipping cream
3 tablespoons dairy sour cream
3 tablespoons mayonnaise
1/3 cup vegetable oil

In a food processor fitted with the steel blade and with motor running, add garlic through feed tube to mince. Add all ingredients except oil. Process until combined. Stop machine; scrape side of bowl. With motor running, add oil through feed tube in a slow, steady stream. Process until combined. Pour dressing into a jar with a tight-fitting lid. Refrigerate until chilled or up to 3 days. Makes about 1-1/4 cups.

Pecan-Garlic Dressing

South Louisiana is blessed with a bountiful pecan crop. Ancient pecan groves line the bottom land along the Mississippi. We use pecans in any course of the meal. This uniquely different salad dressing is one of my favorite uses for this delicious nut.

3 large garlic cloves
1/4 cup coarsely chopped pecans
1/2 teaspoon salt
1/4 teaspoon freshly ground pepper

1/2 teaspoon sugar
1/4 cup red-wine vinegar
3/4 cup olive oil

In a food processor fitted with the steel blade and with motor running, drop garlic through feed tube to mince. Add pecans, salt, pepper and sugar. Stop machine; scrape side of bowl. Add vinegar; process until blended, turning on and off 3 or 4 times. With motor running, add olive oil through feed tube in a slow, steady stream. Process until combined. Toss dressing with your favorite combination of greens. Makes about 1 cup.

Strawberry-Cream Dressing

This versatile dressing can even be served as a cold soup garnished with strawberry halves or as a dip with a platter of fresh fruit tidbits!

1/2 cup mayonnaise
1 (8-oz.) pkg. cream cheese,
   room temperature
1 (3-oz.) pkg. cream cheese,
   room temperature

1/2 pint dairy sour cream (1 cup)
1 cup fresh strawberries
1/2 cup powdered sugar

Place all ingredients in a food processor fitted with the steel blade. Process until smooth and creamy. Serve over fresh fruit. Thin slightly with milk to use as a soup. Covered and refrigerated, dressing will keep up to 3 days. Makes 2-1/2 cups dressing.

Variation
Substitute 1 (10-oz.) pkg. frozen sweetened strawberries that have been thawed and well drained for fresh strawberries. Decrease sugar, if desired.

How to Make Strawberry-Cream Dressing

1/Place all ingredients in a food processor fitted with the steel blade.

2/Serve dressing over fresh fruit.

Poultry & Meat

The time is not long past when every respectable rural Cajun home would have its supply of chickens and three or four pigs. These animals made a large contribution to the family's diet. Many grown Cajun men remember the childhood chore of wringing chicken's necks and dressing them out for mama to work her magic for supper.

Both chickens and pigs were fairly self-sufficient animals and kept things going nicely for the Cajun families. Chickens and pigs lived on the family's scraps, and the family lived on the chickens and pigs! Hog-butchering was a time for celebration. Called a *boucherie,* it started early in the morning with the killing and butchering of the pig. Sausages of several varieties were made and stuffed into the cleaned intestines or wrapped in the caul fat from the stomach area. Lard was rendered. Feet were pickled. The poor-quality spare parts such as shoulder meat were rubbed with a mixture of spicy seasonings and put in the smokehouse to slowly smoke down into *tasso,* the delicious Cajun seasoning meat still in use today. It is said that the Cajuns use every part of the pig but the squeal!

Chicken in the hands of a Cajun cook can become a magnificent work of art. Good South Louisiana Chicken Fricassee is so sublime that it is difficult to perceive that intensity of flavor stemming from the barnyard clucker! In the United States we are blessed with a bounty of excellent quality chickens. They are raised on large chicken farms all over the country and are, for the most part, plump, juicy and quite flavorful. Chickens are also inexpensive, nutritious, low in fat and readily available. Now don't get me wrong—NOTHING will replace the taste of yard chickens that feed on whole corn and peck around the family garden. If you're blessed with a farmer or market that supplies fresh-killed chickens, it will be worth the time and the extra money to purchase them.

Ducks are staple fare in South Louisiana. Any person who is not a hunter probably lives next door to one, which means that both houses have freezers full

---

Dinner for a Winter Night

Oysters Rousseau, page 86
Spinach, Orange & Onion Salad,
page 46
Boned Stuffed Duck with Wine Sauce, page 66
Three-Layer Vegetable Casserole, page 98
Spinach & Artichoke Stuffed Tomatoes,
page 104
Hearty Country Bread, page 41
Cajun-Country Bread Pudding, page 109

---

of ducks. I don't think I've ever met a Cajun who, when the subject of food was mentioned, didn't want to give me his or her recipe for duck. There are certainly as many recipes for duck as there are Cajuns. Being an ardent lover of duck, I have tried every recipe shared with me. I can't recall that I've ever had a bad one! When preparing wild duck for cooking, it is important

that you remove the small bony "nub" at the tail. At the base of this appendage, there are ducts which secrete oil with which the duck preens or lubricates its feathers. If the ducts are not removed, the meat will acquire an unpleasant musky taste from the oil. If you do not have a duck hunter in your house, you may substitute domestic ducks in any of the recipes and obtain admirable results. Keep in mind, however, that domestic ducks, especially young ducklings, are very fatty. A single domestic duckling can easily render 1-1/2 cups fat during roasting.

Stuffed meats are very popular in South Louisiana; some of the most memorable

Cajun and Creole dishes are stuffed, roasted meats. One word of caution is in order when stuffing meats: Be certain that the stuffing is thoroughly cooled before using. Do not allow it to sit at room temperature for an extended period of time.

Veal has been an important part of the haute-Creole cuisine of New Orleans throughout the city's history. Local chefs have always seemed to possess a natural penchant for creating combinations of veal with seafood, such as Veal with Crabmeat, or veal with veal, such as Veal Scallops with Sweetbread Sauce. When selecting veal, look for meat that is a very pale pinkish-white color with no visible marbling of fat.

Sweetbreads were very popular in New Orleans fine cuisine in the mid-1800s and continued to be used extensively until well after the turn of the century. Today the delectable Ris de Veau are featured on only a few of the city's finest restaurant menus. To clear the air about sweetbreads once and for all, let me give a quick course on sweetbread-ology! True sweetbreads are the thymus gland of young calves. The gland lies in the neck of the animal and consists of two lobes, one slightly rounded, the other elongated. As the animal matures, the thymus decreases in size until it finally disappears. The pancreas is often referred to as the "stomach sweetbread". It bears no resemblance in taste to the thymus, which is the sweetbread most often available in the market and always used in restaurants featuring sweetbread dishes.

Beef is not as popular as other meats or fish in South Louisiana. Little beef is produced in the area. When beef is eaten, however, it is serious business. Second-best beef simply will not do. Steaks are the most popular cut of beef, and the rib-eye reigns as the number-one steak. Locals like them cut into 1-1/2- to 2-inch-thick slabs and charcoal grilled or pan broiled.

When selecting steaks, look for a good marbling of white fat throughout the meat. Each of these little veins of fat will melt into the meat, adding juicy flavor to the steak.

Magic Steak Dip

My friend and well-known television personality Merle Ellis discovered this unholy-sounding concoction somewhere in his travels. Merle advises mixing it in something like stainless steel or glass. He says it might eat the finish off anything else, even your porcelain bathtub! BUT SERIOUSLY, this dip will produce the most incredible char-grilled steak you have ever had in your whole lifetime. The recipe makes 2 quarts, which may seem like a lot, but it keeps forever in the refrigerator, and once your friends taste it, you'll find you're giving away as much as you keep, so you might want to go ahead and share the recipe with them.

1 (20-oz.) bottle good-quality soy sauce
1 (10-oz.) bottle Worcestershire sauce
1 (10-oz.) bottle A-1 Steak Sauce
1 (10-oz.) bottle Heinz 57 Sauce
1 lb. light-brown sugar
2 teaspoons granulated garlic or
  garlic powder

2 teaspoons onion powder
1 teaspoon freshly ground pepper
1 teaspoon salt
2 teaspoons fresh lemon juice
1/3 cup prepared mustard
2 teaspoons Tabasco sauce

Mix all ingredients together in a large bowl. Whisk until well blended. Store in tightly sealed jars in refrigerator. To use, pour a small amount of the dip in a non-porous baking dish and dip the steaks in it, coating both sides well. Marinate about 30 minutes before cooking, turning often. Grill or broil to desired degree of doneness. Makes 2 quarts.

Rib-Eye Steak With Merlot-Mushroom Sauce

Among beef eaters in South Louisiana, the rib-eye reigns as the king of steaks. Well-marbled beef is cut into thick slabs, 1-1/2 to 2 inches. Grill, broil or pan-grill to individual perfection. Serve the steaks topped with the mushroom sauce, if desired, a green salad and potatoes for a great sample of Cajun-Creole Saturday night supper fare.

4 (12-oz.) beef rib-eye steaks, cut about
  1-1/2 inches thick

Magic Steak Dip, see recipe above
Merlot-Mushroom Sauce, see below

Merlot-Mushroom Sauce:
1/2 cup unsalted butter
1/2 lb. sliced mushrooms
8 medium garlic cloves, peeled and cut
  into thin slices
3/4 teaspoon freshly ground pepper

2 cups Merlot wine, or Burgundy
2 cups Brown Veal & Pork Stock, page 15, or
  rich canned beef broth
Additional 1/2 cup beef stock, blended
  with 1 tablespoon cornstarch

Pat steaks dry with paper towels. Pour a small amount of the Magic Steak Dip into a non-porous baking dish. Lay the steaks in a single layer, turning to coat both sides well. Marinate for 30 minutes before grilling, turning often. Grill to desired degree of doneness. Using tongs, turn steaks several times during cooking. For rare steaks, grill for a total of about 5 to 6 minutes. For medium steaks, cook 7 to 8 minutes. For well-done steaks, cook 9 to 10 minutes. Place steaks on individual serving plates and top with a portion of the Merlot-Mushroom Sauce. Enjoy. Makes 4 servings.

To prepare Merlot-Mushroom Sauce, melt butter in a heavy 12-inch skillet over medium heat. Add mushrooms, garlic and pepper. Cook, stirring often, until mushrooms are very wilted and liquid has evaporated. Stir in wine, scraping up browned bits from bottom of pan. Cook, stirring often, until wine is reduced almost to a glaze, about 10 minutes. Stir in the 2 cups of stock. Add stock and cornstarch mixture to the skillet, stirring rapidly. Bring the sauce to a boil, stirring constantly. Cook just to thicken sauce. Remove from heat and serve hot.

Boiled Beef with Parsnips

Boiled beef and lunch time go hand-in-hand in New Orleans. No respectable luncheon restaurant in town would dare run out of it! The vegetables literally cook away to nothing and become part of the stock. Parsnips were popular in New Orleans in the late 1800s but are seldom cooked today. This is unfortunate because they are very good indeed.

2 large onions, coarsely chopped
4 medium carrots, peeled and sliced
6 garlic cloves, peeled and smashed
4 celery stalks, chopped, including
  leafy tops
1 (5- to 6-lb.) boneless beef brisket
4 parsley sprigs

3 bay leaves
1 tablespoon whole peppercorns
1 teaspoon whole cloves
2 teaspoons salt
12 parsnips, peeled and cut into
  2-inch lengths
Horseradish Sauce, see below

Horseradish Sauce:
1 (8-oz.) pkg. cream cheese, softened and
  cut into 1-inch cubes
1 tablespoon powdered sugar
1 tablespoon fresh lemon juice

1 tablespoon Worcestershire sauce
1 teaspoon liquid beef extract
1/4 cup prepared horseradish
1/2 cup whipping cream, whipped

Place onions, carrots, garlic and celery in bottom of a heavy 6- to 8-quart soup pot. Trim fat and tendons from brisket, then add meat to the pot. Add enough cold water to cover meat by about 2 inches. Bring to a rapid boil. Skim the foam from the surface, continuing to skim until no more foam appears. Add parsley, bay leaves, peppercorns, cloves and salt. Reduce heat. Cover and simmer about 2-1/2 hours, or until meat is very tender. Add parsnips and cook until parsnips are tender, about 45 minutes. Remove beef from cooking liquid, reserving liquid for another use. Place cooked beef on a cutting board and slice into 1/2-inch-thick slices; arrange on a platter. Remove parsnips from pot and arrange around the beef. Pass Horseradish Sauce separately. Makes 6 to 8 servings.

To prepare Horseradish Sauce, combine all ingredients except whipped cream in a food processor fitted with steel blade; process until smooth. Spoon into a medium bowl; fold in whipped cream. Cover tightly and refrigerate until ready to serve. Makes about 1 to 1-1/2 cups.

Orange-Glazed Pork Roast

This dish, an elegant and flavorful presentation for a humble pork roast, provides an exciting contrast of tastes and features a seldom-mentioned Louisiana crop, oranges. Modern guidelines for cooking pork advise that today's leaner pork is at its best when cooked to an internal temperature of 155 to 160 degrees. The pork will be moist and tender.

1 (3-1/2- to 4-lb.) boneless pork loin top loin roast
4 large garlic cloves, cut into slivers
1 tablespoon dried rosemary or 2 tablespoons minced fresh rosemary
2 teaspoons rubbed sage or 2 tablespoons minced fresh sage

1 teaspoon salt
1 teaspoon freshly ground pepper
Orange Glaze, see below
Pan Sauce, see below
2 navel oranges, thinly sliced
Curly-parsley sprigs

Orange Glaze:
1/4 cup orange marmalade
1/4 cup orange juice

1/4 cup Creole mustard or other stone-ground mustard
2 tablespoons light-brown sugar

Pan Sauce:
1/4 cup Grand Marnier or other orange-flavored liqueur

1 cup orange juice

Preheat oven to 350F (175C). Place roast on a cutting board, fat side up; make small slits in the fat with a paring knife. Insert garlic slivers in slits. In a small bowl, combine rosemary, sage, salt and pepper; pat onto roast. Place meat in a large roasting pan. Roast in preheated oven to an internal temperature of 155 to 160F (70C), about 1 hour. Meanwhile, prepare glaze. About 15 minutes before meat is done, brush glaze over roast; roast 15 minutes more. Place roast on a carving board while preparing Pan Sauce. Prepare sauce. Slice roast into 1/2-inch-thick slices; arrange, slightly overlapping, on a platter. Drizzle sauce over slices; garnish platter with orange slices and parsley sprigs. Makes 6 to 8 servings.
To prepare Orange Glaze, in a small bowl, combine glaze ingredients.
To prepare Pan Sauce, skim all fat from roasting pan; place pan over medium-high heat. Add Grand Marnier and orange juice; scrape up browned bits from bottom of pan. Cook 5 minutes.

Zest is the colored part of citrus-fruit peels. It contains the rich, full-flavored oils. It is a very thin layer that is joined to the white bitter pith. When a recipe calls for grated citrus peel or zest, grate only deep enough to remove the colored outer skin.

Opposite: Orange-Glazed Pork Roast

Veal Scallops with Sweetbread Sauce

Sweetbreads, prepared in a variety of ways, were very popular in both Creole homes and restaurants in the late 19th and early 20th centuries. However, they have become a much-maligned and misunderstood variety of meat among present-day diners. Little do they know what they are missing. This recipe combines sweetbreads with veal scallops, Marsala wine and mushrooms in a dish of memorable delight.

1 lb. veal sweetbreads
4 cups Brown Veal & Pork Stock, page 15,
    or canned beef broth
1 lb. veal scallops
Salt to taste
Freshly ground pepper
About 1 cup all-purpose flour
1/4 cup unsalted butter or margarine

3 garlic cloves, minced
1/4 lb. mushrooms, sliced
2 teaspoons dried leaf basil or
    2 tablespoons minced fresh basil
1/4 cup all-purpose flour
2/3 cup dry Marsala
4 green onions, chopped
1/4 cup unsalted butter or margarine
Curly-parsley sprigs

Place sweetbreads in a medium bowl; add cold water to cover. Refrigerate 1 hour. Drain sweetbreads; set aside. In a heavy 4-quart saucepan, bring stock or broth to a boil; add sweetbreads. Reduce heat. Simmer sweetbreads 10 minutes. Remove sweetbreads with a slotted spoon. Place on a plate; cover with a second plate. Place a heavy object such as a pitcher of water on top of the second plate; set aside until sweetbreads are cool. Return cooking stock to heat; cook until reduced by 1/2. Trim veal scallops to remove any tendons from edges. Using a meat mallet, pound veal until very thin and almost doubled in size. Salt and pepper both sides of scallops; dredge in about 1 cup flour to coat, shaking off excess. Set aside. When sweetbreads are cool, remove and discard all large membranes; slice meat into thin slices. Melt 1/4 cup butter or margarine in a heavy 10-inch skillet over medium heat. Add sliced sweetbreads; cook until lightly browned, about 5 minutes, stirring often. Stir in garlic, mushrooms and basil; cook 4 minutes. Add 1/4 cup flour all at once; stir until combined, 3 to 4 minutes. Slowly stir in Marsala. Add reduced cooking stock; bring to a boil. Reduce heat. Add green onions, salt and pepper to taste. Simmer sauce while cooking veal. In a heavy 12-inch skillet over medium heat, melt 1/4 cup butter or margarine; quickly sauté floured veal scallops 2 minutes per side, turning once with tongs. To serve, place veal scallops on individual plates; top with sauce. Garnish with parsley sprigs. Makes 4 servings.

Breaded Veal Panné

Pannéed veal is one of the most popular of all veal dishes served in major New Orleans restaurants. The dish is a combination of three simple ingredients—veal, a light breading and white wine. The results are delicious and refreshingly satisfying. Serve with your choice of pasta and a green salad.

1 lb. veal scallops, cut very thin, about 1/4 inch
1-1/2 cups Italian-seasoned bread crumbs
1/3 cup grated Parmesan cheese
2 teaspoons freshly ground pepper
2 teaspoons salt
1/4 cup olive oil
1-1/2 cups all-purpose flour, seasoned with 2
    teaspoons salt and 2 teaspoons freshly ground
    pepper

1 egg, beaten with 1 cup milk
1 cup dry white wine
2 tablespoons fresh lemon juice
8 tablespoons unsalted butter, cut into chunks
Minced flat-leaf parsley

Trim veal scallops to remove any tendons from edges. Using a flat veal pounder, pound veal until very thin and almost doubled in size. Take care not to tear the meat. Pat dry with paper towels; set aside. In a medium bowl, combine bread crumbs, Parmesan cheese, salt and pepper; set aside. Heat olive oil in a heavy 12-inch skillet over medium-high heat. When oil is hot, dredge veal scallops first in seasoned flour, coating well and shaking off all excess flour. Next dip in the egg wash, coating well. Dredge in bread crumb mixture, coating well. Shake off all excess crumbs. Lay breaded scallops in the hot oil. Sauté very quickly, about 1-1/2 minutes per side, turning once with tongs. Drain on paper towels and keep warm. Carefully pour off any remaining oil from skillet and return to medium-high heat. Add the white wine and lemon juice, quickly scraping up any browned bits from bottom of skillet. Cook to reduce liquid by half. Pour liquid into a small saucepan over medium-low heat. Add the butter chunks all at once, whisking rapidly to blend. As soon as the sauce is smooth, remove from heat. Serve at once. The sauce cannot be reheated. Place veal scallops on individual serving plates and top each serving with a portion of the sauce and a sprinkling of minced parsley. Makes 4 to 6 servings.

Oyster-Stuffed Beef Fillet

Even steaks get stuffed in South Louisiana. This is one of my favorites—with a rich surprise of cheese and the silky smoothness of hidden oysters.

4 (8-oz.) beef loin tenderloin steaks, 1-1/2 inches thick
4 large oysters or 8 small to medium oysters, shucked, liquor reserved
1/3 cup crumbled Roquefort cheese (about 1-3/4 oz.)
Salt to taste
Freshly ground pepper

1 tablespoon unsalted butter or margarine
3 tablespoons vegetable oil
1/4 cup brandy
1/2 cup Brown Veal & Pork Stock, page 15, or canned beef broth
1/2 pint whipping cream (1 cup)
8 smoked oysters, drained, patted dry
Minced parsley, preferably flat-leaf

Using a sharp knife, cut a 2-inch slit into side of each steak. Carefully extend cut about three-fourths of way through steaks. Gently make opening within steak large enough for an oyster and cheese. Do not cut through sides at any other point. Stuff each steak with 1/4 of cheese and 1 large oyster or 2 smaller ones. Pat steaks dry on paper towels. Salt and pepper both sides. Heat butter or margarine and oil in a heavy 12-inch skillet over medium-high heat. When oil mixture is hot, add steaks; cook to desired doneness, using tongs to turn every minute during cooking. For a rare steak, cook a total of 7 to 8 minutes. For a medium steak, cook 10 to 11 minutes. For a well-done steak, cook 13 to 14 minutes. Place steaks on individual plates; keep warm. Pour off oil from skillet; place skillet over medium-high heat. Add brandy; flame, gently swirling pan until flame goes out. Cook, scraping up browned bits from bottom of pan, until brandy has evaporated to a thin film. Add oyster liquor and stock or broth; cook until reduced to a thick glaze, 4 to 5 minutes. Add cream; cook until slightly thickened, 3 to 4 minutes. Add smoked oysters; stir to heat through. To serve, spoon sauce over each steak; top each steak with 2 smoked oysters. Sprinkle with minced parsley. Makes 4 servings.

Veal Cutlets with Crabmeat & Creolaise Sauce

4 baby veal cutlets, about 1-1/4 lbs. total
1 cup all-purpose flour, seasoned with
    2 teaspoons salt and 2 teaspoons freshly
    ground black pepper
1 cup Italian-seasoned bread crumbs, seasoned
    with 2 teaspoons granulated garlic,
    2 teaspoons salt and 2 teaspoons freshly
    ground black pepper
1/3 cup grated Parmesan cheese

1 egg, beaten with 1 cup milk
1/4 cup olive oil
1/2 lb. jumbo lump crabmeat
4 tablespoons unsalted butter
1 red bell pepper, roasted, peeled and chopped
4 green onions, chopped
Creolaise Sauce, see below
Hungarian paprika
Curly parsley sprigs

Creolaise Sauce:

5 egg yolks
1 oz. Cajun Tasso, roughly chopped, or
    substitute good-quality smoked ham, such as
    Hormel Cure-81
1 tablespoon fresh lemon juice

1/2 teaspoon salt
1/4 teaspoon red (cayenne) pepper
1 heaping tablespoon Creole mustard or other
    whole-grain mustard
1-1/2 cups melted unsalted butter, heated until hot

Prepare Creolaise Sauce; keep warm. Pat veal cutlets dry on paper towels. Combine seasoned bread crumbs and grated Parmesan cheese; set aside. Heat olive oil in a heavy 12-inch skillet over medium heat. When oil is hot, dredge cutlets first in the seasoned flour, coating well and shaking off all excess flour. Next dip in the egg wash, coating well. Coat with bread crumb mixture, shaking off all excess. Add cutlets to the hot oil and cook until golden brown on both sides, turning once, about 8 minutes. Set aside to keep warm. In a separate skillet, heat butter over medium heat. Carefully pick through crabmeat to remove any bits of shell or cartilage, taking care not to break up the lumps; set aside. Add bell pepper to the skillet and toss to heat through. Add crabmeat and cook just to heat through. Stir in green onions and remove pan from heat. To serve, place a cutlet on each serving plate and top with a portion of the crabmeat mixture. Spoon Creolaise Sauce over the top. Garnish with a sprinkling of Hungarian paprika and parsley sprigs. Makes 4 servings.

To prepare Creolaise Sauce, place egg yolks in top of a double boiler over hot water. Whisk until thickened and light lemon in color. Remove from heat. Combine tasso or smoked ham, egg yolks, lemon juice, salt, red (cayenne) pepper and Creole mustard in a food processor fitted with steel blade. Process 2 minutes, or until mixture is smooth. With machine running, add the hot butter in a slow, steady stream through the feed tube. When all has been added, process an additional 10 seconds to form a smooth emulsion. Cover sauce with plastic wrap and set aside to keep warm until ready to serve. Sauce cannot be reheated. Makes about 2-1/4 cups.

Cajun Corn-Bread Dressing

Hearty is the word for this corn-bread-based, rich dressing which contains almost everything but the kitchen sink.

1/2 cup unsalted butter or margarine
1 medium onion, chopped
1 large green bell pepper, chopped
4 celery stalks, chopped, including leafy tops
5 bacon slices, diced
1 tablespoon chopped fresh sage or 1 teaspoon rubbed sage
1 tablespoon chopped fresh thyme or 1 teaspoon dried leaf thyme
1 teaspoon dried leaf oregano
1 teaspoon minced fresh rosemary or 1/2 teaspoon crumbled dried rosemary

1 teaspoon salt, or to taste
1 teaspoon freshly ground black pepper
4 oz. smoked ham, finely chopped
4 cups French-bread cubes, lightly packed, about 4 oz.
6 cups crumbled corn bread, lightly packed, about 8 oz.
3 eggs, beaten
About 1-1/2 cups Louisiana Brown-Poultry Stock, page 14, or canned chicken broth, using enough for a moist dressing

Melt butter or margarine in a heavy 10-inch skillet over medium heat. Add onion, bell pepper, celery, bacon, seasonings and ham. Sauté, stirring often, until vegetables are wilted and bacon is cooked, but not browned, about 10 minutes. Place French bread and corn bread in a large bowl. Pour vegetable mixture over bread; toss to combine. Stir in eggs. Add enough stock or broth to make a moist dressing, stirring to break up corn bread and French bread. Refrigerate until ready to bake. When ready to bake, preheat oven to 350F (175C) and bake dressing for 1 hour, or until golden brown and set. Add additional stock or broth as necessary while baking to keep the dressing moist. Makes about 8 cups.

Creole Oyster Dressing

In South Louisiana, oyster-dressing devotees will argue its merits to the death. Indeed it is hard to dispute its one-of-a-kind taste. For the most delicious results, start with genuine French bread.

9 cups French-bread cubes, lightly packed (1/2 lb.)
1/4 cup unsalted butter or margarine
Heart, gizzard and liver from 1 chicken, minced
1 small onion, chopped
1/4 cup celery, chopped
4 green onions, chopped
3 garlic cloves, minced
1/4 cup minced parsley, preferably flat-leaf
1/2 teaspoon dried leaf thyme or 1-1/2 teaspoons chopped fresh thyme

1/2 teaspoon rubbed sage or 1-1/2 teaspoons chopped fresh sage
1/4 teaspoon dried leaf marjoram or 3/4 teaspoon chopped fresh marjoram
1/4 teaspoon red (cayenne) pepper
1 teaspoon salt
1/2 teaspoon freshly ground black pepper
12 small to medium oysters and their liquor (about 1 pint)
2 eggs, slightly beaten
About 1 cup Louisiana Brown-Poultry Stock, page 14, or canned chicken broth

Preheat oven to 350F (175C). Spread French bread on a baking sheet. Dry in preheated oven 10 minutes. Place dried bread cubes in a large bowl; set aside. Melt butter or margarine in a heavy 10-inch skillet over medium heat. Add heart, liver, gizzard, onion, celery, green onions, garlic, parsley and seasonings. Sauté until wilted, about 5 minutes. Pour cooked vegetables over bread cubes; toss until combined. Add oysters, their liquor and eggs; stir until blended. Add enough stock or broth to make a moist dressing, stirring to break up French bread. Bake about 1 hour or until golden-brown and firm. Makes about 1 pound or 8 cups.

How to Make Boned & Stuffed Chicken

1/Using a thin-bladed knife or boning knife, cut down length of backbone, cutting all the way to the bone.

2/Lay out boned chicken on a flat surface. Spread stuffing over chicken, leaving a 1-1/2-inch border.

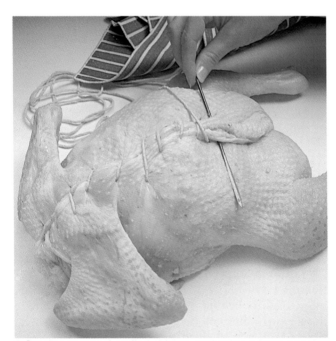

3/Starting at top of stuffed chicken and using a large trussing needle and kitchen twine, sew chicken together. Reshape chicken as you sew.

4/Remove stitches. Place roasted chicken on a platter. Surround with sautéed vegetables.

Chicken Fricassee

Chicken Fricassee is one of those subjects that can incite people to ugly behavior in our part of country. When conversations turn to food, as they invariably do among Cajuns and Creoles, the subject of fricassee is bound to come up, and battle lines are drawn with one utterance: "But you should taste MY fricassee…" Chicken Fricassee is traditional fare among Cajuns—an economical meal that cooks with little supervision. It is a good example of the Cajun *cooking-down* method of food preparation. Serve with rice for a simple and delicious meal.

1 cup lard or vegetable oil
2 (1-1/2- to 2-lb.) broiler-fryer chickens,
   cut up
Salt to taste
Freshly ground black pepper
Red (cayenne) pepper
1 cup all-purpose flour
5 medium onions, halved lengthwise, sliced
3 celery stalks, chopped

3 large garlic cloves, minced
2 bay leaves, minced
1/2 teaspoon red (cayenne) pepper
1 teaspoon freshly ground black pepper
1/2 teaspoon dried leaf thyme or
   1-1/2 teaspoons chopped fresh thyme
3 cups Louisiana Brown-Poultry Stock,
   page 14, or canned chicken broth
6 green onions, chopped

Heat lard or vegetable oil in a heavy 14-inch skillet over medium heat. Season chicken pieces with salt, black pepper and cayenne. When fat is hot, add seasoned chicken. Quickly brown chicken on both sides. Drain on paper towels. Add flour to fat in skillet; whisk until combined. Cook, whisking constantly, until peanut-butter-colored, about 25 minutes. Stir in onions, celery, garlic, bay leaves, 1/2 teaspoon cayenne, 1 teaspoon black pepper and thyme. Cook, stirring, until onions are wilted and transparent, about 10 minutes. Slowly stir in stock or broth. Return chicken to skillet; season with salt. Reduce heat. Simmer 1 hour. To serve, place chicken on a large platter; stir green onions into sauce. Serve vegetables and sauce in a separate bowl. Makes 4 to 6 servings.

Boned & Stuffed Chicken

The procedure for boning a chicken is exactly the same as for boning a duck, page 66.

1 (5-lb.) baking chicken
1 recipe Hearty Poultry Stuffing, page 63,
   or 1 recipe Creole Oyster Stuffing,
   page 63

1 recipe Wine Sauce, from Boned Stuffed Duck
   with Wine Sauce, page 66
Sautéed vegetables

Bone, stuff and bake chicken following directions for Boned Stuffed Duck with Wine Sauce, page 66, leaving in leg and wing bones. Substitute 1 of the above stuffings from page 63 for pâté and duxelles. Prepare Wine Sauce from pan drippings. Serve with sautéed vegetables. Makes 4 to 6 servings.

Variation
You may use boning instructions to bone a turkey; leave wing and leg bones for a nicer presentation. Increase quantity of stuffing in relation to size of turkey. Spread softened butter or margarine over surface of stuffed turkey. Roast boned, stuffed turkey, covered, in a preheated 325F (165C) 20 minutes per pound. Remove cover during last 45 minutes to brown turkey.

Boned Stuffed Duck with Wine Sauce

Duck and pork just seem to have a natural affinity for each other. The combination is a taste favorite in Cajun country, where both are treasured foods. This dish is impressive for a special occasion.

Sausage Pâté, see below
Duxelles, see below
1 (4- to 5-lb.) domestic duck
Olive oil

2 cups Louisiana Brown-Poultry Stock,
    page 14, or canned chicken broth
Wine Sauce, see below

Sausage Pâté:
6 oz. chicken livers
6 oz. bulk pork sausage
8 juniper berries, mashed
4 green onions, coarsely chopped
1/4 cup Madiera
2/3 cup cognac or other brandy
1 teaspoon salt
1/2 teaspoon freshly ground pepper
1/4 teaspoon dried leaf thyme or
    3/4 teaspoon chopped fresh thyme

1 bay leaf, crushed
1/4 teaspoon dried leaf basil or
    3/4 teaspoon chopped fresh basil
1/2 teaspoon rubbed sage or
    1-1/2 teaspoons chopped fresh sage
1/4 teaspoon ground coriander
1/4 teaspoon ground mace

Duxelles:
3 tablespoons unsalted butter or margarine
1/2 lb. mushrooms, minced
4 green onions, minced
2 garlic cloves, minced

1/2 teaspoon salt
1 teaspoon freshly ground pepper
1 tablespoon all-purpose flour
1/2 cup dry white wine

Wine Sauce:
1-1/2 cups dry white wine
2 garlic cloves, mashed
3 green onions, minced
2-1/2 cups Louisiana Brown-Poultry Stock,
    page 14, or canned chicken broth

Salt to taste
Freshly ground pepper
1/2 cup unsalted butter or margarine,
    cut into 1-inch cubes

To prepare Sausage Pâté, combine all pâté ingredients in a medium bowl, adding liver and fat from duck. Cover with plastic wrap; refrigerate 24 hours. Drain marinated pâté ingredients, pressing down to remove moisture. Place drained ingredients in a food processor fitted with the steel blade; process until smooth.
To prepare Duxelles, melt butter or margarine in a heavy 10-inch skillet over medium heat. Add mushrooms, green onions, garlic, salt and pepper. Sauté until mixture is dry and starting to stick to pan slightly, 10 minutes. Stir in flour; cook 3 to 4 minutes. Stir in wine; cook, stirring often, until wine evaporates, 7 to 8 minutes. Refrigerate until chilled.
To bone duck, place duck on a cutting board, breast-side-down. Using a sharp, thin-bladed knife or boning knife, cut down length of backbone, cutting all the way to bone. Working down right side first, carefully cut your way toward breast, always keeping knife against bone and taking care not to puncture skin. When you get to thigh joint, use tip of knife to expose ball-and-socket joint. Cut meat away from it, leaving meat attached to skin. Lay knife down; using your right hand, get a good grip on thigh bone. Twist thigh and leg free from carcass. Now, take knife and begin to scrape meat away from thigh bone toward leg. Carefully cut around leg joint; scrape meat off leg toward end of leg. Cut to within 1 inch of end, grasp leg bone with a paper towel; pull hard until bone pulls free. Feel end of leg skin and cut off hard, cartilaginous knob on end. The leg will now be turned completely inside-out. Carefully turn it back right-side-out, leaving some of end of leg skin tucked in to seal end opening. Now carefully cut meat away from ribs, always keeping knife

against bones, until you reach breast meat. Be sure to sever membranous-appearing meat, which will be attached to ribs, toward tail end. This is meat and should stay with skin. When you reach wing joint, follow same procedure as for disjointing thigh bone. When wing has been broken free, carefully cut meat away from ribs toward middle of breast bone. Continue toward tail, removing all breast meat from bones, until you reach middle of breast bone. Now remove all meat from first bone of wing. Disjoint bone; discard. Leave remaining wing bones attached. You are now halfway through! Place duck back on its breast. Go back to backbone where you started, working to left this time and following same procedure. When you reach middle of breast bone, very carefully sever meat from cartilage; remove entire carcass. Reserve carcass for making stock. Spread now flattened duck on cutting board, skin-side-down. Feel carefully over meat and remove any small fragments of bone or cartilage.

To assemble and cook, preheat oven to 400F (205C). Spread out duck on a flat surface; spread with a layer of pâté, leaving a border of 1-1/2 inches. Spread a layer of duxelles over pâté. Fold skin from neck down over stuffings; fold bottom skin up. Bring sides of duck together, overlapping 1 side. Starting at top of duck and using a large trussing needle and kitchen twine, sew duck back together using over and under stitches. Draw seam together tightly as you sew, using your hands to reshape duck. Truss duck. Heat 1/4 inch of olive oil in a heavy 12-inch skillet over medium heat. When oil is hot, add duck; quickly brown on all sides. Remove browned duck; place in a roasting pan. Add stock. Roast in preheated oven until juices run clear when duck is pierced, about 1 hour, basting often. Carefully remove twine. Place roasted duck on a platter. Reserve pan drippings for sauce. Cover; keep warm while preparing sauce. Prepare sauce. To serve, slice duck into 1/2-inch-thick slices using a serrated knife. Pass sauce separately. Makes 4 to 6 servings.

To prepare Wine Sauce, skim and discard fat from surface of pan drippings. Place pan over medium-high heat. When pan drippings are hot, add wine. Scrape up all browned bits from bottom of pan; add garlic and green onions. Cook until reduced by 1/2, about 15 minutes. Add stock; reduce again by 1/2. Strain mixture into a 2-quart saucepan. Season with salt and pepper. Over low heat, whisk butter or margarine cubes into sauce, 1 or 2 at a time, until each is blended before adding more.

Mesquite-Smoked Duck

If you are a lover of duck, you will find true happiness in the taste of this sausage-stuffed, slowly-smoked version prepared in a home smoker.

2 (4- to 5-lb.) domestic ducks or	12 bacon slices
6 wild ducks	1 gallon jug-wine-quality Burgundy wine
1 lb. sage-flavored bulk sausage	2 tablespoons peppercorns
1 celery stalk, chopped	2 large onions, coarsely chopped
1 medium onion, chopped	5 to 6 mesquite-wood pieces, soaked in
1/4 cup minced parsley, preferably flat-leaf	water 30 minutes, patted dry
Salt to taste	
Freshly ground black pepper	

Prepare a charcoal fire in bottom pan of a home smoker; place racks in proper position. Remove and discard tails from ducks. In a medium bowl, combine sausage, celery, 1 chopped onion and parsley. Stuff body cavity of each duck with sausage mixture. Salt and pepper skin. Wrap ducks in bacon slices; tie securely, using kitchen twine. In drip pan of smoker, combine part of wine and all of peppercorns and coarsely chopped onions. Place mesquite wood in charcoal fire; place ducks on upper grill racks. Smoke 6 hours. Alternately add remaining wine and water to drip pan throughout smoking period. The pan should never be allowed to cook dry. The moisture is necessary to insure a juicy and tender finished product. The combined tastes of the ever-concentrating wine mixture are an integral part of this dish. The duck should be well done. Remove kitchen string; carve. Serve hot. Makes 4 to 6 servings.

Barbecued Pork Spareribs

There are few taste experiences more soul-satisfying than juicy, falling-off-the-bone tender spareribs dripping with barbecue sauce. The Fourth of July in the South just wouldn't be the same without them. This barbecue sauce is a staple around my house. The recipe makes a large quantity, so you'll have plenty on hand to share with good friends.

5 to 6 racks pork baby back ribs
Barbecue Basting Sauce, see below

Louisiana Barbecue Sauce, see below

Barbecue Basting Sauce:
1 (8-oz.) bottle Italian salad dressing
1 cup cider vinegar
1 cup prepared yellow mustard
1/2 teaspoon red (cayenne) pepper

1-1/2 teaspoons freshly ground black pepper
1/2 teaspoon salt
1 tablespoon Worcestershire sauce
1 teaspoon Tabasco sauce

Louisiana Barbecue Sauce:
1/4 cup unsalted butter or margarine
6 green onions, minced
1/4 cup granulated garlic
1/4 cup chili powder
3 tablespoons finely ground black pepper
1 tablespoon dried leaf oregano
1-1/2 teaspoons red (cayenne) pepper
4 fresh bay leaves or 2 dried bay leaves
1/4 cup Worcestershire sauce

2 (32-oz.) bottles ketchup
2 qts. water
1/4 cup Tabasco sauce
3/4 cup prepared yellow mustard
1-1/2 cups firmly packed light-brown sugar
2 cups apple cider vinegar
1 (12-oz.) can beer
1/2 cup Burgundy wine

Prepare basting sauce and barbecue sauce. Let stand several hours before using. Prepare a charcoal fire in an outdoor grill; position grill 8 inches above coals. When coals are evenly burning and covered with a fine, white ash, place ribs on grill. Brush with a liberal amount of basting sauce. Cook ribs until the bones are beginning to separate from the meat, about 1- to 1-1/2 hours. Turn every 15 minutes, basting each time with basting sauce. When ribs are done, remove from grill and slice into individual pieces between the bones. Place in deep-sided baking pan and pour desired amount of barbecue sauce over the top. Cover tightly with foil and place in preheated 325F (165C) oven 25 minutes while assembling the rest of the meal. Serve hot, passing additional sauce at table, if desired. Makes 6 to 8 servings.
To prepare Barbecue Basting Sauce, combine all ingredients in a medium bowl and whisk to blend well. Refrigerate until ready to use.
To prepare Louisiana Barbecue Sauce, in a heavy 6-quart saucepan over medium heat, melt butter or margarine; add remaining ingredients. Cook, stirring occasionally, 1 hour. Cool; discard bay leaves. Pour into jars with tight-fitting lids and refrigerate. Makes about 5 quarts.

Lee Hebert's Braised Wild Duck

Lee Hebert is a Cajun hunter and fisherman extraordinaire. In South Louisiana it is an accepted fact that such a person invariably works magic in the kitchen, turning hunting bounty into irresistible and mouthwatering dishes fit for royalty. Lee is no exception and I am forever in his debt for sharing this very old duck-and-fishing-camp recipe with me. The dish is sublime and embodies the Cajun philosophy on eating: "Things just can't get no better."

4 large wild ducks, such as mallards
1 large onion, quartered
8 large garlic cloves
3/4 lb. andouille sausage or kielbasa,
    cut into 4 pieces
3 medium onions, chopped
4 large garlic cloves, minced
1 medium, green bell pepper, chopped
3 celery stalks, chopped
1/4 cup minced parsley,
    preferably flat-leaf
1/2 lb. andouille sausage or kielbasa,
    sliced into rounds

1 lb. mushrooms, sliced
1-1/2 teaspoons red (cayenne) pepper
1/3 cup Worcestershire sauce
3 bay leaves
1 teaspoon dried leaf thyme or
    1 tablespoon chopped fresh thyme
1 teaspoon rubbed sage or
    1 tablespoon chopped fresh sage
1/2 cup dry vermouth
1 (14-oz.) can artichoke hearts, quartered
Salt to taste
Hot cooked white rice

Remove and discard tails from ducks. Stuff each duck with 1 onion quarter, 2 garlic cloves and 1 sausage piece. To truss, place ducks on a surface with legs pointing toward you. Thread a trussing needle with kitchen string; thrust needle through lower part of carcass—the area where tail was removed. Bring twine back over 1 leg through tip of breast bone. Stretch twine over second leg; tie with other end of string. Thread needle again; thrust needle completely through carcass where thigh joins legs, coming out at same spot on other side. Turn ducks breast-side down. Fold wings against body; push needle through closest wing. Pull neck skin up over backbone; secure by passing needle through it, into skin of back and out same spot on other wing. Pull twine taut; tie securely. Place ducks, breast-side down, in a flameproof 13-quart Dutch oven or roasting pan. Add all ingredients except artichoke hearts and rice. Add enough cold water to cover ducks. Place pan on medium-high heat; bring to a boil. Reduce heat. Simmer until liquid is reduced by 3/4, about 1 hour and 15 minutes. Add water to cover again; repeat reduction. Check often to prevent sticking. Carefully turn ducks onto their backs; add enough water to come halfway up side of ducks. Add artichoke hearts and salt to taste. Cook until liquid is reduced by 1/2, 30 to 45 minutes. Place ducks on a carving board; remove trussing strings. Carve ducks. Serve on individual plates with rice. Skim any fat from surface of liquid; discard bay leaves. Spoon liquid and artichoke hearts over rice. Serve hot. Makes 4 servings.

Fish & Shellfish

Shellfish are an integral part of the lifestyle in South Louisiana. Some of the oldest and most deeply rooted social customs center around the eating of different varieties of shellfish. The crab, shrimp or crawfish boil, for instance, has become an institution reaching every level of society. It is served by the bayou-dwelling Cajun who caught the crawfish himself and cooked them over a butane burner on his back porch to the New Orleans Garden District gentleman who had the whole affair catered. No matter how it's done, everyone gets good and messy and shares some of the best food to be had anywhere on this earth.

"If it swims, we'll eat it" is the Cajun policy concerning fish. But then anyone living in South Louisiana who doesn't like fish is in a serious dilemma, because we are literally surrounded by them! Our bayous, marshlands, rivers, lakes, streams and the Gulf of Mexico are teeming with hundreds of species of fresh and saltwater fish. Many species are held in great esteem by gourmets the world over.

Fish and fishing are the basis for a unique South Louisiana social institution known as the *fishing camp*. Many families of avid fishermen own one somewhere. It's usually a dilapidated little house on pilings, sitting on the banks of a bayou, lake, river, brackish marshland or gulf inlet.

Come Friday afternoon when work is done and the fish are biting, the car is loaded and the family heads for the camp. Perhaps on Saturday, friends and relatives come, and the weekend is spent fishing, fellowshipping, swatting horseflies and mosquitoes and telling tales. But, most importantly, the weekend is actively dedicated to cooking and eating the catch of the day. I wish to tell you, fishing-camp cooking has produced some of the finest food you could ever aspire to eat. Fish recipes that could make a food writer rich and bring tears of joy to the eyes of a gourmet

Birthday Dinner

Acadian Crabmeat Tarts
Spinach Salad Vermillion, page 45
Shrimp Bisque, page 34
Pompano en Papillote with
Champagne Sauce
Creole Spinach Mousse, page 102
New Orleans French Loaves, page 42
Bittersweet Chocolate Cake, page 118
Cafe Brulot, page 172

have been passed down through generations of fishing-camp cooks.

If you catch your own fish, gut them as soon as possible after taking them off the hook and store on ice until they can be refrigerated. Use fresh fish within two days or freeze immediately.

If you buy your fish at the market, select a reputable market that is clean and pleasant-smelling. You should not have to hold your nose inside a fish market! Whenever possible, make your selections from whole, uncut fish and have the market fillet and skin them, if desired.

When purchasing whole fish to fillet, you will lose about 70 to 75 percent of the weight in the head and bones, depending on the species. The average serving of filleted fish is 6 to 8 ounces per person. When serving whole fish, allow 12 to 16 ounces per person. When selecting a fresh fish, look at it closely. The eyes should be clear and protruding from the sockets, not clouded and sunken. The flesh should be firm to the touch and never "mushy." It

should not be slimy feeling. It should be moist with no signs of dryness. The gills should be bright red in color. Be sure to get the carcasses to use in making stock. After all, if you buy a whole fish, you have paid for those bones! If your market has only filleted fish or steaks from which to choose, select those fillets which have moist translucent flesh, and let your nose be your guide.

If fresh Gulf fish is not available, I urge you to experiment with the recipes, substituting your local fresh fish. If you live in the Pacific Northwest, but you are literally dying to try Blackened Redfish, let me say that one of the best dishes I have ever cooked was Blackened Salmon. Use fresh Pacific salmon and substitute dill for the thyme in the Blackened Redfish recipe.

Even if you live in the Midwest, you needn't despair. If the selection of fresh fish is limited, select frozen fish fillets. Most major supermarket chains carry a selection of unbreaded frozen fish fillets, such as ocean perch, halibut, catfish and haddock. I have had great success in preparing many of the recipes in this chapter using frozen fish fillets from local supermarkets.

Ideally, fish should never be cooked to an internal temperature over 131F (55C). There is a very simple formula that will insure perfectly cooked fish every time: Fish should be cooked at 375F (190C) 10 MINUTES PER INCH OF THICKNESS. This rule applies to fillets, whole fish, steaks, stuffed fish, fish with toppings or fish any way. Stand a ruler on end next to the fish to be cooked; measure its height. If it's 3 inches thick, it cooks 30 minutes. If it's 1 inch thick, it cooks 10 minutes. If it's 1/2 inch thick, it cooks 5 minutes.

Please don't overcook fish. You will be doing yourself a great favor. Throughout my years of teaching cooking, I have found countless students who are amazed and delighted when they taste properly cooked fish.

Boiled Shrimp   *Photos on cover and page 73.*

Boiled shellfish is probably the number one company dish in South Louisiana, and what could be easier? No need to set a table. Just cover the kitchen table or backyard picnic table with several layers of newspaper. Spread the boiled seafood out along the length of the table directly on the newspaper. When dinner is over, simply roll up the newspaper with the peeled shells, and toss it all away! To make a real meal out of boiled seafood, drop whole ears of shucked corn, whole new potatoes and whole onions into the water 20 minutes before adding shellfish. The vegetables soak up the seasonings and are almost as good as the shellfish!

1 (3-oz.) pkg. crab and shrimp boil	**2 tablespoons peppercorns**
3 lemons, cut into quarters	**3 lbs. uncooked heads-on shrimp**
3 bay leaves	**2 tablespoons salt**
1-1/2 tablespoons red (cayenne) pepper	**2 qts. ice cubes**
3 tablespoons salt	

In a heavy 12- to 15-quart stockpot, combine crab and shrimp boil, lemons, bay leaves, cayenne, 3 tablespoons salt, peppercorns and 2 gallons water. Bring to a boil over high heat. Reduce heat to low. Simmer 20 minutes to develop flavor. Bring back to a boil. Add shrimp; stir in quickly, Cook just until all shrimp turn coral pink, 3 to 4 minutes. Drain immediately. While shrimp are cooking, combine 2 gallons water and 2 tablespoons salt in sink with stopper in place. Stir to dissolve salt; add ice cubes. Place drained shrimp in ice bath; let stand until shrimp are well chilled, about 10 minutes. Drain and refrigerate if not using at once. Makes 2 to 3 servings.

Boiled Blue Crabs   *Photos on cover and page 73.*

Pack live crabs on ice in a cooler 2 to 3 hours before cooking. This will make them sluggish and easy to handle. And they will not lose their claws during cooking!

2 (3-oz.) pkgs. crab and shrimp boil	**1/4 cup red (cayenne) pepper**
1/2 cup seasoned salt	**1 tablespoon peppercorns**
4 bay leaves	**24 live blue crabs**
4 lemons, cut into quarters	

In a heavy 25- to 30-quart stockpot, combine crab and shrimp boil, seasoned salt, bay leaves, lemons, cayenne and peppercorns. Add 3 gallons water; bring to a boil over high heat. Reduce heat to low. Simmer 20 minutes to develop flavor. Bring back to a boil; add live crabs, pushing them into water with a large spoon. Boil 15 minutes. Drain crabs. Serve hot. To serve chilled, cool in ice bath as for Boiled Shrimp, above, then refrigerate until chilled. Makes 4 servings.

Boiled Crawfish   *Photos on cover and opposite.*

In Cajun Country during crawfish season, the restaurants serve up plastic trays piled high with steaming, hot and spicy boiled crawfish. Serve these boiled "mudbugs" this way at your house for a great casual dinner.

2 (3-oz.) pkgs. crab and shrimp boil
1/2 cup seasoned salt
4 bay leaves
4 lemons, cut into quarters

1/2 cup red (cayenne) pepper
1 tablespoon peppercorns
2 tablespoons whole cloves
20 lbs. live crawfish

In a heavy 35- to 40-quart stockpot over high heat, combine crab and shrimp boil and all seasonings. Add 5 gallons water; bring to a boil over high heat. Reduce heat to low; simmer 20 minutes to develop flavor. Sort through crawfish; remove and discard any dead ones. Bring water back to a boil; add crawfish. Boil 10 minutes. Drain; serve hot. Makes 4 servings.

Red Cocktail Sauce

Serve this piquant red sauce with boiled shellfish cocktails. Or for a tasty finger food, use it as a dip with chilled, boiled shrimp.

1-1/2 cups ketchup
1/2 cup bottled chili sauce
1/2 teaspoon granulated garlic
1/2 teaspoon onion powder
1/4 cup prepared horseradish

2 tablespoons fresh lemon juice
2 tablespoons Worcestershire sauce
1/2 teaspoon Tabasco sauce
1/4 teaspoon freshly ground pepper
Salt to taste

In a medium bowl, combine all ingredients and whisk until well blended. Cover and refrigerate until well chilled before serving. Makes about 2-1/4 cups.

Mustard Sauce   *Photos on cover and opposite.*

This tasty sauce is an alternative to the traditional red sauce for seafood. Or serve both kinds!

1-1/4 cups Creole mustard or
**   other stone-ground mustard**
2/3 cup mayonnaise

4 teaspoons prepared horseradish
1/4 teaspoon red (cayenne) pepper

In a small bowl, whisk all ingredients until combined. Cover and refrigerate until chilled before serving. Makes about 2 cups.

Clockwise from top: Boiled Blue Crabs, page 71; Boiled potatoes and corn; Mustard Sauce; Boiled Shrimp, page 71; Boiled Crawfish

Crawfish Dauphine

If you could taste this dish, you would never guess it was the easiest recipe in the book. It's one of the best!

1/4 cup extra-virgin olive oil
1 lb. peeled crawfish tails
4 French shallots, minced
3 large garlic cloves, minced
1/2 lb. sliced mushrooms
2 celery stalks, chopped
1/4 cup all-purpose flour
2 cups Seafood Stock, page 14, bottled clam juice or stock made from Knorr fish bouillon cubes

1 cup (1/2 pint) whipping cream
Salt to taste
Freshly ground black pepper to taste
Red (cayenne) pepper to taste
1-1/2 tablespoons minced flat-leaf parsley
3 green onions, chopped
1 lb. fettucine, cooked al dente and drained
Parsley sprigs as garnish, if desired

Heat olive oil in a heavy 12-inch skillet over medium-high heat. Add crawfish and sauté 5 minutes, stirring often. Remove crawfish with slotted spoon and set aside. Add the shallots, garlic, mushrooms and celery to skillet; sauté until mushroom liquid has evaporated and mushrooms have a caramelized appearance, about 10 minutes. Add the flour all at once and stir to blend well. Cook, stirring constantly, 3 or 4 minutes. Add the Seafood Stock and stir to blend well, scraping up any browned bits from bottom of pan. Cook over medium heat until thickened. Add the whipping cream and stir to blend well. Add crawfish back to the pan; cook just to heat through. Stir in the seasonings, parsley and green onions. Remove from heat and spoon mixture over pasta. Serve hot. Makes 4 to 6 servings.

Acadian Crabmeat Tarts

This dish makes one of the most elegant first courses imaginable. When you are planning one of those pull-out-all-the-stops dinner parties, be sure to make this your first course. The pastries may be made ahead of time, even frozen and gently reheated prior to serving.

1-1/2 recipes Flaky Pie Pastry, page 110
1/4 cup unsalted butter
6 green onions, chopped

1/2 green bell pepper, chopped
1 lb. backfin lump crabmeat

Creole Béarnaise Sauce:
2 tablespoons minced green onions
1-1/2 teaspoons dried leaf tarragon
1-1/2 teaspoons dried leaf chervil
1 tablespoon·minced shallots
1/4 teaspoon salt
1/4 teaspoon freshly ground black pepper
3 garlic cloves, minced
1/4 cup fresh lemon juice

1/4 cup dry white wine
1 teaspoon Tabasco sauce
3 egg yolks
1/4 teaspoon red (cayenne) pepper
1 teaspoon Creole mustard or other stone-ground mustard
3/4 cup unsalted butter, melted
Minced fresh parsley, preferably flat-leaf

Preheat oven to 375F (190C). Place 10 (3-inch) tart pans on a baking sheet. On a lightly floured surface, roll out pastry. Cut 10 (6-inch) rounds from dough, re-rolling scraps. Carefully fit pastry into tart tins. Trim pastry even with edges of tins. Prick pastry with a fork. Bake in preheated oven until golden brown, about 10 minutes. Remove from tins and cool on a wire rack. Prepare Creole Béarnaise Sauce. Place a tart shell on each of 10 individual 6-inch plates. In a heavy 12-inch skillet, melt butter. Add onions and bell pepper; sauté until slightly wilted, about 5 minutes. Add crabmeat; toss quickly, but gently, to avoid breaking up the lumps. Cook just to heat through. Place warm crabmeat mixture in tart shells. Spoon a portion of the sauce over each; garnish with minced parsley. Makes 10 first-course servings.
To prepare Creole Béarnaise Sauce, combine all ingredients through Tabasco sauce in a heavy saucepan over medium-high heat. Cook until about 1 tablespoon of liquid remains, about 10 minutes. Transfer

mixture to work bowl of food processor fitted with steel blade. Add remaining ingredients, except melted butter. Process for about 2 minutes, or until mixture has thickened and egg yolks are light lemon-yellow in color. With machine running, add the melted butter in a slow, steady stream through the feed tube. When all has been added, process an additional 10 seconds to form a smooth emulsion.

Crabmeat au Gratin

This traditional dish never seems to lose its popularity in South Louisiana. It's an easy-to-prepare and delicious one-dish meal. Serve with a salad and French bread.

1 lb. lump crabmeat
1/4 cup unsalted butter or margarine
1 medium onion, chopped
1 large celery stalk, chopped
1 small green bell pepper, chopped
2 medium garlic cloves, minced
4 green onions, chopped
1/4 cup all-purpose flour

2 cups milk
1/4 cup dry bread crumbs
1 teaspoon salt
1/4 teaspoon red (cayenne) pepper
1/4 teaspoon freshly ground black pepper
2 egg yolks, well beaten
3/4 cup shredded Cheddar cheese (3 oz.)

Preheat oven to 375F (190C). Lightly grease a 13'' x 9'' baking dish or 4 to 6 individual au gratin dishes. With your fingertips, carefully pick through crabmeat; remove and discard any bits of shell or cartilage. Do not break up lumps of meat. Set aside. In a heavy 12-inch skillet over medium heat, melt butter or margarine. Add onion, celery, bell pepper, garlic and green onions. Sauté until onions are wilted and transparent, about 5 minutes. Stir in flour. Cook, stirring, 3 to 4 minutes. Slowly stir in milk. Cook, stirring constantly, until thickened, 5 minutes. Stir in bread crumbs, salt, cayenne and black pepper until moist. Stir in egg yolks; cook 5 minutes, stirring. Remove pan from heat; gently fold in crabmeat; do not break up lumps. Spoon mixture into greased baking dish or au gratin dishes. Sprinkle cheese over top. Bake in preheated oven until cheese is light golden brown and bubbly, 15 to 20 minutes. Serve hot. Makes 4 to 6 servings.

Shrimp Creole

Shrimp Creole is one of the most well-known of the classic old Creole dishes. Rightfully so, because when you get right down to it, it's still one of the best.

1/4 cup extra-virgin olive oil
1/4 cup all-purpose flour
2 medium onions, chopped
3 medium garlic cloves, minced
1 large green bell pepper, chopped
1 large red bell pepper, chopped
2 celery stalks, chopped, including leafy tops
1 tablespoon minced flat-leaf parsley
2 (16-oz.) cans stewed tomatoes, diced, liquid reserved
1 tablespoon fresh lemon juice

1/2 teaspoon red (cayenne) pepper
Salt to taste
3 fresh bay leaves, minced, or 2 dried bay leaves, crumbled
1/2 teaspoon celery seed
2 lbs. (peeled weight) raw peeled and deveined small shrimp
1 tablespoon Worcestershire sauce
4 green onions, chopped, including green tops
Cooked white rice

Heat olive oil in a heavy 12-inch Dutch oven over medium heat. Add flour all at once and stir to blend. Cook, stirring constantly, to form a rich, peanut-butter-colored roux. Add onions, garlic, bell peppers, celery and parsley. Cook until onions are wilted and transparent, about 8 minutes. Stir occasionally. Add tomatoes and their liquid, lemon juice and all seasonings, except Worcestershire sauce. Stir to blend well. Bring to a full boil to thicken. Reduce heat to low and cover pan. Simmer 30 minutes. Stir in shrimp and Worcestershire sauce. Replace cover and cook an additional 30 minutes. Remove cover and stir in green onions; cook 5 minutes. Remove from heat and serve over rice. Makes 4 to 6 servings.

Stuffed Crabs Lafitte

Knowing that I have a dozen stuffed crabs in the freezer brings me inner peace. I am assured that as long as I have a supply, a rave-review meal is only 15 minutes from the table. A meal of stuffed crab, green salad and French bread is very hard to beat. The crabmeat mixture may be served in real crab shells which have been well scrubbed, in ceramic crab shells, in scallop shells, or if you prefer, in individual au gratin dishes.

1 lb. backfin lump crabmeat
3 eggs, well beaten
1 cup evaporated milk
6 (1-inch-thick) French-bread slices
1/2 cup unsalted butter or margarine
1 large onion, chopped
2 large celery stalks, chopped
1 small green bell pepper, chopped
2 medium garlic cloves, minced

1-1/2 teaspoons Worcestershire sauce
3 tablespoons dry sherry
1/2 teaspoon freshly ground black pepper
1/2 teaspoon red (cayenne) pepper
Salt to taste
5 green onions, finely chopped
1/4 cup minced fresh parsley,
    preferably flat-leaf
About 3/4 cup dry bread crumbs

Preheat oven to 375F (190C). Using your fingers, carefully pick through crabmeat; remove and discard any bits of shell and cartilage. Do not break up lumps of meat; set aside. In a flat baking dish, whisk eggs and milk until blended; place bread slices in mixture, breaking up slices. Set aside. In a heavy 12-inch skillet over medium heat, melt butter or margarine. Add onion, celery, bell pepper and garlic; cook, stirring often, until vegetables are wilted, about 5 minutes. Add Worcestershire sauce, sherry, black pepper, cayenne, salt and crabmeat to skillet. Stir gently to combine; simmer mixture 10 minutes. Add green onions and parsley; cook 5 minutes. Add bread-and-egg mixture, completely breaking up bread and combining thoroughly with crab mixture. Grease 12 baking dishes if using. Use crab mixture to stuff 12 individual crab shells or greased baking dishes. Sprinkle tops of stuffed shells with bread crumbs; place on a baking sheet. Bake in preheated oven until golden brown on top, 10 minutes. Serve hot. To make ahead, wrap stuffed crab shells individually in a double layer of plastic wrap, then foil. Freeze up to 3 months. Bake in preheated oven, frozen, 15 to 20 minutes. Makes 12 stuffed crab shells or 6 to 12 servings.

Garlic-Broiled Shrimp

A garlic-lover's delight, this dish is so easy to prepare you can serve it to company after a full day's work!

3 lbs. medium uncooked shrimp, peeled and
    deveined, leaving tails
2/3 cup unsalted butter or margarine
2/3 cup extra-virgin olive oil
4 green onions, chopped, including green tops
6 large garlic cloves, minced
1-1/2 tablespoons fresh lemon juice

1 tablespoon White Wine Worcestershire sauce
1/2 teaspoon Tabasco sauce
Salt to taste
1/4 cup dry white wine
1 tablespoon minced flat-leaf parsley
Grated Parmesan cheese
Parsley sprigs for garnish, if desired

Divide shrimp equally among 6 small au gratin dishes; place on baking sheets and set aside. In a heavy saucepan, heat butter or margarine and olive oil. Add all remaining ingredients except cheese and parsley sprigs. Cook 5 minutes over medium heat. Position oven rack 4 inches below heat source and preheat broiler. Pour the garlic-butter sauce over shrimp; top with a generous scattering of Parmesan cheese. Broil under preheated broiler until shrimp are coral pink and sauce is bubbly and lightly browned, about 4 minutes. Garnish with parsley sprigs, if desired. Makes 6 servings.

How to Make Stuffed Crabs Lafitte

1/Using your hands, stuff crab mixture firmly into shells or baking dishes.

2/Serve 1 or 2 baked stuffed crabs per person.

Acadian Peppered Shrimp

Every South Louisiana cook has a recipe for barbecued shrimp which never see a grill! These tasty concoctions are based on butter and perhaps stock, but always have enough seasoning to bring tears to the eyes of mere mortals. People ask "Why on earth do I keep eating these things?" as they reach for another. Be sure to use *unpeeled* shrimp, or you won't be able to eat them.

1-1/2 cups unsalted butter or margarine
1-1/2 cups extra-virgin olive oil
1 cup Seafood Stock, page 14, bottled clam juice
  or stock made from Knorr fish bouillon cubes
5 large garlic cloves, minced
6 fresh bay leaves or 3 dried bay leaves
1/4 cup minced fresh basil or 1 tablespoon dried
  leaf basil
2 teaspoons dried leaf oregano

1 teaspoon red (cayenne) pepper
2 teaspoons freshly grated nutmeg
1 tablespoon Hungarian paprika
1/2 cup very finely ground black pepper
1/4 cup fresh lemon juice
Salt to taste
6 lbs. uncooked, unpeeled medium-sized shrimp,
  preferably with heads on, if available

In a heavy 10-quart Dutch oven, combine butter and olive oil. Cook over medium heat to melt butter. Add all remaining ingredients except shrimp. Cook, uncovered, stirring occasionally, about 25 minutes, or until sauce is a rich, hazelnut-brown color. Add the shrimp to sauce; stir to coat evenly with sauce. Cook over medium heat, stirring often, until all shrimp are coral pink, about 25 minutes. Ladle shrimp into individual soup plates; spoon a liberal amount of the buttery sauce over each portion. Serve with plenty of French bread for sopping up the sauce and lots of napkins. (Note: the shrimp are eaten with the fingers!) Makes about 8 to 10 servings.

Trout Marguery

The origin of this dish is often mistakenly attributed to New Orleans, where it has long been popular. The dish actually originated in France and is believed to have been introduced to New Orleans by Jean Galatoire when he came from France around the turn of the century. Today, the dish remains on the menu of his famous Galatoire's restaurant. Two schools of thought exist regarding the sauce for this dish. One sauce is based on a basic bechamel, or cream sauce, with fish stock and shrimp added. The other is based on a hollandaise sauce with seafood stock, white wine and shrimp added. I prefer the rich latter version.

6 (4- to 6-oz.) Gulf speckled trout fillets, skinned
3 cups Seafood Stock, page 14, bottled clam juice or stock made from Knorr fish bouillon cubes
1 cup dry white wine
1 teaspoon salt
1/2 teaspoon freshly ground white pepper

1 tablespoon fresh lemon juice
2 flat-leaf parsley sprigs, coarsely chopped
4 green onions, coarsely chopped
1/4 teaspoon red (cayenne) pepper
Marguery Sauce, see below
Parsley sprigs as garnish, if desired
Hungarian paprika

Marguery Sauce:
1/4 cup extra-virgin olive oil
1 lb. peeled and deveined small shrimp
1 tablespoon all-purpose Cajun seasoning blend
3 egg yolks

1 teaspoon Dijon-style mustard
1/4 teaspoon red (cayenne) pepper
2 teaspoons fresh lemon juice
1/2 cup melted unsalted butter
1 cup reserved poaching stock

Preheat oven to 375F (190C). Place fish fillets in a 14" x 10" baking dish; set aside. Combine stock, wine, salt, white pepper, bay leaf, parsley, green onions, lemon juice and red (cayenne) pepper in a 2-quart saucepan over medium heat; bring to a boil. Pour the boiling liquid over the fish fillets. Bake in preheated oven until fish turns from transparent to opaque, about 10 minutes. Place fillets on individual serving plates. Cover to keep warm. Strain the poaching broth, reserving 1 cup for the sauce. Prepare Sauce. To serve, spoon a portion of the sauce over each fillet and garnish with parsley sprigs and a light dusting of paprika. Makes 6 servings.

To prepare Marguery Sauce, heat olive oil in a heavy 12-inch skillet over medium heat. When oil is hot, add the shrimp and Cajun seasoning, stirring well. Cook until shrimp are a rich, coral-pink color and very lightly browned, about 7 minutes. Remove from heat and strain shrimp; set aside to keep warm. Place egg yolks in top of a double boiler over hot water. Whisk until thickened and light lemon in color. Remove from heat. Combine the egg yolks, mustard, red (cayenne) pepper and lemon juice in work bowl of food processor fitted with steel blade. Process for 2 minutes, or until mixture has thickened. With machine running, add the melted butter in a slow, steady stream through the feed tube. When all has been added, process an additional 10 seconds to form a smooth emulsion. Next add the reserved poaching liquid in a slow, steady stream through the feed tube. When all has been added, process for about 1 minute. Remove from work bowl and stir in the shrimp.

Trout with Roasted Pecans

This innovative and delicious dish, made popular in New Orleans by Commander's Palace Restaurant, is a wonderful combination of two native favorites, Gulf speckled trout and pecans butter-toasted to deep-brown perfection.

Roasted Pecans, see below
6 (4- to 6-oz.) Gulf speckled trout fillets, skinned
2 cups all-purpose flour, seasoned with
  2 teaspoons each: salt, freshly ground black
  pepper, red (cayenne) pepper and granulated
  garlic

3 tablespoons unsalted butter
1/4 cup extra-virgin olive oil
2 eggs beaten with 1 cup milk
Parsley sprigs as garnish, if desired

Roasted Pecans:
3/4 cup unsalted butter
3 large garlic cloves, minced
1 cup chopped pecans
1 tablespoon White Wine Worcestershire sauce

1/2 teaspoon Tabasco sauce
1 tablespoon fresh lemon juice
1/2 teaspoon salt

Prepare Roasted Pecans and set aside to keep warm. Pat fish fillets dry using paper towels; set aside. Toss flour with the seasonings to blend well. In a heavy 12-inch skillet over medium heat, combine butter and olive oil. When oil is hot, dredge fish fillets in the seasoned flour, turning to coat well and shaking off all excess flour. Next dredge in egg wash, then again in the flour, coating well and shaking off all excess flour. Place fillets, skin-side-down, in skillet and cook about 4 minutes per side, turning once, until golden brown. Place fillets on individual serving plates and top with a portion of the Roasted Pecans and their buttery sauce. Garnish with parsley sprigs, if desired. Makes 6 servings.
To prepare Roasted Pecans, melt butter in a heavy 12-inch skillet over medium heat. Add the garlic cloves and pecans. Cook, stirring, until garlic is transparent and pecans are lightly toasted, about 5 minutes. Stir in remaining ingredients and cook just to heat through. Remove from heat.

Grilled Red Snapper with Mango Salsa

Today's creative Creole chefs are experimenting with combinations of fish, shellfish and fruits in response to the public demand for dishes lower in fat. The results are adding a new dimension to Creole cuisine. Taste for yourself.

6 (4- to 6-oz.) red snapper fillets, skinned
Olive oil

Cajun seasoning blend
Mango Salsa, see below

Mango Salsa:
1/4 cup extra-virgin olive oil
2 large mangoes, peeled and chopped into tiny dice
3/4 cup diced cantaloupe
3/4 cup diced honeydew melon

1 large red bell pepper, roasted, peeled and diced
2 serrano chilies, seeds and veins removed, minced
3 tablespoons light-brown sugar
1/4 cup apple cider vinegar
1 tablespoon chopped fresh cilantro

Prepare a charcoal fire in outdoor grill. Position grill rack about 8 inches above coals. While you wait for the fire to cook down until all coals are evenly burning and covered with a light white ash, prepare the salsa and set aside to keep warm. When the fire is ready, brush the fillets with olive oil and place on grill. Season with Cajun seasoning blend. Grill the fish about 5 minutes per side, turning once, or until fillets have turned completely opaque. Place on individual serving plates and top with a portion of the Mango Salsa. Makes 6 servings.

To prepare Mango Salsa, heat olive oil in a heavy 12-inch skillet over medium heat. When oil is hot, add the diced mango, cantaloupe, honeydew, red bell pepper and serrano chilies. Cook, stirring often, until the mixture is very wilted, about 8 minutes. Add the brown sugar and cider vinegar. Cook, stirring often, until liquid is reduced by 3/4. Stir in cilantro and remove from heat. Serve warm.

Baked Crab Cakes with Roasted Red Bell Pepper & Pineapple Salsa

These mouth-watering crab cakes and their light and tangy topping are yet another example of the ongoing evolution of the cuisine.

Crab Cakes:
1/2 lb. lump crabmeat
1/2 lb. claw crabmeat
1/3 cup rich mayonnaise
2 teaspoons Worcestershire sauce
2 teaspoons Creole mustard, or substitute another whole-grain mustard

1/4 teaspoon red (cayenne) pepper
1 tablespoon minced flat-leaf parsley
1/2 cup chopped green onions, including green tops
2 eggs, beaten
2 cups Italian-seasoned bread crumbs

Roasted Red Bell Pepper & Pineapple Salsa:
1/4 cup extra-virgin olive oil
2 large red bell peppers, blistered, peeled and seeded, cut into small dice
1-1/2 cups diced fresh pineapple
2 serrano chilies, seeds and veins removed, minced
2 tablespoons minced fresh pineapple sage

1 tablespoon chopped cilantro
1/2 teaspoon freshly ground black pepper
1/4 cup fresh lime juice
2 tablespoons apple jelly
Salt to taste
1 teaspoon Tabasco sauce

Preheat oven to 375F (190C). Carefully pick through the crabmeat to remove any bits of shell or cartilage; set aside. In a medium bowl, combine mayonnaise, Worcestershire sauce, mustard, cayenne, parsley, green onions, beaten eggs and 1 cup of the bread crumbs. Whisk to form a smooth batter. Stir in the crabmeat, blending well. Using the palms of your hands, form the mixture into 6 crab cakes. Roll the cakes in the remaining cup of bread crumbs, coating both sides well. Pat the bread crumbs gently into the cakes. Glaze a heavy baking sheet with olive oil and place the sheet in preheated oven about 8 minutes. When the olive oil is hot, lay the crab cakes on the baking sheet. Bake 10 minutes, turn the cakes and bake an additional 10 to 15 minutes, or until light golden brown. Serve hot, topped with a portion of the salsa. Makes 6 servings.

To prepare Salsa, heat the olive oil in a heavy 12-inch skillet over medium heat. When the oil is hot, add all remaining ingredients and cook just to melt the jelly, stirring often. Remove from heat and set aside to keep warm until ready to use.

Red Snapper a la Creole

This dish is probably more representative of the type of food that would be served in a Creole home than any other dish. It is impressive when served on an attractively garnished platter and placed in the center of the table with pride.

1 (5-lb.) whole red snapper, cleaned
1/2 cup vegetable oil
2 large onions, quartered, thinly sliced
2 medium, green bell peppers, chopped
4 celery stalks, chopped
4 garlic cloves, minced
2 bay leaves, minced
1/2 teaspoon dried leaf thyme or
   1-1/2 teaspoons chopped fresh thyme
1/2 teaspoon dried leaf oregano or
   1-1/2 teaspoons chopped fresh oregano
1/2 teaspoon freshly ground black pepper
1/2 teaspoon red (cayenne) pepper

1 tablespoon brown sugar
5 large tomatoes, peeled, chopped
1 (6-oz.) can tomato paste
1/4 cup fresh lemon juice
2 cups Seafood Stock, page 14, or
   2 (8-oz.) bottles clam juice
1/4 cup minced parsley, preferably flat-leaf
6 green onions, chopped
2 lbs. small uncooked shrimp,
   peeled, deveined
Salt to taste
Lemon slices
Curly-parsley sprigs

Place red snapper in a large baking dish or roasting pan. Cover and refrigerate while preparing sauce. In a heavy 12-inch skillet over medium heat, heat oil until hot. Add onions, bell peppers, celery and garlic. Cook until vegetables are wilted and transparent, about 8 minutes. Stir in seasonings, sugar and tomatoes. Cook 10 minutes. Stir in tomato paste, lemon juice and stock or clam juice. Reduce heat. Simmer, partially covered, 45 minutes. Add parsley and green onions; stir until distributed. Add shrimp and salt; cook 5 minutes. Preheat oven to 375F (190C). Pour sauce over fish. Bake in preheated oven until fish turns from transparent to opaque, 40 minutes. To serve, place fish in center of a large platter; spoon sauce around fish. Place lemon slices and parsley sprigs around edge of platter. Makes 6 to 8 servings.

New Orleans Oyster Loaf

No visit to New Orleans would ever be complete without at least one oyster loaf. It's a 6-inch length of crusty French bread stacked with oysters fried just long enough to be crispy on the outside but still almost liquidy-smooth on the inside. An oyster loaf is some of the best eating New Orleans has to offer. To be native, have yours "dressed" with all the toppings.

Tartar Sauce, see below
Vegetable oil
8 shucked medium oysters, well drained
3 cups yellow cornmeal
1-1/2 teaspoons salt
1-1/2 teaspoons freshly ground black pepper
1 teaspoon red (cayenne) pepper

2 cups all-purpose flour
2 eggs beaten with 2 cups milk
1 (6-inch-section) toasted French bread
4 pickled okra pods,
 sliced into thin rounds
Shredded lettuce
3 tomato slices

Tartar Sauce:
1-1/4 cups mayonnaise
1/3 cup chopped dill pickles
1/4 cup chopped pimento-stuffed olives
1/2 small onion, minced

1 tablespoon fresh lemon juice
1/2 teaspoon salt
1/2 teaspoon freshly ground pepper
1/2 teaspoon sugar

Prepare Tartar Sauce; cover and refrigerate until served. Heat 3 inches oil in a large saucepan to 365F (185C) or until a 1-inch bread cube turns golden brown in 60 seconds. Pat oysters dry on paper towels. In a shallow bowl, combine cornmeal, salt, black pepper and cayenne. Place flour in a shallow bowl. Dredge dried oysters in flour; shake off excess. Dip each floured oyster into egg-and-milk mixture. Then dredge in seasoned cornmeal to coat well; shake off excess. Fry oysters in hot oil, 2 or 3 at a time, just until crust is golden brown and crisp, 3 to 4 minutes. Drain on paper towels. Using a serrated knife, slice bread in half lengthwise. Generously coat inside of top and bottom of bread with Tartar Sauce. Arrange oysters on bottom; top with okra rounds. Sprinkle with shredded lettuce; add tomato slices. Replace top. Makes 1 serving.
To prepare Tartar Sauce, combine all ingredients in a 2-quart bowl. Cover with plastic wrap; refrigerate until ready to serve or up to 2 days. Makes 2 cups.

Oysters en Brochette

This is one of Louisiana's best oyster dishes. It is so easy to prepare that you can have dinner for company in the time it takes to cook the rice. This dish can also be served as a first course by deleting the rice and placing 3 to 4 cooked oysters and mushrooms in individual au gratin dishes and drizzling the sauce over the top.

12 bacon slices, cut in half	1/4 teaspoon red (cayenne) pepper
1/2 cup unsalted butter or margarine	1/2 teaspoon freshly ground black pepper
1 tablespoon White Wine Worcestershire sauce	24 shucked oysters, about 2 pints, drained
1/8 teaspoon liquid smoke	24 medium-sized mushrooms
1 tablespoon fresh lemon juice	Cooked white rice
1/2 teaspoon granulated garlic	Caper-Butter Sauce, see below
1/2 teaspoon salt	

Caper-Butter Sauce:

2 tablespoons capers, minced	1/2 teaspoon salt
4 green onions, minced	1/4 cup whipping cream
1/4 cup fresh lemon juice	12 tablespoons unsalted butter, cut into 1-inch
Pinch of red (cayenne) pepper	cubes

Preheat oven to 350F (175C). Lay bacon pieces on a heavy baking sheet and bake in preheated oven until half-cooked, about 4 minutes. Drain on paper towels and set aside. Combine remaining ingredients, except oysters, mushrooms and rice, in a small saucepan over medium heat. Whisk to blend ingredients well and cook 5 minutes. Remove from heat and set aside to cool slightly. Dredge the oysters in the buttery sauce and wrap each oyster in a half slice of bacon. Dredge the mushrooms in the buttery sauce. Alternate the bacon-wrapped oysters and mushrooms on skewers, placing 6 oysters and 6 mushrooms on each skewer. Lay the skewers across a baking sheet and set aside. Preheat broiler and position oven rack 5 inches below heat source. When broiler is hot, brush the oysters and mushrooms with more of the buttery sauce and place under broiler. Cook about 5 minutes, or until bacon is cooked and oysters are curled at the edges. Place a portion of rice on each serving plate and slide the oysters and mushrooms off of the skewers onto the rice, 1 skewer per plate. Whisk the pan drippings into the Caper-Butter Sauce and spoon a portion of the sauce over each serving. Makes 4 servings.

To prepare Caper-Butter Sauce, combine all ingredients except cream and butter cubes in a saucepan over medium-high heat. Cook until liquid is reduced to about 1 tablespoon, 5 or 6 minutes. Add the cream and reduce by half. Reduce heat to low and add the butter cubes all at once. Whisk rapidly to incorporate the butter. As soon as the butter is incorporated, remove pan from heat. Continuing to whisk, add the buttery drippings from the baking sheet to the sauce. Whisk until well blended. Serve at once. Do not allow the sauce to boil. The sauce cannot be reheated.

Oysters Bienville

This egg-rich shrimp topping is named for the city's founder, Jean Baptiste le Moyne, Sieur de Bienville.

1/4 cup unsalted butter or margarine	**1/4 cup dry sherry**
4 green onions, minced	**1/2 teaspoon freshly ground black pepper**
2 tablespoons minced parsley,	**1/2 teaspoon red (cayenne) pepper**
preferably flat-leaf	**Salt to taste**
2 garlic cloves, minced	**1/3 cup grated Parmesan cheese (1 oz.)**
1/3 cup minced mushrooms	**1/4 cup dry bread crumbs**
1/2 lb. deveined, peeled boiled shrimp,	**1/2 teaspoon salt**
minced	**24 shucked oysters, well drained**
1/4 cup all-purpose flour	**24 well-scrubbed oyster shells**
1/2 pint whipping cream (1 cup)	**Rock salt**
2 egg yolks, beaten until frothy	

In a heavy 10-inch skillet over medium heat, melt butter or margarine. Add green onions, parsley, garlic, mushrooms and shrimp. Cook until vegetables are wilted and transparent and liquid has evaporated, 8 to 10 minutes. Stir in flour until blended; cook 3 to 4 minutes, stirring. Slowly stir in cream; stir until combined. Stir in egg yolks, sherry, black pepper, cayenne and salt until combined. Cook until mixture thickens, 5 to 6 minutes. Set aside. In a small bowl, combine cheese, bread crumbs and 1/2 teaspoon salt; set aside. Preheat oven to 400F (205C). Line a large baking pan with rock salt. Pat oysters dry on paper towels. Place a dried oyster in each shell; nest shells into rock salt. Spoon a portion of shrimp mixture over each oyster; sprinkle with cheese mixture. Bake in preheated oven until bubbly and browned on top, 10 to 15 minutes. Serve hot. Makes 6 to 8 first-course servings or 4 light entrees.

Oysters Rockefeller

This classic oyster dish has become one of New Orleans signature dishes.

1 (10-oz.) pkg. frozen chopped spinach,	**1/2 teaspoon dried leaf basil**
cooked	**1/2 teaspoon red (cayenne) pepper**
6 tablespoons unsalted butter or margarine	**Salt to taste**
1 bunch watercress, finely chopped	**1 tablespoon Herbsaint**
1/4 cup minced parsley, preferably flat-leaf	**About 1/2 cup whipping cream**
6 green onions, minced	**Rock salt**
2 teaspoons finely minced green bell pepper	**24 shucked oysters, well drained**
1/2 teaspoon freshly ground black pepper	**24 well-scrubbed oyster shells**
1/2 teaspoon dried leaf marjoram	

Press spinach until very dry; set aside. Melt butter or margarine in a heavy 10-inch skillet over medium heat. Add spinach, watercress, parsley, green onions and bell pepper; sauté until vegetables are slightly wilted, about 5 minutes. Stir in black pepper, marjoram, basil, cayenne, salt, Herbsaint and 1/2 cup whipping cream. Cook, stirring, until mixture is thick and creamy, 5 minutes. Add additional cream if mixture is too thick to spoon easily. Set aside. Preheat oven to 400F (205C). Line a large baking pan with rock salt. Pat oysters dry on paper towels; place 1 dried oyster in each shell. Nest shells into rock salt. Divide topping among oysters, placing an even layer on top of each. Bake in preheated oven until bubbly and lightly browned on top, 10 to 15 minutes. Makes 6 to 8 first-course servings or 4 light entrees.

Top to bottom: Oysters Rockefeller; Oysters Rousseau, page 86; Oysters Bienville

Oysters Rousseau   *Photo on page 85.*

A light and zesty oyster dish perfect for the cocktail hour, this one is easy to prepare.

1 (16-oz.) can peeled tomatoes and their liquid	2 heaping tablespoons tomato paste
1/4 cup olive oil	1 tablespoon fresh lemon juice
1/2 medium onion, chopped	1 tablespoon Worcestershire sauce
3 medium garlic cloves, minced	1/2 teaspoon salt
1 small green bell pepper, chopped	1/2 teaspoon freshly ground black pepper
1 tablespoon minced fresh basil or 3/4 teaspoon dried leaf basil	1/4 teaspoon red (cayenne) pepper
1/2 teaspoon dried leaf oregano	8 bacon slices
1 teaspoon minced fresh marjoram or 1/2 teaspoon dried leaf marjoram	Rock salt
	24 shucked oysters, well drained
1 tablespoon minced flat-leaf parsley	24 well-scrubbed oyster shells
1/2 dried bay leaf, crumbled	Grated Parmesan cheese

In a food processor fitted with the steel blade, puree tomatoes in their liquid; set aside. Heat olive oil in a heavy 10-inch skillet over medium heat. Add onion, garlic, bell pepper and herbs. Sauté until onion is wilted and transparent, about 5 minutes. Stir in tomato paste and cook, stirring constantly, 2 to 3 minutes. Stir in the pureed tomatoes. Add lemon juice, Worcestershire sauce, salt, black pepper and cayenne. Simmer 15 to 20 minutes. Taste for seasonings and adjust if necessary; sauce should be slightly piquant. Set aside. Preheat oven to 400F (205C). Cut bacon slices into thirds; lay pieces in a baking pan. Bake in preheated oven until half cooked, 4 to 5 minutes. Remove from pan and drain on paper towels. Line a large baking pan with rock salt. Pat oysters very dry on paper towels. Place 1 oyster in each shell; nest shells into rock salt. Divide the tomato sauce among oysters. Place a bacon strip on each oyster. Top liberally with grated Parmesan cheese. Bake in preheated oven until bacon is crisp and cheese is bubbly and light golden brown, about 10 minutes. Serve hot. Makes 6 appetizers or 4 light entrees.

Fried Crawfish Tails

This is one of the best ways to eat crawfish—it's no wonder that these tidbits are so popular.

Vegetable oil for deep-frying	1 tablespoon granulated garlic
4 eggs beaten with 3 cups milk	1 tablespoon paprika
2 cups yellow cornmeal	4 cups all-purpose flour
2 cups corn flour, page 16	3 lbs. peeled crawfish tails
2 tablespoons red (cayenne) pepper	Tartar Sauce, page 82, or Creole Mayonnaise, page 83
1 tablespoon ground black pepper	
1 tablespoon salt	

In a heavy, deep-sided 12-inch skillet, heat 3 inches of oil to 365F (185C), or until a 1-inch bread cube turns golden brown in 65 seconds. Get out 3 medium wire-meshed strainers. In a large bowl, whisk eggs and milk until well blended; set aside. In a medium bowl, combine cornmeal, corn flour and seasonings, tossing with a fork to blend well. Place all-purpose flour in a third bowl. Place a small portion of the crawfish tails in the flour and toss to coat well. Scoop the tails out with one of the fine strainers and shake to remove all excess flour. Transfer tails to a second strainer and dip them into the egg wash, coating well and shaking off excess egg wash. Transfer tails to the seasoned cornmeal and toss to coat well. Remove the tails using the third strainer, shaking off all excess cornmeal. Transfer to a baking sheet in a single layer; set aside while breading remaining crawfish. Be sure that you use the same strainers in the flour, egg wash and cornmeal. Carefully place coated crawfish in batches into preheated oil. Do not crowd the pan or tails will stick together. Fry just until crisp, about 3 minutes per batch. Drain on paper towels. Repeat until all crawfish have been fried. Serve hot with Tartar Sauce or Creole Mayonnaise. Makes 4 to 6 servings.

Grilled Bacon-Wrapped Shrimp

This easy-to-fix dish is perfect for lazy summer evenings when the weather is perfect for cooking and even eating outside. Be forewarned, however, that some people like the shrimp so much they even brave winter's cold to make them!

2 lbs. large peeled and deveined shrimp
1/2 lb. unsalted butter
5 large garlic cloves, minced
1/2 cup bottled Italian salad dressing
2 teaspoons Creole mustard or other
   whole-grain mustard

1/4 cup White Wine Worcestershire sauce
1/2 teaspoon salt
1/2 teaspoon black pepper
1/4 teaspoon red (cayenne) pepper
About 20 bacon slices, cut in half

Wash shrimp thoroughly and pat dry, using paper towels; set aside. Combine remaining ingredients, except bacon slices, in a medium saucepan over medium-low heat. Cook, whisking often, until butter is melted and sauce is well blended. Remove from heat and cool to lukewarm. Arrange the shrimp in a shallow baking pan and pour the sauce over them, making sure all shrimp are coated well. Remove shrimp one by one from sauce and wrap each in a half-slice of bacon. Thread onto skewers and set aside on baking sheets. Pour remaining sauce back into saucepan or bowl. Grill shrimp over a medium-hot charcoal fire until they are opaque and bacon is lightly charred, about 8 minutes, turning twice. Brush shrimp often with the butter sauce while grilling. Serve hot, drizzling each portion with remaining butter sauce. Makes 4 to 6 servings.

Sweet & Spicy Hush Puppies

No meal of fried fish and tartar sauce is complete without hush puppies, and every Louisiana cook thinks he or she makes the best. Each one is probably right! I never tire of the story of the origin of hush puppies. It so fits the slow way of life we enjoy. South Louisiana has always had an over-abundance of yapping, precious little yellow mongrel dogs. Because kitchens on big plantations did not have doors, dogs would come begging when dinner preparation started. There was always more than enough corn bread batter waiting to be baked and always a great pot of hot lard hanging in the fire. The cook would take several handfuls of batter and throw them into the hot fat. When they floated to the top, she would fish them out and toss them to the dogs with the stern admonishment "Hush, puppy!"

1-1/2 cups water
3/4 cup unsalted butter or margarine
2 cups plus 2 tablespoons yellow cornmeal
1/2 cup sugar
2 teaspoons salt

3 large garlic cloves, minced
2 medium pickled jalapeño chilies, minced
2 teaspoons baking powder
1/3 cup minced green onions
Vegetable oil for deep-frying

In a heavy 2-quart saucepan over medium heat, combine water and butter or margarine. Bring to a full boil. Meanwhile, blend cornmeal, sugar, salt, garlic, jalapeños, baking powder and green onions in a large bowl. Stir boiling water mixture into cornmeal mixture until all dry ingredients are moist. Let mixture stand until cool enough to handle. Heat 3 inches of oil to 350F (175C), or until a 1-inch bread cube turns golden brown in 65 seconds. Form dough into 2-inch-long ovals by rolling between the palms of your hands. Put 8 or 9 at a time into the hot oil; do not crowd the pan. Cook, turning once, until deep golden brown, 4 to 5 minutes total. Drain on paper towels. Repeat until all batter has been used, making sure that oil maintains a consistent temperature. Serve hot. Makes about 24 hush puppies.

Mustard-Fried Catfish

Mustard-battered catfish is very popular in Cajun country. Some of the best catfish I've ever had was cooked by this method at a fishing camp deep in the Atchafalaya Basin, a tranquil and primeval marshland wilderness outside of Henderson, Louisiana.

6 (10- to 12-oz.) catfish, cleaned,
   beheaded, skinned
Vegetable oil
2 cups prepared yellow mustard
3 eggs, well beaten
1 teaspoon Tabasco sauce
1 cup corn flour, page 16, or
   very finely ground cornmeal
1 cup yellow cornmeal

1 cup all-purpose flour
1 cup Italian-seasoned bread crumbs
2 teaspoons salt
1 teaspoon garlic powder
1 teaspoon freshly ground pepper
1 teaspoon Hungarian paprika
Lemon wedges
Green onions

Pat fish dry with paper towels; set aside. In a heavy 12-inch skillet, heat 1 inch of oil to 350F (175C) or until a 1-inch bread cube turns golden brown in 65 seconds. In a medium bowl, combine mustard, eggs and Tabasco sauce. Pour mixture into a 13'' x 9'' baking dish. In a medium bowl, combine all remaining ingredients except lemon wedges; pour into another 13'' x 9'' baking dish. Dredge fish in mustard mixture, turning to coat all surfaces. Dip fish in cornmeal mixture, turning to coat well. Shake off excess. Gently place fish, 2 or 3 at a time, in preheated oil. Fry until golden brown and crispy, 6 to 7 minutes on each side, turning once. Drain on paper towels. Serve hot with lemon wedges. Makes 4 to 6 servings.

Baked Flounder & Tomatoes

In summer, when tomatoes reach ripe perfection in the garden next to the basil, and flounder are plentiful, this dish can't be beat for taste and ease of preparation.

1 (3- to 3-1/2-lb.) whole flounder,
   head removed, cleaned
1/2 cup unsalted butter or margarine, melted
Salt to taste
Freshly ground black pepper
1 medium onion, halved lengthwise, sliced
3 tablespoons minced fresh basil or
   1 tablespoon dried leaf basil

2 large ripe tomatoes, sliced
1 tablespoon Creole mustard or
   other stone-ground mustard
1/4 teaspoon red (cayenne) pepper
2 cups dry white wine
Lemon slices
Basil sprigs or curly-parsley sprigs

Preheat oven to 375F (190C). Lightly butter bottom of a 13'' x 9'' baking pan. Place flounder in buttered baking pan; drizzle melted butter or margarine over surface. Season with salt and pepper. Spread onion over fish; scatter basil over onions. Top with sliced tomatoes. In a small bowl, combine mustard, cayenne and wine; pour into baking pan. Bake in preheated oven until fish turns from transparent to opaque, 20 minutes. Using 2 long spatulas, place fish on a serving platter; keep warm. Place baking pan over high heat; rapidly reduce pan juices by 1/2. Pour reduced sauce over fish; serve hot. Garnish with lemon slices and basil or parsley sprigs. Makes 4 to 6 servings.

How to Make Mustard-Fried Catfish

1/Dredge fish in mustard mixture, turning to coat all surfaces.

2/Dip mustard-coated fish in cornmeal mixture, turning to coat well.

3/Fry coated fish in hot oil until golden brown and crispy.

4/Drain cooked fish on paper towels. Serve hot with lemon wedges.

Flounder Rockefeller with Crawfish-Buttercream Sauce

The rich and delicate taste combinations in this dish make it simply divine. The sauce, made from butter ground with whole boiled crawfish—shells, heads and all—is so delicious you'll want to use it with other fish dishes too.

6 (6- to 8-oz.) flounder fillets, skinned
Rockefeller Filling, see below
2 tablespoons fresh lemon juice
3 tablespoons unsalted butter or margarine, melted

Crawfish-Buttercream Sauce, see below
Spinach leaves
Lemon slices

Rockefeller Filling:
2 (10-oz.) pkgs. frozen chopped spinach, thawed
2 tablespoons unsalted butter or margarine
3 large garlic cloves, minced
1 tablespoon all-purpose flour
1/2 cup whipping cream

1 teaspoon Herbsaint or other anise-flavored liqueur
1/4 teaspoon red (cayenne) pepper
1/2 teaspoon freshly ground black pepper
Salt to taste
2 eggs, slightly beaten

Crawfish-Buttercream Sauce:
1/2 pound cooked crawfish in shells
1/2 cup unsalted butter or margarine, cut into 1-inch cubes
1/2 pint whipping cream (1 cup)
1/2 cup Seafood Stock, page 14, or bottled clam juice

1 teaspoon Worcestershire sauce
1/4 teaspoon freshly ground black pepper
1/4 teaspoon red (cayenne) pepper
Salt to taste

Pat flounder fillets dry with paper towels; set aside. Make Rockefeller Filling. Lay fillets on a work surface; place equal amounts of filling in center of each fillet. Fold both ends of fish over filling, overlapping at center. Lift carefully; place, seam-sides-down, in an ungreased 13'' x 9'' baking pan. Drizzle fish bundles with lemon juice, then with melted butter or margarine. Refrigerate until ready to bake, if making ahead. Preheat oven to 375F (190C). Bake in preheated oven until fish turns from transparent to opaque, 15 minutes. Meanwhile, prepare Crawfish-Buttercream Sauce. Carefully place cooked fish on individual plates. Top with sauce; serve hot. Garnish plates with fresh spinach leaves and lemon slices. Makes 4 to 6 servings.

To prepare Rockefeller Filling, press out all moisture from spinach. In a heavy 10-inch skillet over medium heat, melt butter or margarine. Add drained spinach and garlic; saute 2 minutes over medium heat, stirring often. Sprinkle with flour; stir in flour. Stir in whipping cream, liqueur, cayenne and black pepper. Season with salt. Cook 3 to 4 minutes, stirring. Cool spinach mixture slightly. Stir eggs into warm filling mixture; set aside.

To prepare Crawfish-Buttercream Sauce, in a food processor fitted with the steel blade, combine crawfish in shells and butter or margarine. Process until pureed, stopping to scrape down side of bowl often. Set aside. In a heavy 2-quart saucepan over medium-high heat, reduce whipping cream by 1/2. Add Seafood Stock or clam juice; reduce by 1/2. While cream and stock are reducing, press crawfish butter through a very fine strainer or tamis, using a rubber spatula or the palm of your hand. Extract as much pure butter as possible, leaving minute particles of shell behind in strainer. Reduce heat; whisk strained crawfish butter into reduced mixture, a spoonful at a time, continuing until all butter has been added. Remove from heat; whisk in Worcestershire sauce. Season with black pepper, cayenne and salt. Make about 3 cups.

Pompano en Papillote with Champagne Sauce

Pompano was elevated to regal status with the creation of this impressive dish at the turn of the century by Jules Alciatore, then proprietor of Antoine's Restaurant. Ask the fish market to save you the pompano carcasses for the sauce.

Unsalted butter for buttering papillotes
8 (4- to 6-oz.) skinned pompano fillets, or
   substitute another fish fillet

1/2 cup unsalted butter or margarine, melted
   with 2 tablespoons fresh lemon juice
Salt and freshly ground pepper
3 egg whites, beaten until very frothy

Champagne Sauce:
1/2 cup unsalted butter
3 tablespoons minced French shallot
8 oz. sliced mushrooms
8 oz. lump crabmeat
1 teaspoon minced fresh tarragon or 1 teaspoon
   dried leaf tarragon
1/2 teaspoon salt
1/4 teaspoon freshly ground black pepper
1 tablespoon White Wine Worcestershire sauce

2/3 cup dry Champagne
1/2 cup Seafood Stock, page 14, bottled clam
   juice or stock made from Knorr fish bouillon
   cube
2 cups whipping cream
3 tablespoons unsalted butter, softened, and well
   blended with 3 tablespoons all-purpose flour so
   that no unblended traces of flour remain
1 teaspoon Tabasco sauce

Cut 6 (15" x 12") parchment paper sheets. Fold parchment sheets in half on the 15-inch side. Using a pencil, draw half-heart shapes starting at folds. The hearts should extend from top to bottom and side to side of folded sheets. Using scissors, cut out hearts. Lay the hearts open on work surface so that heart shapes open to the left like a book. Butter the right-hand portion of the heart to within 1-1/2 inches of the edge. Lay a pompano or other fish fillet on each buttered papillote and brush fish with the butter and lemon mixture. Salt and pepper each fillet. Using a pastry brush, paint the unbuttered edges of papillotes with egg white. Fold the left half of heart over, sealing the 2 halves at egg-white border. Starting at the top center of heart, on the fold, seal papillotes using overlapping pleats, continuing to bottom tip of heart. Paint the pleated edge liberally with egg whites and repeat the pleating a second time. When you reach the bottom tip of the heart, twist the paper 3 or 4 times, corkscrew fashion. Give pleats a final coat of egg white to form a tight seal. Lay sealed papillotes in a single layer on baking sheets. Refrigerate up to 12 hours before baking. Prepare sauce. Preheat oven to 375F (190C). Bake the papillotes 15 minutes, or until they are puffed and paper is golden brown. Place on individual serving plates. Using a sharp knife, slit each papillote down the middle and spoon a portion of the sauce inside. Serve hot. Makes 6 servings.

To prepare Champagne Sauce, melt butter in a heavy 12-inch skillet over medium heat. Add shallots and mushrooms; cook, stirring often, until mushroom liquid has evaporated, about 10 minutes. Add crabmeat, tarragon, salt, pepper and White Wine Worcestershire sauce to skillet. Stir to blend well. Add Champagne and Seafood Stock; cook until reduced to a glaze. Add whipping cream and stir thoroughly. Cook just to bring to a full boil. Add the blended butter and flour mixture and whisk until sauce has thickened. Stir in Tabasco sauce and remove pan from heat.

Blackened Redfish

This now-world-famous dish certainly needs no introduction. Since the original edition of this book was written, "blackening" has become an accepted cooking method for just about every kind of food from potatoes to prime rib, and I heartily support it. The initial rage of blackened redfish almost decimated the supply of redfish and resulted in significant regulations on the harvesting of the fish. Now, redfish are being farmed and a good supply of those perfectly sized, 6-oz. fillets are available on a regular basis, with no guilt attached! Or, you may substitute another fish with firm flesh and strong connective tissue, such as red snapper, grouper, tilefish or drum. I have also used salmon fillets with great-tasting results. If you try salmon, substitute dill weed for the thyme in the butter sauce. A few pointers are still in order for the home cook preparing blackened anything.

The fish fillets must be no thicker than 1/2 inch. You MUST use a solid cast-iron skillet to cook this dish. Do not attempt to use any other type of skillet, or you will ruin the skillet and possibly create a serious fire hazard. The best way to blacken is on an open-flame butane burner outside. If this is not possible, be forewarned that the cooking process will create great clouds of smoke. Two precautions: (1) If you have smoke detectors, disarm them before proceeding; (2) if you have a cooktop with a space-saver microwave/vent-hood overhead, do not attempt to prepare this dish. The butter sauce from the fish may ignite because of the intense heat; it almost always does when using electric heat, on the first fish cooked. The flames, of course, would ruin the microwave. Keep a snug-fitting lid for your skillet close at hand. Should flaming occur, do not panic! Merely place the lid on the skillet momentarily to smother the flames and proceed with cooking. Even if you are ardently devoted to using fresh herbs, as I certainly am, it is important to use dried herbs in this recipe. The minced particles of fresh herbs char and burn immediately in the intense heat involved, giving the fish an acrid and bitter taste.

6 redfish fillets, about 1/2- to 3/4-inch thick, skinned	1 teaspoon salt
2-1/2 cups unsalted butter or margarine	2 teaspoons freshly ground black pepper
1/2 cup fresh lemon juice	1 tablespoon dried leaf thyme
1-1/2 teaspoons red (cayenne) pepper	Curly-parsley sprigs
	Lemon wedges

Place fish fillets on a cutting board; trim off any thin edges and very thin tip of tail. If left on, these thin areas will char and break away. Pat fillets dry with paper towels; cover and refrigerate until ready to cook. The butter sauce adheres better to cold fillets. In a heavy 3-quart saucepan over medium heat, melt butter; add lemon juice, cayenne, salt, black pepper and thyme. Stir to blend seasonings; cool to lukewarm. Place an EMPTY 10-inch cast-iron skillet over HIGH heat until bottom has a definite white haze and begins to smoke slightly. Remove fish from refrigerator; dip 1 fillet in warm butter sauce, coating well. Place fish in hot skillet, taking care that spits and spatters do not burn you. The fish will sear and cook almost immediately. Turn fillet over; blacken other side. Repeat with remaining fillets, cooking no more than 2 at a time. Reserve remaining butter sauce. As fillets are cooked, place them on individual plates; keep warm. Remove and discard any accumulated butter sauce and charred bits between batches. When all fish have been cooked, quickly remove skillet from heat; discard any accumulated butter sauce and charred bits. Immediately place empty skillet back on heat. Add reserved butter sauce; carefully swirl skillet 5 or 6 times to blacken butter. Remove pan from heat; drizzle butter over each fillet. Garnish with parsley sprigs and lemon wedges. Serve hot. Makes 4 to 6 servings.

Crabmeat-Stuffed Flounder

Stuffed flounder has long been a popular dish on New Orleans restaurant menus. The fish may be completely assembled ahead, refrigerated and baked when ready to serve.

1 (2-1/2- to 3-lb.) flounder, head removed, cleaned	**1 teaspoon red (cayenne) pepper**
3/4 lb. backfin lump crabmeat	**1-3/4 cups shredded Monterey Jack cheese (7 oz.)**
1/4 lb. mushrooms, chopped	**1 cup unsalted butter or margarine**
3/4 cup dry bread crumbs	**Juice of 1 lemon**
6 green onions, chopped	**12 lemon slices**
1/4 cup minced parsley, preferably flat-leaf	**Hungarian paprika**
1 teaspoon salt	**Curly-parsley sprigs**

Preheat oven to 350F (175C). Lightly grease a baking sheet; set aside. Lay flounder, dark-side up, on a cutting board with tail nearest to you. Using a sharp, thin-bladed knife or boning knife, start about 3/4-inch from head, make a slit down midline to one-half inch from where tail begins. Cut into fish until you feel knife touch bone in middle. Now, starting at top, carefully work knife into slit, keeping knife against bones and working toward outside edge. Separate flesh from bones all way to outside fins on both sides of center slit, taking care not to pierce skin. Turn fish over so that white side is facing up. Starting at head end, carefully slip knife between bones and bottom fillet of fish. Working toward tail and both sides with knife always against bones, separate fillet from bones. The bones should now be completely separated from meat on both sides. Working from slit on top and from head end, use your fingers to gently tear bones loose from side fins. When you reach tail end, snip bones free using kitchen shears. Use tweezers or small pliers to remove any bones remaining at side edges. Place fish on greased baking sheet; refrigerate while preparing stuffing. Place crabmeat in a medium bowl. With your fingers, carefully pick through crabmeat; remove and discard any bits of shell or cartilage. Do not break up lumps of crabmeat. Add mushrooms, bread crumbs, green onions, parsley, salt, cayenne and cheese. Toss gently to combine ingredients. Melt butter or margarine in a small saucepan; set aside 1/3 cup. Add remaining melted butter or margarine to crabmeat mixture; toss gently to blend. Carefully stuff crabmeat mixture into boned flounder, mounding it toward middle. Pat top down over filling. Drizzle lemon juice over fish and exposed stuffing. Using a pastry brush, brush fish with reserved butter or margarine. Place lemon slices, slightly overlapping, down center of fish; lightly dust top with paprika. Bake in preheated oven until stuffing is light golden brown and fish turns from transparent to opaque, 25 minutes. Using 2 long spatulas, carefully place fish on a serving platter. Garnish with parsley sprigs. Makes 4 to 6 servings.

If fish smells a little *fishy*, try this. Place fish in a shallow dish; add enough milk, blended with a tablespoon or two of fresh lemon juice, to cover. Cover tightly and refrigerate for an hour. Do not leave the fish in the milk bath for longer than an hour, because the lactic acid in the milk will break down the connective tissue in the fish and it will tend to fall apart when cooked. Drain fish, pat dry on paper towels and use as desired. This step can often salvage fish that you have kept a bit too long before using.

How to Make Crabmeat-Stuffed Flounder

1/Carefully work knife into center slit, keeping knife against bones and working toward outside edge.

2/Using your hand, remove loosened bones through front opening.

3/Stuff flounder with crabmeat mixture, mounding it toward middle.

4/Use 2 long spatulas to place baked flounder on a platter. Garnish with parsley.

Vegetables & Rice

South Louisiana is richly blessed with a growing season that extends throughout most of the year. What a treat it is to wander through the stalls at the French market and see the colorful patterns formed by the bins of fresh vegetables. There are golden yellow kernels of corn peeking out of fresh green husks, brilliant, scarlet-red Creole tomatoes lined up in row after row, shiny green bell peppers piled precariously high—all just waiting to be chopped and tossed into a big pot.

Cajun-Creole vegetable-cooking methods have really "taken it on the chin" from the nutrition-conscious, al dente-vegetable advocates. It is quite true that most Cajun-Creole home-cooked vegetables are overcooked and that they are cooked in large quantities of water into which all of their nutrients leach. Ah, but the taste of those vegetables will provide the victor's edge in any such discussion. It is that magical and complex taste created by combinations of vegetables and seasonings cooking down for hours that forms an integral part of *la bouche Creole,* or the Creole mouth.

In defense of the Cajun-Creole method of overcooking vegetables, let me say that even though most of the vitamins and minerals do leach out into the excessive liquid during the long cooking times, they are not completely lost. In fact, that excessive liquid, which becomes a rich and flavor-packed broth, is one of the most important taste aspects of the dish. In South Louisiana it is called *pot likker,* and is usually served in bowls with the vegetable.

When cooking any type of dried beans, the Cajuns and Creoles like to cook them until they start to break down to a pulpy consistency. What a delicious and smooth

Lousiana "Down-Home" Sunday Supper

New Orleans Seafood Filé Gumbo, page 31
Chicken Fricassee, page 65
Marinated Carrot Salad, page 49
Creole Sweet-Potato Pone
Creole Corn Pudding
New Orleans French Loaves, page 42
Ponchatoula Strawberry Shortcake, page 117

gravy-like sauce they make. Some of us believe that the bean gravy is the best part, especially when combined with rice.

All members of the onion family are aromatic vegetables. The leek, like the true shallot, is rarely used in Cajun-Creole cooking. The yellow onion is the most bold-flavored member of the family and should be used in dishes that will be cooked. In uncooked dishes such as potato salad or sandwiches, use either white onions or red onions.

Greens are a mainstay of the Cajun-Creole diet. The most commonly used varieties are spinach, turnip, mustard and collard greens. Often supper consists of a big pot of mixed greens with onions, turnips and a bit of seasoning meat, cooked for several hours and served in a big bowl with corn bread on the side. The most important thing to remember in preparing greens is that they are generally grown in slightly sandy soil and must be washed thoroughly.

South Louisianans eat a great many of the old-fashioned, or non-trendy vegetables, transforming the dull tastes of strange-looking things, such as turnips, rutabagas and kohlrabi, into something mighty good, using a pinch of this and a dab of that.

The Cajuns and Creoles prepare dishes from the lowly sweet potato that are so delicious that they must be divinely inspired. Louisiana is second only to North Carolina in sweet-potato production. There's even a Yamboree each year in Opelousas to celebrate the harvest and give an opportunity to sample sweet potatoes prepared by every method under the sun.

One of the best-kept vegetable-seasoning secrets is the pinch of sugar that the Cajuns add to their vegetables! Sugar acts as a marvelous flavor enhancer, adding a definite flavor perk. There is never enough sugar to make the vegetables taste sweet, but enough to let you know that there is something very unique about those vegetables!

The Cajuns and Creoles use herbs extensively to flavor vegetables. If you have fresh herbs available, all the better! If you gain nothing else from this chapter, I hope that you will be inspired to experiment with vegetables. Who knows, you may gain so much love for down-home vegetables that you will feel compelled to serve Mixed Greens with Turnips & Tasso at your next sit-down dinner for 12. Just discreetly tuck a bib under the edge of the bowl and tell your guests that greens are "in" this year.

Mixed Greens with Turnips & Tasso

Greens are good for you, everybody's heard that one. But not everybody knows that greens are just plain good, too. They're an institution in Cajun country. The best way to enjoy them is to serve them on the side in a bowl with lots of juice. The Cajuns call this juice *pot likker*. It is the custom to pick up the bowl and drink the likker after the greens have been eaten. For a real down-home meal, serve a large soup plate of greens and pot likker with Cajun Corn Bread, page 126. Be sure each bowl gets some tasso or ham.

1 large bunch each: fresh collard greens, mustard greens, turnip greens and kale, or any combination
2 medium onions, halved lengthwise, sliced thin
2 medium turnips, peeled, halved lengthwise, sliced thin

4 oz. tasso, below, or substitute a good-quality smoked ham, such as Hormel Cure-81
3 tablespoons sugar
1/2 cup picante sauce
1 tablespoon salt
1 tablespoon freshly ground pepper

Place all greens in sink or a large pot; fill to brim with lukewarm water. Let greens stand 15 minutes. Carefully remove greens from water without disturbing sandy silt which has settled to bottom. Wash leaves under running water; tear leaves into small pieces, removing tough ribs. Place torn greens, onions, turnips and tasso or ham in a 10- to 12-quart soup pot; fill to top with water. Add sugar, picante sauce, salt and pepper. Bring to a boil over medium-high heat; boil 5 minutes. Reduce heat. Barely simmer, stirring occasionally, 3 hours. Taste for seasoning; adjust if necessary. Greens should have lots of liquid left; add more water if necessary. Serve hot; enjoy one of the greatest Cajun treats. Makes 8 to 10 servings.

Creole Stewed Okra & Tomatoes

In South Louisiana, stewed okra with tomatoes is like an old shoe—good and comfortable. Serve with grilled, broiled or roasted meats, poultry or fish.

2 tablespoons vegetable oil
2 tablespoons bacon drippings
1 medium onion, halved lengthwise, sliced thin
3 large garlic cloves, minced
1 (28-oz.) can peeled tomatoes, diced, and their liquid

2 (10-oz.) pkgs. frozen sliced okra
1/2 teaspoon freshly ground black pepper
1 teaspoon sugar
Salt to taste

Heat vegetable oil and bacon drippings in a heavy 3-quart saucepan over medium heat. When fat is hot, add remaining ingredients and stir to blend well. Cook, stirring often, for about 1 hour, or until mixture is very wilted. Taste for seasoning and adjust if necessary. Skim any fat from surface and serve hot in small side dishes. Makes 4 to 6 servings.

Tasso is a smoked pork or beef seasoning meat made from poor-quality meat cuts. The meat is coated with a very spicy seasoning mixture and slow smoked until hard and very flavorful.

Rosemary Potatoes

This delicious dish, which makes use of leftover baked potatoes, is sure to become a house favorite. Fresh rosemary, if available, is an added enhancement. The dish is great with steaks, or serve with any grilled or broiled meats, fish or poultry.

2-1/2 lbs. small red new potatoes, scrubbed and halved
1/2 cup extra-virgin olive oil
1 tablespoon all-purpose Cajun seasoning blend

1/2 teaspoon minced fresh rosemary
1 tablespoon sugar
1 large onion, halved lengthwise, sliced thin

Preheat oven to 350F (175C). Place potatoes in a single layer in a shallow baking pan. Pour olive oil over potatoes and toss to coat well. Combine the Cajun seasoning, fresh rosemary and sugar. Scatter half of the mixture over the potatoes. Bake in preheated oven about 25 minutes, stirring occasionally. Scatter the sliced onions over the potatoes and stir to coat with oil. Scatter the remaining seasoning blend over the top and bake an additional 25 minutes, or until potatoes are tender. Serve hot. Makes 4 to 6 servings.

Three-Layer Vegetable Casserole

This recipe was adapted from one given to me by Peg Lee, Director of the Rice Epicurean Cooking School in Houston, Texas. It originally came from France and is very similar in nature to casseroles which I have eaten in Cajun homes. The assertive seasonings make this dish an excellent accompaniment to game dishes. Use fresh herbs if at all possible; the difference in taste is pretty remarkable.

1 (16-oz.) can navy beans and their liquid
12 medium garlic cloves, minced
1 tablespoon minced fresh thyme or 1 teaspoon dried leaf thyme
2 tablespoons minced fresh basil or 2 teaspoons dried leaf basil
1 tablespoon minced fresh savory or 1 teaspoon dried leaf summer savory
1/4 cup olive oil

1 bunch fresh spinach, washed and torn into bite-size pieces
1 large red bell pepper, blistered, peeled and diced
1 medium zucchini, sliced
1 medium yellow squash, sliced
6 large mushrooms, sliced
1/3 cup Italian-seasoned bread crumbs, mixed with 3 tablespoons grated Parmesan cheese

Preheat oven to 400F (205C). Transfer navy beans to a small bowl and stir to separate beans; set aside. Combine the minced garlic and herbs in a small bowl and toss to blend well; set aside. Heat the olive oil in a heavy 12-inch skillet over medium heat. Add the beans and one-third of the garlic and herb mixture. Cook, stirring often, until bean gravy has reduced by about half, about 8 minutes. Turn the beans out into a 10-inch au gratin dish or casserole, spreading them evenly over the bottom; set aside. Add a little more olive oil to the skillet and return pan to medium heat. When oil is hot, add the spinach, diced bell pepper and another third of the garlic and herb mixture. Stir-fry just until spinach is wilted, about 2 minutes. Spread the spinach mixture evenly over the beans. Again, add more olive oil to the skillet and return to medium heat. When oil is hot, add the zucchini, yellow squash, mushrooms and the remaining garlic and herb mixture. Cook, stirring often, until squash is barely wilted, about 7 minutes. Spread the mixture over the spinach layer. Scatter the bread-crumb mixture over the top of the squash. Bake in preheated oven for 20 minutes, or until bubbling and golden brown on top. Serve hot. Makes 4 to 6 servings.

Vegetable Jambalaya

This tasty dish makes an excellent one-dish accompaniment to a simple meat or fish dish, providing starch and vegetables in a single dish.

1/2 cup extra-virgin olive oil
1 medium onion, chopped
1 small green bell pepper, chopped
1 celery stalk, chopped
3 medium garlic cloves, minced
1/2 cup finely diced yellow squash
1/2 cup finely diced peeled eggplant
1/2 cup frozen green peas
2 teaspoons sugar

2 cups long-grain white rice
1 large tomato, peeled and chopped
3 cups beef or chicken stock
1 teaspoon minced fresh marjoram or
    1/2 teaspoon dried leaf marjoram
1/2 teaspoon freshly ground black pepper
1/4 teaspoon red (cayenne) pepper, or to taste
3 green onions, chopped, including green tops
2 tablespoons minced flat-leaf parsley

In a heavy, deep-sided skillet, heat olive oil. Add onions, bell pepper, celery, garlic, squash, eggplant, peas and sugar; cook until vegetables are wilted, about 5 minutes, stirring occasionally. Add the rice and cook, stirring constantly, until grains are lightly browned, about 7 minutes. Add tomato and stir to blend. Cook 2 minutes. Stir in stock. Add marjoram, black pepper and cayenne. Reduce heat, cover and simmer until rice is tender and no liquid remains, about 40 minutes. Taste for seasonings and adjust if needed. Add green onions and parsley, stirring to combine. Cover and cook an additional 10 minutes. Serve hot. Makes 6 to 8 servings.

Cajun Maque-Chou

Maque-chou (pronounced *mock-shoe*), is a wonderful Cajun dish based on corn. When preparing this dish, the Cajuns always use the kernels from young, tender corn, scraped fresh from the cob.

2 tablespoons vegetable oil
2 tablespoons bacon drippings
4 cups fresh corn kernels, scraped from about
    6 large cobs, or substitute 2 (10-oz.) pkgs.
    frozen corn kernels
1 large onion, chopped

1 medium green bell pepper, chopped
1 teaspoon salt
1/2 teaspoon freshly ground black pepper
1 tablespoon sugar
1/4 teaspoon red (cayenne) pepper
1-1/2 cups whipping cream

Heat vegetable oil and bacon drippings in a heavy 12-inch skillet over medium heat. Add remaining ingredients except whipping cream and stir to blend well. Sauté, stirring often, until corn kernels have started to brown lightly, about 15 minutes. Do not let kernels stick to bottom of pan. Add the whipping cream and stir to blend, scraping up browned bits from bottom of pan. Cook just until cream has reduced to form a gravy, about 10 minutes. Serve hot. Makes 4 to 6 servings.

To peel tomatoes easily, drop the whole tomato into a deep pot of boiling water for about 20 seconds. Remove and run under cold water. The skin should now slip off quite easily.

Creole Sweet-Potato Pone

This classic Cajun dish is a must at holiday meals and the perfect accompaniment to any baked poultry dish.

4 large sweet potatoes (about 2 lbs.),
  peeled, quartered
1/2 cup unsalted butter or margarine
2 eggs, slightly beaten
1/2 pint whipping cream (1 cup)
1 teaspoon vanilla extract
2 tablespoons light-brown sugar
1/2 teaspoon ground cinnamon
1/2 teaspoon ground allspice

1/2 teaspoon ground cloves
Dash of freshly grated nutmeg
1/2 cup golden raisins
1/2 cup flaked coconut
1 teaspoon grated orange zest
1 teaspoon grated lemon zest
1/2 cup all-purpose flour
1 tablespoon baking powder
Topping, see below

Topping:
1 cup firmly packed light-brown sugar
1/2 cup unsalted butter or margarine,
  room temperature

1/2 cup finely chopped pecans
1/2 cup Grape Nuts cereal

Place quartered sweet potatoes in a heavy 5- to 6-quart saucepan; add enough water to cover. Bring to a boil over high heat. Reduce heat; simmer until potatoes are very tender, 20 minutes. Drain well; mash. Preheat oven to 350F (175C). Lightly butter a 13'' x 9'' baking dish. In a heavy 1-quart saucepan, melt butter or margarine over medium heat; cook until nut-brown in color, about 7 minutes. Stir browned butter or margarine and remaining ingredients except Topping into mashed sweet potatoes, blending well. Spread mixture into buttered baking dish; set aside. Prepare Topping. Sprinkle Topping evenly over sweet-potato mixture. Bake in preheated oven until golden brown and bubbly, 30 minutes. Serve hot. Makes 6 to 8 servings.
To prepare Topping, in a medium bowl, combine all topping ingredients.

Creole Corn Pudding

Corn Pudding is a delicious vegetable side dish that is very traditional in the Deep South. It is a perfect accompaniment to roast pork or poultry.

1 (20-oz.) can cream-style corn
1 tablespoon sugar
1 teaspoon salt
1/2 teaspoon freshly ground pepper
1/4 cup unsalted butter or margarine, melted

5 eggs, well beaten
1 cup milk
1/2 pint whipping cream (1 cup)
1 tablespoon cornstarch mixed with
  1 tablespoon cold water

Preheat oven to 350F (175C). Lightly butter a 13'' x 9'' baking dish. In a medium bowl, combine all ingredients. Spoon into buttered baking dish. Bake in preheated oven until custard is firm and knife inserted off center comes out clean, 1 hour. Serve hot. Makes 6 to 8 servings.

Sweet-Potato Puffs

For years this recipe has been served to dignitaries from around the globe. Its creation is attributed to Blanche Long, wife of former Louisiana governor, Earl K. Long. The puffs are made ahead and baked while still frozen.

**4 large sweet potatoes (2 lbs.),
 peeled, quartered**
1/4 cup unsalted butter or margarine, melted
1/2 teaspoon salt
2 tablespoons light-brown sugar
1 teaspoon ground nutmeg

1 teaspoon ground cinnamon
2 egg yolks, slightly beaten
12 large marshmallows
2 cups cornflake crumbs
1/4 cup unsalted butter or margarine, melted

Place sweet potatoes in a heavy 5- to 6-quart saucepan; add enough water to cover. Bring to a boil over high heat. Reduce heat; simmer until potatoes are very tender, 20 minutes. Immediately drain well; cool slightly. Mash cooled potatoes. In a medium bowl, combine mashed sweet potatoes, 1/4 cup butter or margarine, salt, brown sugar, nutmeg, cinnamon and egg yolks. If mixture is too soft to shape, refrigerate until chilled. Flatten 1/3 cup sweet-potato mixture into a 3-inch circle; place a marshmallow in center. Gather sweet-potato mixture around marshmallow to enclose, leaving a small hole at top. Set aside. Repeat with remaining sweet-potato mixture and marshmallows. In a medium bowl, combine cornflake crumbs with remaining 1/4 cup butter or margarine. Roll puffs in buttered crumbs, turning to coat well. Place on a baking sheet; freeze until solid. If not baking immediately, place frozen puffs in a plastic freezer container; store up to 2 months. To bake, preheat oven to 350F (175C). Bake frozen puffs 20 minutes; serve hot. Makes 12 puffs.

How to Make Sweet-Potato Puffs

1/Place a marshmallow in center of sweet-potato mixture. Gather mixture around marshmallow to enclose.

2/Roll puffs in buttered crumbs, turning to coat well.

Creole Spinach Mousse   *Photo on page 105.*

These tasty individual mousses will add an elegant touch to any meal. They are simple to prepare.

1-1/2 (10-oz.) pkgs. frozen chopped spinach
2 tablespoons unsalted butter or margarine
1 large garlic clove, minced
2 green onions, minced
1 tablespoon all-purpose flour
1/2 cup milk

1/2 cup whipping cream
1 teaspoon Herbsaint
1/2 teaspoon salt
1/4 teaspoon freshly ground black pepper
1/4 teaspoon red (cayenne) pepper
2 eggs

Preheat oven to 350F (175C). Thoroughly butter 6 (1/2-cup) ramekins; set aside. Butter 1 side of a 13'' x 9'' parchment-paper sheet. Thaw spinach completely; press out all moisture from spinach. In a heavy 10-inch skillet over medium heat, melt butter or margarine; add pressed spinach, garlic and green onions. Cook 5 minutes; add flour, stirring to blend well. Cook 4 minutes, stirring constantly. Combine milk and cream; add to spinach mixture in a slow, steady stream. Add Herbsaint and seasonings; cook 5 minutes. Cool slightly. Lightly beat eggs; fold beaten eggs into spinach mixture. Pour into buttered ramekins. Place ramekins in a 13'' x 9'' baking dish. Add about 3 cups boiling water; put parchment paper, buttered-side-down, on ramekins. Bake in preheated oven until mousses are set, 25 to 30 minutes. Remove from water bath; unmold carefully onto serving plates. Serve hot. Makes 6 servings.

Variation
Sprinkle two sieved, hard-cooked egg yolks on a serving plate. Place mousses on egg yolks. Decorate with fresh thyme leaves and lemon-peel twists.

Chili-Cheese Grits Piquant

Grits are by no means just for breakfast in Cajun-Creole country. They're too good to be so limited! This spicy casserole makes an excellent vegetable dish for a buffet.

2-1/4 cups water
3/4 cup slow-cooking grits
6 tablespoons unsalted butter or margarine, room temperature
6 oz. processed cheese, cut into 1/2-inch chunks

3 jalapeño peppers, seeds and veins removed, minced
1 medium, red bell pepper, chopped
4 green onions, chopped
1 teaspoon salt
2 eggs, slightly beaten

Preheat oven to 325F (165C). Butter a 13'' x 9'' baking dish. In a heavy 2-quart saucepan over medium-high heat, bring water to a boil; add grits. Reduce heat to medium; cook, stirring often, until mixture begins to thicken, about 20 minutes. Remove from heat; stir in butter or margarine, cheese, jalapeño peppers, bell pepper, green onions and salt. Blend well. Fold in eggs; spoon mixture into buttered baking dish. Bake in preheated oven until bubbly and lightly browned, 45 minutes. Makes 4 to 6 servings.

To easily remove moisture from thawed frozen spinach, place spinach in a pie pan. Set another pie pan over spinach. Over the sink, holding pie pans vertically in your hands, press pans together. Liquid will be pressed from spinach and drain into the sink!

Sweet-Sour Rutabagas

The rutabaga, like its cousin, the turnip, is not a front-runner among trendy foods—and what a shame. It's delicious and a nice change of pace.

4 medium rutabagas
1/2 cup bacon drippings
1 large onion, chopped
1 teaspoon salt

1/2 teaspoon freshly ground pepper
1 tablespoon sugar
1/4 cup cider vinegar
6 green onions, chopped

Fill a 5-quart saucepan half full of water; bring to a boil over medium-high heat. Add rutabagas; cook until almost tender, about 10 minutes. Drain and cool to room temperature. Dice cooled rutabagas into 1/2-inch cubes; set aside. Heat bacon drippings in a heavy 12-inch skillet over medium heat. Add rutabaga cubes and onion; cook, stirring often, until onion is wilted and golden brown, about 15 minutes. Add salt, pepper and sugar; cook 5 minutes. Add vinegar; stir quickly, scraping up browned bits from bottom of pan. Cook until liquid has evaporated to a glaze, 6 to 7 minutes. Stir in green onions. Serve hot. Makes 4 to 6 servings.

Broccoli & Rice Casserole with Cress Sauce

Serve this robust-flavored vegetable dish with grilled steak, broiled fish or baked chicken for a most enjoyable meal.

3 cups tightly packed broccoli flowerets or
   2 (10-oz.) pkgs. frozen chopped broccoli
1/2 cup unsalted butter or margarine
3 large garlic cloves, minced
1 large bay leaf, minced

1/2 cup dry bread crumbs
3 cups cooked white rice
3 hard-boiled eggs, sliced
Cress Sauce, see below

Cress Sauce:
1 cup packed watercress leaves and
   tender stems
1/4 cup chopped parsley,
   preferably flat-leaf
3 green onions, coarsely chopped
1/2 teaspoon dill weed or
   1-1/2 teaspoons minced fresh dill

1/2 teaspoon dried leaf basil or
   1-1/2 teaspoons chopped fresh basil
1/2 cup mayonnaise
1 teaspoon Creole mustard or
   other stone-ground mustard
1/8 teaspoon curry powder
1/4 teaspoon red (cayenne) pepper
Salt to taste

Preheat oven to 350F (175C). Lightly grease a 3-quart casserole dish. Steam broccoli flowerets over rapidly boiling water until almost tender, 4 to 5 minutes. Cool slightly; coarsely chop. Or thaw and drain frozen broccoli. Set aside. In a medium saucepan, melt butter or margarine. Add garlic and bay leaf; cook over medium-low heat 5 minutes. Fold in bread crumbs, tossing to coat bread crumbs well. Stir in rice and chopped broccoli; turn into prepared casserole. Top with sliced eggs. Bake in preheated oven 20 minutes. While casserole is cooking, prepare sauce. Top casserole with sauce; bake 5 minutes. Serve hot. Makes 4 to 6 servings.
To prepare Cress Sauce, in a food processor fitted with the steel blade, combine all sauce ingredients. Process until pureed, stopping 2 or 3 times to scrape down side of bowl.

Scalloped Onion & Almond Casserole

Another great make-ahead dish for your next buffet dinner, this dish has a unique and delicate taste.

20 small pearl onions (about 1/2 lb.)
6 tablespoons unsalted butter or margarine
4 celery stalks, chopped
5 green onions, chopped
5 tablespoons all-purpose flour
1 teaspoon salt
1/2 teaspoon freshly ground pepper

1 teaspoon Tabasco sauce
2-1/4 cups half and half
2/3 cup sliced blanched almonds
1/2 cup grated Parmesan cheese (1-1/2 oz.)
Toasted sliced almonds, if desired
Celery leaves, if desired

Preheat oven to 350F (175C). Lightly butter a 1-1/2-quart casserole dish. Using a sharp knife, cut off and discard root end from each onion; set onions aside. Fill a 4- to 6-quart saucepan half full of water; bring to a boil over medium-high heat. Add onions; parboil 1 minute. Drain into a colander; place under running water to cool. When onions are cool enough to handle, peel by grasping between your thumb and forefinger at stem end and squeezing lightly. The peel should slip off easily. Set peeled onions aside. In a heavy 12-inch skillet over medium heat, melt butter or margarine. Add celery; cook 5 minutes. Add peeled onions and green onions; stir to blend. Sprinkle flour into skillet; stir until combined. Cook 3 to 4 minutes, stirring. Blend in salt, pepper and Tabasco sauce. Slowly stir in half and half. Cook about 5 minutes; fold in 2/3 cup almonds and cheese. Pour into buttered baking dish. Bake in preheated oven until bubbly and lightly browned, 25 minutes. Top with toasted almonds and celery leaves, if desired. Makes 6 to 8 servings.

Spinach & Artichoke Stuffed Tomatoes

This colorful vegetable dish is an excellent accompaniment to grilled fish, such as Grilled Shark Steak, page 81. The tomatoes can be completely prepared ahead of time and baked when ready to serve.

3 large, firm tomatoes
Salt to taste
Freshly ground black pepper
1 (6-oz.) jar marinated artichoke hearts
1 (10-oz.) pkg. frozen chopped spinach,
    thawed
4 green onions, chopped
2/3 (3-oz.) pkg. cream cheese,
    room temperature

1 tablespoon unsalted butter or margarine
2 tablespoons dairy sour cream
1 teaspoon dried leaf oregano or
    1 tablespoon chopped fresh oregano
1/2 teaspoon salt
1/2 cup grated Parmesan cheese (1-1/2 oz.)
2 tablespoons unsalted butter or margarine,
    melted
1/2 cup dry bread crumbs

Preheat oven to 350F (175C). Halve tomatoes crosswise. Carefully scoop out and discard pulp and seeds, taking care not to puncture shells. Sprinkle inside of each tomato with salt and pepper; set aside. Drain artichoke hearts; chop drained artichokes. Press out all moisture from spinach. In a medium bowl, combine pressed spinach, chopped artichoke hearts and green onions. In a food processor fitted with the steel blade, combine cream cheese, 1 tablespoon butter or margarine, sour cream, oregano, 1/2 teaspoon salt and Parmesan cheese. Process until pureed. Fold cream-cheese mixture into vegetables until blended. In a small bowl, combine 2 tablespoons butter or margarine and bread crumbs with a fork. Stuff tomato halves with spinach filling; top with buttered bread crumbs. Place in 13'' x 9'' baking dish; bake in preheated oven until heated through, 10 minutes. Do not overcook. Serve hot. Makes 6 servings.

Clockwise from top left: Scalloped Onion & Almond Casserole; Spinach & Artichoke Stuffed Tomatoes; Creole Spinach Mousse, page 102

Spinach Rice

Trust this easy-to-fix dish to add the perfect touch to any meal.

1 (10-oz.) pkg. frozen chopped spinach
1/2 cup unsalted butter or margarine
1 small onion, chopped
4 green onions, chopped
2 tablespoons minced parsley,
  preferably flat-leaf
1 teaspoon freshly ground black pepper

1/4 teaspoon red (cayenne) pepper
1/2 teaspoon ground ginger
Salt to taste
3 cups cooked white rice
1/4 cup dry sherry

Thaw frozen spinach thoroughly; press out all moisture. In a deep 12-inch skillet over medium heat, melt butter or margarine. Add onion; cook until slightly wilted and transparent, about 5 minutes. Add drained spinach, green onions, parsley, black pepper, cayenne, ginger and salt. Cook, stirring, 5 minutes. Add rice; stir until combined. Add sherry; cook until heated through and bubbly, about 5 minutes. Spoon into a serving dish. Makes 4 to 6 servings.

Cajun "Dirty" Rice

Cajuns and Dirty Rice are like pancakes and syrup—they just belong together. There is rarely an occasion involving food where Dirty Rice is not served. The dish meets the basic requirements for Cajun family fare: It is filling, it is cooked in one big pot, it will feed a lot of people for a little money and, most important, it is delicious. The authentic cooking method given here is time-consuming but well worth the effort. Even if you despise chicken livers and gizzards, you will love Dirty Rice. Neither livers nor gizzards are detectable as such. They become a part of the overall taste. Serve Dirty Rice as a side dish or as the main dish.

1 lb. chicken or turkey gizzards
1/2 lb. chicken, duck or turkey livers,
  or a combination
1 cup sausage or bacon drippings
2 medium onions, finely chopped
1 large green bell pepper, finely chopped
2 celery stalks, finely chopped
4 large garlic cloves, minced
3 cups Louisiana Brown-Poultry Stock,
  page 14, or canned chicken broth

1 teaspoon freshly ground black pepper
3/4 teaspoon red (cayenne) pepper or
  to taste
Salt to taste
1/4 cup minced parsley, preferably flat-leaf
6 green onions, chopped
4 cups cooked white rice

Using a small, sharp knife, remove tough outer skin from gizzards by scraping meat from skin. Keep blade of knife at an angle against skin as you scrape. Place gizzards and livers in a food processor fitted with the steel blade; process until pureed. Heat drippings in a heavy 5- to 6-quart Dutch oven over medium heat; add gizzard-liver mixture. Cook, stirring, until mixture is browned, about 10 minutes. Add additional drippings, if necessary, to prevent sticking. Add onions, bell pepper, celery and garlic; cook until vegetables are slightly wilted and transparent, about 5 minutes. Add stock or broth, black pepper, cayenne and salt, scraping bottom of pan to release any browned bits of meat. Reduce heat to low; cook, stirring often, until thickened, about 45 minutes. Fold in parsley, green onions and rice, blending well. Cook just to heat through. Serve hot. Makes 6 to 8 servings.

Stir-fried Spinach with Squash & Pine Nuts

This zesty and colorful vegetable dish is one of my favorite examples of the great flavor combinations being introduced into Cajun-Creole foods.

1/4 cup olive oil
4 oz. sliced mushrooms
4 large garlic cloves, minced
2 large red bell peppers, roasted, peeled and diced
1 medium yellow squash, halved lengthwise, sliced thin
1 medium zucchini, halved lengthwise, sliced thin

5 green onions, sliced on the diagonal
1/2 teaspoon salt
1/2 teaspoon freshly ground black pepper
1/3 cup julienne strips of fresh basil
1 pkg. fresh spinach, washed, dried and torn into bite-size pieces
1/4 cup toasted pine nuts
1/4 cup grated Parmesan cheese

Heat olive oil in heavy 14-inch skillet over medium heat. Add mushrooms and garlic; cook, stirring often, until mushrooms are wilted and liquid has evaporated. Stir in red bell peppers, yellow squash and zucchini. Cook, stirring constantly, to barely heat the squash through. Add green onions and seasonings; stir to blend. Add basil strips, spinach and pine nuts. Toss and cook just to barely wilt (NOT COOK) the spinach. Remove from heat and toss in the Parmesan cheese, blending well. Serve at once. Makes 10 to 12 servings.

Cooking Great Rice!

Rice is not only a mainstay of the diet in South Louisiana. Rice production accounts for a large portion of the state's economy, too. Cooking perfect rice, with slightly firm grains that don't stick together (even when reheated) is very easy if you follow the guidelines that I learned many years ago from Kristen O'Brien of the Rice Council of America.

Here's a couple of handy pointers to help in multiplying rice quantities. Always use one part rice to two parts liquid. The liquid can be anything! If you are serving rice with a chicken dish, use chicken broth—beef broth for a beef dish, etc. Add a little salt and melted butter to the cooking liquid.

When you come across one of those maddening recipes that call for a certain amount of *cooked* rice and you need to know how much raw rice to start with, use this formula: divide the amount of cooked rice indicated in the recipe by three. This will give you the amount of raw rice which you need. The remaining portion will be your liquid. For example, if the recipe calls for 6 cups of cooked rice, one-third would be 2 cups of raw rice, leaving 4 cups of liquid!

When estimating the quantity of rice you need to cook, use the following guideline: each cup of raw rice will produce 3 cups of cooked rice (1 cup of rice plus 2 cups of liquid). The following recipe will make 3 cups of cooked rice.

2 cups liquid, such as water or stock
1 tablespoon unsalted butter or margarine

1/2 teaspoon salt
1 cup long-grain white rice

Combine the liquid, butter or margarine and salt in a heavy, 2-quart saucepan over high heat. Bring to a full boil, then stir in the rice. Cover and reduce heat to lowest setting. Set a timer for exactly 15 minutes. When the timer buzzes, transfer the rice to a serving dish and cover until ready to serve, *even if there is still a small portion of liquid remaining.* By the time you have put the rest of the meal together, the rice will be perfect.

Desserts

The subject of desserts in South Louisiana needs no long-winded introduction. The Cajuns and Creoles like desserts. Fine restaurants throughout the area have extensive dessert menus offering a vast array of sinfully delicious, cream-and-butter-laden goodies. New Orleans' fine hotels and restaurants have been training grounds for some of the country's finest dessert and pastry chefs.

Fresh fruit is a favorite dessert ingredient, with the emphasis on Louisiana-grown varieties. Plaquemines Parish oranges, Ruston peaches and Ponchatoula strawberries are sliced, diced, mashed, pureed, sectioned and cooked into hundreds of irresistibly mouth-watering dessert dishes. Chocolate is another popular ingredient.

Many desserts which are considered passé in other areas of the country have never lost popularity in South Louisiana. This is a fact for which I give thanks each time I indulge in one of the dozens of rich and gooey crepe dishes popular in the area. Humble bread pudding is far and away the number-one dessert, and there are as many recipes for it in South Louisiana as there are stoves. Each version has its own delightful personality.

One of the best desserts ever born of South Louisiana's cuisine is found only in Creole homes—which is unfortunate, because visitors rarely get to taste it. It is

Frozen Creole Cream Cheese. It is one of the few dishes that will cut through the ravages of the unbearably hot and humid weather of South Louisiana to really cool your bones! It is like ice cream, but much richer. It is like frozen yogurt, but much better.

Of course, to make frozen Creole Cream Cheese, you must first have Creole cream cheese! The bad news is that it is usually not available outside of the New Orleans area. Produced by several of New Orleans' oldest creameries, Creole cream cheese is similar in taste and consistency to a combination of sour cream and cream cheese. It

is often served for breakfast—right out of the container or topped with fresh fruit.

For years I have talked about Frozen Creole Cream Cheese all over the country—and I've fed it to anybody who came to visit, always with the underlying frustration of knowing they couldn't have it again. I finally took matters into my own hands and made a frontal assault on the creameries of New Orleans, "How is Creole Cream Cheese made?" I cried. Most, believe it or not, were very cooperative. After much testing—scaling things down from 500 gallons to 3 cups and substituting readily available ingredients—I determined that it is possible for anyone to make Creole Cream Cheese, and therefore, Frozen Creole Cream Cheese. The recipes repose quietly in the pages of this chapter—sleeping giants of taste.

Although the Cajun-Creole cuisine does indeed boast some very elegant and complicated dessert preparations, it is also loaded with rich-and-enticing down-home desserts, the likes of which can make a grown man cry. To ferret out the secrets of these desserts, I turned once again to the ultimate sources of great regional food—the covered-dish suppers, church socials, country fairs and treasured meals in private homes of every social strata. Researching this chapter I added 15 pounds, but I enjoyed every butter-dripping ounce of it!

Crepe Soufflé with Custard Sauce

Here is a delightfully light dessert that is the perfect ending to an elegant meal.

Custard Sauce, from Bittersweet-Chocolate Cake, page 118

Filling, see below
8 Sweet Crepes, page 120

Filling:
6 egg whites, room temperature
3 cups powdered sugar, sifted

Grated zest of 1 large orange

Prepare Custard Sauce as directed on page 118. Prepare Filling. Preheat oven to 400F (205C). Place crepes on a large ungreased baking sheet. Spread filling mixture over 1/2 of each crepe, then fold remaining half over to cover filling. Bake in preheated oven until filling has risen and browned lightly, about 10 minutes. Immediately place 2 crepes on each serving plate; cover with Custard Sauce. Serve immediately. Makes 4 servings.

To prepare Filling, in a medium bowl, beat egg whites with an electric mixer until very soft peaks form. Beat in sugar until smooth and glossy and stiff peaks form. Beat in orange zest.

Cajun-Country Bread Pudding with Rum Sauce & Chantilly Cream

1 (16-oz.) loaf French bread, cut into
  1-inch cubes and dried
3 eggs
1-1/2 cups sugar
3/4 cup unsalted butter, melted
2 tablespoons vanilla extract
1 teaspoon freshly grated nutmeg

1-1/2 teaspoons ground cinnamon
3 cups milk
3/4 cup golden raisins
3/4 cup flaked coconut
1/2 cup coarsely chopped toasted pecans
Rum Sauce, see below
Chantilly Cream, see below

Rum Sauce:
1 cup unsalted butter, softened
1-1/2 cups sugar

2 eggs, beaten until frothy
1/2 cup dark rum

Chantilly Cream:
1 pint (2 cups) whipping cream
1/3 cup powdered sugar, sifted
1 tablespoon vanilla extract

2 tablespoons cognac or other brandy
2 tablespoons Frangelico liqueur
1/4 cup dairy sour cream

Put dried bread cubes into a 14" x 10" baking pan; set aside. Combine eggs and sugar in bowl of electric mixer. Beat at medium speed until thickened and light lemon-yellow in color, 3 to 4 minutes. Add melted butter, vanilla, nutmeg, cinnamon and milk. Beat to blend well. Add the raisins, coconut and pecans; beat to incorporate. Pour the mixture evenly over the bread cubes in the baking pan and stir to distribute the raisins, nuts and coconut throughout. Press the bread cubes down into the liquid using the back of a large spoon. Set the pudding aside until all liquid has been absorbed by the bread, about 30 minutes. Preheat oven to 350F (175C). Bake in preheated oven until crusty and golden brown on top, 45 to 50 minutes. While pudding is baking, prepare Rum Sauce and Chantilly Cream. Cool bread pudding to lukewarm. Slice into squares. Place a portion of rum sauce in bottom of each serving bowl; add a square of bread pudding. Top with a generous dollop of chantilly cream. Makes about 15 servings.

To prepare Rum Sauce, using an electric mixer, cream butter and sugar at medium speed until light and fluffy, about 5 minutes. Using a rubber spatula, transfer creamed butter to the top of a double boiler. Place over simmering water and cook 20 minutes, whisking often and vigorously, until mixture is smooth and silky in texture. Whisk 1/4 cup of the butter mixture into the beaten eggs, then whisk the now-warmed eggs into the double boiler, beating vigorously. Continue to cook, whisking constantly, until mixture is thickened, about 3 to 4 minutes. Whisk in rum and remove from heat. Serve hot. The rum sauce may be prepared ahead of time, refrigerated and reheated when ready to serve.

To prepare Chantilly Cream, chill beaters and mixer bowl until very cold. Place all ingredients in bowl and beat at medium-high speed until soft, loose peaks form, 3 to 4 minutes. The cream should have a slightly runny, cloudlike consistency that softly drapes over the bread pudding. Do not overbeat. Cover tightly with plastic wrap and refrigerate until ready to serve.

Fresh Peach Pie

You have to go far and wide to find a dessert better than peach pie made from ripe and juicy peaches just a few hours off the tree. If you do find such a dessert, I'll wager it's much more difficult to prepare than this one!

Double recipe Flaky Pie Pastry, below
1/2 pint whipping cream (1 cup)
1/4 cup all-purpose flour
1 cup sugar
1/2 teaspoon ground cinnamon

1/2 teaspoon freshly grated nutmeg
6 large peaches, peeled, sliced,
   tossed with lemon juice
Vanilla ice cream or Frozen Creole Cream
   Cheese, page 114, if desired

Preheat oven to 350F (175C). Prepare pastry as directed below; divide into 2 equal pieces. Wrap 1 pastry piece in plastic wrap; refrigerate until ready to use. On a lightly floured surface, roll out remaining pastry to a 1/16-inch-thick circle. Roll pastry loosely around rolling pin; unroll into a 9-inch pie pan. Gently lower pastry into bottom of pan; lightly press against side. Do not stretch pastry. Cut away excess pastry, leaving a 1/2-inch overhang at edge; set aside. In a medium bowl, whisk cream, flour, sugar, cinnamon and nutmeg until smooth. Pour 1/2 of cream mixture into prepared pie shell. Add sliced peaches, spreading evenly; pour remaining cream mixture over top. On a lightly floured surface, roll out remaining pastry as directed above. Place pastry over filling. Cut off excess pastry, leaving about a 1-inch overhang at edge. Tuck edge of top pastry securely under edge of bottom pastry. Flute edges, if desired, or press pastry against edge of pan using tines of a fork. Cut 2 rows of steam vents in top of pastry. Bake in preheated oven until golden brown, 35 to 40 minutes. Cool slightly. Serve hot. For a sinfully rich addition, top each slice with a scoop of vanilla ice cream or Frozen Creole Cream Cheese. Makes 8 servings.

Flaky Pie Pastry

To make flaky pie pastry in a food processor, the butter or margarine must be frozen.

1 cup all-purpose flour
1/2 cup frozen unsalted butter or margarine,
   cut into 1-inch chunks

Pinch of salt
3 to 4 tablespoons iced water

Place flour, butter or margarine and salt in a food processor fitted with the steel blade. Turning on and off, process just until butter or margarine is in pea-sized chunks. With machine running, slowly add enough water through feed tube to form a soft, moist dough. Do not process until mixture forms a ball. Turn mixture out onto a lightly floured surface; using your hands and a pastry scraper, bring mixture together to form a ball. Do not overwork. Wrap in plastic wrap; refrigerate 30 minutes. Use as directed in recipe. Or roll out chilled dough and bake as directed below. On a lightly floured surface, roll out chilled dough in 1 direction only to 1/16-inch thick circle. Loosely roll pastry around rolling pin; unroll into an 8- or 9-inch pie pan, letting pastry fall into place. Gently ease pastry into bottom of pan; pat against side. Do not stretch. If stretched, pastry will shrink when baked. Preheat oven to 400F (205C). If baking pastry blind or without filling, prick pastry with a fork. Line with foil; fill with rice, dried beans or metal pie weights. Bake in preheated oven 15 minutes. Carefully remove foil and weights; bake until golden brown on bottom. Makes 1 (8- or 9-inch) pie crust.

Variation
For a sweet crust, add 2 teaspoons sugar along with flour, butter and salt.

Sweet Potato-Pecan Pie

The best of two South Louisiana favorites, sweet potatoes and pecans, are baked up into one delicious pie in this easy to prepare recipe.

1 recipe Flaky Pie Pastry, opposite
Filling, see below

Topping, see below

Filling:

2 tablespoons unsalted butter or margarine, melted
1 cup cooked, mashed sweet potatoes (1 large sweet potato)
2 eggs, slightly beaten
3/4 cup firmly packed light-brown sugar
1/2 teaspoon ground ginger

1/2 teaspoon ground cinnamon
1/2 teaspoon freshly grated nutmeg
1 teaspoon vanilla extract
1/2 teaspoon salt
1/2 cup dark corn syrup
1 cup evaporated milk
1-1/2 cups coarsely chopped pecans

Topping:

1 pint whipping cream (2 cups)
3 tablespoons powdered sugar

1/4 cup Praline Liqueur or Frangelico
Pecan halves

To prepare Pastry, prepare pastry and chill as directed opposite. Preheat oven to 375F (190C). On a lightly floured surface, roll out chilled pastry into a 1/16-inch-thick circle. Gently roll pastry around rolling pin; unroll into a 9-inch pie pan. Gently ease pastry into bottom of pan; pat against side. Do not stretch pastry. Trim off and discard excess pastry. Flute edges, if desired. Refrigerate until ready to bake.

To prepare Filling, in a large bowl, stir butter or margarine into sweet potatoes. Add all remaining ingredients except pecans; blend well.

To assemble pie, pour sweet-potato filling into prepared pie crust; sprinkle chopped pecans evenly over top. Bake in preheated oven until filling is set and a knife inserted into center comes out clean, 40 to 45 minutes. Cool in pan on a rack to room temperature before slicing. Prepare topping. To serve, top with topping. Top with pecan halves. Makes 8 servings.

To prepare Topping, combine cream, powdered sugar and liqueur in a large bowl. Beat with an electric mixer until large, soft peaks form. Refrigerate, covered, until ready to serve.

New Orleans Butter Pralines

New Orleans pralines—and that's pronounced PRAH-leens, to set the record straight—are unique among pralines. They contain butter and milk to give them a softer, almost chewy texture. The taste is addictive.

2 cups granulated sugar
1 cup firmly packed light-brown sugar
1/2 cup unsalted butter or margarine
1 cup milk

2 tablespoons light corn syrup
3 cups pecan halves
2 teaspoons vanilla extract

Place 2 large parchment-paper sheets on baking sheets; butter parchment paper. Set aside. Combine all ingredients except vanilla in a heavy 2-quart saucepan over medium heat. Bring mixture to a boil, stirring often. Cook to soft-ball stage, 234F (114C). Remove from heat; stir in vanilla. Stir briskly until mixture loses its glossy sheen. **WORKING QUICKLY,** drop mixture by tablespoons onto buttered paper. Let pralines cool completely before removing from paper. Store at room temperature in an airtight container. Makes 24 pralines.

How to Section Oranges

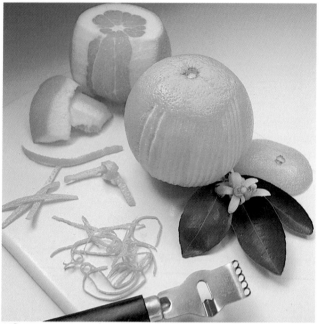

1/Orange zest can be removed with a zester. To peel, remove zest and all bitter, white pith with a vegetable peeler or small knife.

2/To section peeled oranges, with a sharp paring knife, cut down on each side of membranes to free sections. Lift out sections.

Louisiana Lemon Chess Pie

This classic country pie is a snap to prepare and is easy on the budget—two main considerations of its Cajun creators. It also tastes wonderful.

1 recipe Flaky Pie Pastry, page 110
2 cups sugar
1 tablespoon all-purpose flour
1/4 cup cornmeal
4 eggs, slightly beaten

1/4 cup unsalted butter or margarine, melted
1 cup milk
1/4 cup fresh lemon juice
1/4 cup grated lemon zest

Preheat oven to 350F (175C). Prepare pastry and chill according to directions on page 110. On a lightly floured surface, roll out pastry into a 1/32-inch-thick circle. Gently roll crust around rolling pin; unroll into a 9-inch pie pan. Gently ease pastry into bottom of pan; pat against side. Do not stretch pastry. Trim excess pastry off edges and discard. Flute edges, if desired. Refrigerate until ready to bake. In a medium bowl, combine sugar, flour and cornmeal with a fork. Add remaining ingredients; stir until blended. Pour filling into prepared pie crust. Bake in preheated oven until a knife inserted in center comes out clean, 45 minutes. Cool on a rack to lukewarm before slicing. Makes 8 servings.

Satsuma Cake

Satsumas are small, thin-skinned mandarin oranges grown in South Louisiana. They are wonderfully sweet and used in a wide variety of dishes. You may substitute other oranges in the recipe.

2-1/2 cups cake flour, sifted
4-1/2 teaspoons baking powder
1-1/2 cups sugar
1 teaspoon salt
1/2 cup unsalted butter or margarine,
  room temperature
1 tablespoon grated Satsuma zest or
  other orange zest

1 teaspoon orange extract
1 tablespoon vanilla extract
3/4 cup Satsuma or other orange juice
1/4 cup milk
4 egg whites, room temperature
Satsuma Filling, see below
Satsuma Butter Cream, see below
Satsuma or other orange sections

Satsuma Filling:
1/4 cup unsalted butter or margarine,
  room temperature
1-1/4 cups sugar
1/2 cup cornstarch
2 (12-oz.) cans frozen orange-juice
  concentrate, thawed

1 tablespoon grated lemon zest
2 tablespoons grated Satsuma or
  other orange zest
1 pint whipping cream (2 cups)
4 egg yolks, beaten until frothy

Satsuma Butter Cream:
1/3 cup all-purpose flour
1 cup milk
1/2 cup Satsuma or other orange juice

1-1/2 cups sugar
2 teaspoons vanilla extract
1-1/2 cups unsalted butter or margarine

Preheat oven to 350F (175C). Butter and flour 2 (9-inch) springform pans, shake out all excess flour. Cut 2 (9-inch) parchment-paper circles; place circles in pans. Butter and flour circles in pans, again shake out excess flour. Set pans aside. Sift all dry ingredients into a medium bowl. Add all ingredients through milk. Beat on low speed 1 minute to blend. Increase speed to medium; beat 2 minutes, scraping down side of bowl as necessary. Add milk and egg whites. Beat 2 minutes on medium-high. Pour equal amounts of batter into each prepared pan. Bake in preheated oven until center of cake springs back when pressed lightly with fingertips, 20 minutes. Cool in pans on racks 10 minutes. Remove from pans; invert cakes on wire racks. Remove parchment. Cool layers completely. Prepare filling. Prepare butter cream. When layers have cooled completely, cut in half crosswise using a serrated knife. Set 3 layers aside; place last layer on a serving plate; spread with a layer of filling. Carefully place a second cake layer on top. Spread with filling. On top of filling, spread a layer of Satsuma sections. Place a third cake layer over sections. Top with another layer of filling, and finally, place remaining cake layer on top. Frost cake with butter cream; decorate, if desired, with Satsuma sections. Makes 1 (9-inch) layer cake.
To prepare Satsuma Filling, using an electric mixer, in a medium bowl, cream butter or margarine and sugar until light and fluffy. Place mixture in top of a double boiler set over simmering water; melt mixture, whisking often. Meanwhile, in a medium bowl, stir cornstarch and orange-juice concentrate until cornstarch is completely dissolved. Add all remaining ingredients except egg yolks to orange-juice mixture. Add orange-juice mixture to melted butter mixture; whisk over simmering water until thickened. Cover and cook 5 minutes without stirring. Remove orange-filling mixture from heat. Add 1/2 cup hot filling mixture in a slow, steady stream to egg yolks, rapidly whisking yolks while pouring. Whisk warmed egg-yolk mixture slowly into remaining filling mixture; whisk 2 to 3 minutes. Cool slightly. Cover and refrigerate until chilled.
To prepare Satsuma Butter Cream, in a medium saucepan, combine flour and milk; whisk to dissolve flour lumps. Cook over medium heat until thick. Whisk in juice. Cool to room temperature. In a medium bowl, cream sugar, butter or margarine and vanilla with an electric mixer until light and fluffy. Add sugar mixture to flour mixture; beat with electric mixer until light. Cover and refrigerate until slightly chilled.

Homemade Creole Cream Cheese

Creole cream cheese is an old New Orleans treat which is, unfortunately, not usually available outside of South Louisiana. It is eaten for breakfast or dessert topped with fresh fruit. Or it is enjoyed as Frozen Creole Cream Cheese, below, a favorite New Orleans dessert. Making cheese at home is a lengthy procedure, but it is worth the effort. Rennet tablets are available in the baking-supply section in supermarkets.

1/2 gallon skim milk
1 rennet tablet

1/2 cup buttermilk
1 cup nonfat dry milk

In a large saucepan, heat skim milk to 170F (75C); hold at that temperature 20 minutes. This is most easily accomplished in a microwave oven with a temperature probe and HOLD feature. Use a nonmetallic bowl for the microwave. Immediately stir in rennet tablet, buttermilk and nonfat dry milk until blended. Cover with plastic wrap; let stand at room temperature 24 hours to clabber. After 24 hours, carefully drain and discard liquid from cheese. Line a large, fine strainer with a double thickness of cheesecloth; place over a deep bowl. Carefully turn clabber into strainer. Cover with plastic wrap and refrigerate. Let drain 36 hours. Place finished cheese in a bowl; use as desired. Creole cream cheese can be covered and refrigerated up to 2 weeks. Makes 24 ounces.

Frozen Creole Cream Cheese

This dessert, enjoyed in Creole homes as a respite from the beastly hot and humid weather, is one of New Orleans best kept secrets. Enjoy it right out of the ice-cream freezer at backyard cookouts, or serve with sauces for a more elaborate presentation. Recipe can be halved.

3 recipes (72 oz.) Creole Cream
** Cheese, above**
1 qt. milk

1 qt. whipping cream (4 cups)
3 cups sugar
3 teaspoons vanilla extract

Using back of a wooden spoon, mash Creole Cream Cheese through a medium strainer into a large bowl. Add milk, cream and sugar; stir until blended. Stir in vanilla. Pour mixture into an ice-cream freezer; freeze according to manufacturer's directions. Keep frozen until ready to serve. Serve with Easy Strawberry Sauce, page 117, or Chocolate-Sherry Sauce, page 116, if desired. Makes 1 gallon or 12 to 15 servings.

Rennet is an enzyme used in cheese making.

Bananas Foster

Bananas Foster, next to bread pudding, is probably the most well-known of all South Louisiana dishes. Through the years, it has been flamed in some of the finest restaurants. It remains a strong favorite today.

1/3 cup firmly packed light-brown sugar
1 teaspoon ground cinnamon
1/4 cup unsalted butter or margarine
1/2 cup creme de banana or
    other banana liqueur

1/2 cup dark rum
4 bananas, halved lengthwise
4 scoops rich vanilla ice cream
Mint sprigs, if desired

In a small bowl, combine brown sugar and cinnamon with a fork; set aside. In a heavy 12-inch skillet or flambé pan, melt butter or margarine over medium heat. Add cinnamon-sugar mixture; stir until sugar melts. Pour in banana liqueur and 1/4 cup rum; cook, stirring, until syrupy and thickened, about 5 minutes. Add bananas; lightly coat with syrup. Add remaining 1/4 cup rum. Swirl pan; ignite rum. Quickly swirl pan. Cook, basting bananas with sauce, until flame goes out. Remove from heat; place 2 banana slices on each of 4 plates, side by side. Place a scoop of ice cream on top of each serving; drizzle with sauce. Decorate with mint, if desired. Serve immediately. Makes 4 servings.

How to Make Bananas Foster

1/Ignite rum. Cook, basting bananas with sauce, until flame goes out.

2/Place a scoop of ice cream on top of bananas; drizzle with sauce. Decorate with mint, if desired.

Creamy Chocolate & Bourbon Pie

Variations of this rich pie are served throughout the Deep South. It's right at home in South Louisiana, where folks do like their bourbon. The next time you bring dessert, bring this one. It'll be a hit!

Chocolate Crust, see below
Filling, see below

Chocolate Crust:
1-1/4 cups chocolate-wafer crumbs
1 tablespoon sugar

Filling:
21 large marshmallows
1 cup evaporated milk
1/2 pint whipping cream (1 cup)

Topping:
1/2 pint whipping cream (1 cup)
2 tablespoons powdered sugar

Topping, see below
2 oz. semisweet chocolate, grated

3 tablespoons unsalted butter or margarine, melted

3 tablespoons bourbon
1/2 cup chopped pecans

1 teaspoon vanilla extract

To prepare Crust, preheat oven to 350F (175C). In a medium bowl, toss all ingredients with a fork until crumbs are moist. Spoon mixture into a 9-inch pie pan; pat into bottom and side. Bake crust in preheated oven 10 minutes. Cool slightly. Cover and refrigerate until chilled.

To prepare Filling, combine marshmallows and evaporated milk in a heavy 3-quart saucepan over medium heat. Cook until marshmallows melt, about 10 minutes, stirring often. Do not boil. Cool slightly; cover and refrigerate 1 hour. In a medium bowl, with an electric mixer, beat whipping cream and bourbon until medium-stiff peaks form. Fold pecans into chilled marshmallow mixture. Fold in whipped cream until blended.

To assemble pie, pour filling into chilled crust; smooth top. Cover and refrigerate until set, about 4 hours. To serve, prepare topping. Spread on chilled pie; top with chocolate. Makes 8 servings.

To prepare Topping, in a medium bowl, beat cream, sugar and vanilla until stiff peaks form.

Chocolate-Sherry Sauce

This sauce, in various versions, was a staple dessert sauce for cakes or puddings in the Old South. Today it is equally good over store-bought pound cake for a quick and wonderful dessert. It is positively decadent over Frozen Creole Cream Cheese, page 114, or your favorite vanilla ice cream. This is a favorite of one of my bosses, Joe Parlongo, at the lodge where I am the chef.

1/2 lb. unsweetened chocolate
1/2 pint (1 cup) whipping cream
1/2 cup unsalted butter, room temperature

1 (1-lb.) box powdered sugar, sifted
1/2 cup cream sherry

In a heavy 2-quart saucepan over medium heat, combine chocolate and cream. Cook, stirring often, until chocolate melts and mixture is smooth and creamy. Set aside. In a medium bowl, with an electric mixer on medium speed, cream butter or margarine and sugar until light and fluffy, about 5 minutes. Spoon sugar mixture into the top of a double boiler set over simmering water; cook, whisking often, until silken and smooth, 20 minutes. Whisk in chocolate mixture; cook, whisking constantly, 5 minutes. Remove from heat; whisk in sherry. Serve warm. Makes 2 cups.

Ponchatoula Strawberry Shortcake

Ponchatoula strawberries are the best in the land. Grown in a small area around Ponchatoula, Louisiana, they are huge, sweet berries that need no adornment at all. I love to eat them right from the strawberry patch.

Shortcake Base, see below
3 pints strawberries
3/4 cup granulated sugar
1 pint whipping cream (2 cups)

2-1/2 tablespoons powdered sugar
2 teaspoons vanilla extract
2 tablespoons kirsch, if desired

Shortcake Base:
3 cups cake flour, sifted
1-1/4 cups all-purpose flour
**1 tablespoon plus 1-1/2 teaspoons
    baking powder**
2 tablespoons plus 1 teaspoon sugar

1-1/2 teaspoons salt
**1/2 cup plus 1 tablespoon unsalted butter
    or margarine, cut into 1-inch chunks**
1-1/4 to 1-1/2 cups whipping cream

Prepare Shortcake Base. Place 1/2 of berries in a medium bowl; add sugar. Using a potato masher, mash berries with sugar to form a chunky puree. Cut remaining 1/2 of berries into pieces, reserving 5 whole berries for decoration. Stir pieces into puree; set aside. Using an electric mixer, beat cream, powdered sugar, vanilla and kirsch, if desired, until medium-stiff peaks form. To serve, split shortcakes in half horizontally; place 1 bottom in each dessert dish. Spoon berries over bottoms; top with cream mixture. Set top of shortcake over cream. Slice reserved 5 berries in half; place a half berry, cut-side-down on each shortcake. Makes 10 servings.

To prepare Shortcake Base, preheat oven to 425F (220C). Lightly grease 2 heavy baking sheets. Sift flours, baking powder, sugar and salt into a 5-quart bowl; resift. With a pastry blender or 2 knives, cut butter or margarine into flour until mixture resembles coarse oatmeal in texture. Add 1-1/4 cups cream; blend with a fork just until all flour is moist. If mixture is too dry to roll out, add remaining cream until dough forms a ball and is slightly sticky. Turn out dough onto a lightly floured surface. Form dough into a ball; knead gently 2 or 3 times. Roll out into a 1/2-inch-thick circle. Using a 3-inch round cutter, cut dough into 10 circles. Place circles on greased baking sheets. Bake in preheated oven until golden brown and flaky, 12 to 15 minutes. Cool on racks.

Easy Strawberry Sauce

Nothing quite sums up the taste of summer like fresh strawberries. They really shine in this sweet and refreshing sauce.

3-1/2 cups strawberries, fresh or frozen
2/3 cup sugar

1/4 cup kirsch, if desired

Place all ingredients in a food processor fitted with the steel blade. Process until pureed. Pour into a serving bowl. If sugar has not dissolved, let stand a few minutes; stir occasionally. Makes 2 cups.

Bittersweet Chocolate Cake

Chocoholics gather 'round—this is the cake you have been waiting for. Ultimately rich and fudge-like, it is guaranteed to satisfy even the strongest chocolate cravings. It is very attractive nestled in a pool of custard sauce and topped with a strawberry half.

1 lb. bittersweet chocolate, chopped
2 cups unsalted butter
1-3/4 cups sugar
11 eggs, separated, room temperature
1-1/2 tablespoons Grand Marnier or
   other orange-flavored liqueur

1 teaspoon vanilla extract
Custard Sauce, see below
8 large strawberries, with tops,
   if desired

Custard Sauce:
1 cup milk
1/2 pint whipping cream (1 cup)
3/4 cup sugar

6 egg yolks, slightly beaten
2 tablespoons Grand Marnier or
   other orange-flavored liqueur

Butter and flour a 12-inch springform pan; shake out all traces of excess flour. Place rack in middle of oven. Preheat oven to 250F (120C). In a very heavy 3-quart saucepan over medium-low heat, combine chocolate and butter. Stir until melted. Cool to room temperature, stirring occasionally. In a large bowl, combine 1-1/2 cups sugar and egg yolks. Beat with an electric mixer on medium speed until mixture is light, fluffy and lemon-colored, 8 to 10 minutes. Fold in cooled chocolate until blended. Set mixture aside. In a medium bowl, beat egg whites until soft peaks form. Beat in remaining 1/4 cup sugar, liqueur and vanilla. Beat until medium-stiff peaks form, about 3 minutes on medium speed. Using a rubber spatula, fold in 1/4 of beaten whites into chocolate mixture to lighten it. Fold in remaining beaten egg whites. Pour batter into prepared pan. Bake in middle of preheated oven until a wooden pick inserted into center comes out clean, 3 hours. Cool in pan on a wire rack 15 minutes. Remove side of pan; cool completely. When cool, remove bottom of springform pan; invert cake onto a serving plate. Refrigerate until chilled. Prepare sauce. To serve, slice strawberries in half. Cut cake into 16 equal pieces; place a strawberry half, cut-side down, on each slice. Pour some sauce onto each serving plate; arrange a slice of cake in middle of sauce. Serve at once. Makes 16 servings.

To prepare Custard Sauce, in a heavy 3-quart saucepan over medium-high heat, bring milk, cream and sugar to a full boil. Whisking constantly, add 1/4 cup hot cream mixture in a slow, steady stream to egg yolks. Reduce heat to medium. Whisk warmed egg-yolk mixture slowly into remaining cream mixture. Whisking constantly, cook until mixture thickens and coats back of a metal spoon, about 3 minutes. This will happen rapidly; do not overcook and scramble eggs. Remove sauce from heat; whisk 3 minutes to cool slightly. Whisk in liqueur; strain sauce through a fine strainer into a 2-quart bowl. Place plastic wrap over custard; refrigerate until chilled. Custard Sauce will keep in the refrigerator 5 days or in the freezer 3 months. If frozen, thaw completely in refrigerator; whisk to smooth texture before serving.

Chocolate melts more easily if it is grated or chopped before melting. High temperature will cause chocolate to be dry and grainy.

Bittersweet Chocolate Cake with Custard Sauce

Praline Crepes

If you keep a supply of crepes in the freezer, putting this dessert together is a breeze. It is so good that your guests will think you cooked all day.

Praline Sauce, see below
4 Sweet Crepes, below

4 scoops Frozen Creole Cream Cheese, page 114, or rich vanilla ice cream

Praline Sauce:
1/4 cup unsalted butter or margarine
1/2 cup powdered sugar
2 tablespoons dark corn syrup

1/4 cup dark rum
1/2 cup chopped pecans

Prepare Praline Sauce. Working quickly, fill each crepe with a scoop of Frozen Creole Cream Cheese or ice cream. Place 1 filled crepe, seam-side down, on each serving plate. Drizzle sauce over crepes; serve at once. Makes 4 servings.
To prepare Praline Sauce, melt butter or margarine in a heavy 2-quart saucepan over medium heat. Add remaining ingredients; stir until blended. Cook, stirring often, until sauce is thick and syrupy, about 7 minutes. Set aside.

Sweet Crepes

Crepes freeze well. Place a layer of waxed paper between each cooled crepe, stack, and place in zip-sealing plastic freezer bags. The frozen crepes may be peeled off as needed! Thaw completely before using.

1 cup all-purpose flour
2 tablespoons sugar
1/4 teaspoon salt
1 egg
1 egg yolk
1 cup milk

1 tablespoon unsalted butter or margarine, melted
1/2 cup water
1 teaspoon vanilla extract
Unsalted butter or margarine

In a medium bowl, combine flour, sugar and salt with a fork. Make a well in center of flour mixture; add egg and egg yolk. Using a fork, slowly begin to mix egg into flour. Continue until all flour has been moistened. Add milk slowly, stirring constantly to form a smooth batter. Stir in 1 tablespoon butter or margarine, water and vanilla until blended. The batter should be the consistency of light cream. If it is too thick, add 1 or 2 teaspoons more water; stir until blended. Cover and let batter stand at room temperature 30 minutes before using. To cook crepes, melt about 1 teaspoon butter or margarine in a 6-inch crepe pan over medium heat, swirling to coat bottom and side. Pour 3 tablespoons batter into pan all at once; swirl pan very quickly to cover bottom with batter. Cook until bottom of crepe is set and golden brown, about 2 minutes. Turn crepe; cook other side about 30 seconds. Cool crepes on paper towels. Repeat with remaining batter. Separate crepes with small sheets of wax paper, if desired. When serving crepes, fill so that first side cooked will be on outside. Makes 24 (6-inch) crepes.

Sugar-Fried Pecans

These irresistible little snacks will be the hit of your next party. They're guaranteed to be one of the most addictive party finger foods you will ever serve! Or serve them scattered over rich vanilla ice cream for a simple, yet delicious, dessert.

1/4 cup sugar
2 tablespoons water
2 cups water

1 cup pecan halves
2 cups peanut oil

In a heavy 1-quart saucepan, combine sugar and 2 tablespoons water. Bring to a boil. Cover 1 minute to wash down any sugar crystals. Uncover; cook to jelly stage, 220F (105C), on a candy thermometer. While syrup is cooking, bring 2 cups water to a boil in a 2-quart saucepan. Add pecans; blanch 3 minutes. Drain in a colander; pat dry with paper towels. Immediately pour hot pecans into sugar syrup; stir until each piece is coated evenly. Remove nuts with a slotted spoon; place on a baking sheet in a single layer, not touching, to cool and dry, 30 minutes. When nuts are cool and dry, heat oil in deep skillet or wok to 240F (115C). Add pecans; fry until milk-chocolate-colored, 7 minutes, stirring gently and constantly. Remove with a slotted spoon; spread on a baking sheet in a single layer to cool. When cool, place on paper towels to remove excess oil. Store thoroughly cooled nuts in a container with a tight-sealing lid. Makes 1 cup.

Chocolate Marquis with Custard Sauce

This wonderful recipe is manna for the devoted chocoholic. It was adapted from the dessert of the same name served at Billy McKinnon's Louisiana Restaurant in Atlanta.

1 lb. bittersweet chocolate, chopped
3/4 cup unsalted butter, softened
7 egg yolks
1-1/2 cups whipping cream
2 tablespoons vanilla extract

2 tablespoons cognac
3/4 cup chopped hazelnuts
Custard Sauce, page 118, substituting
** Frangelico for Grand Marnier**

Thoroughly grease a 9" x 5" bread loaf pan and line with a double thickness of heavy-duty plastic wrap, allowing the wrap to hang over the top edges of the pan by about 3 inches. Set aside. Combine the chocolate and butter in a heavy saucepan over medium-low heat. Cook, stirring often, until chocolate has melted and mixture is smooth and glossy. Remove from heat and set aside. In bowl of electric mixer, beat the egg yolks with whipping cream at medium speed 5 minutes. Transfer mixture to top of double boiler over simmering water and cook, whisking, until mixture has thickened, about 10 minutes. Do not allow the egg mixture to boil. Remove from water and stir in chocolate, vanilla, cognac and hazelnuts, blending well. Pour the mixture into the prepared loaf pan and freeze until solid. When ready to serve, unmold the Marquis onto serving platter and carefully peel off plastic wrap. Using a heavy slicing knife, slice the loaf into slices approximately 1/4 to 1/2 inch thick. Serve on a bed of Custard Sauce. Makes about 20 servings.

Praline Cheesecake

This wonderfully rich and delicious cheesecake captures the very flavor of New Orleans.

Crust, see below
Filling, see below

Topping, see below

Crust:

1 cup graham-cracker crumbs
6 New Orleans Butter Pralines, page 111,
  or New Orleans-type pralines

3 tablespoons unsalted butter or
  margarine, melted

Filling:

2 (8-oz.) pkgs. cream cheese,
  room temperature
1 cup sugar
1 tablespoon cornstarch
3 eggs

1 tablespoon fresh lemon juice
1-1/2 pints dairy sour cream (3 cups),
  drained
1/2 cup Praline Liqueur or Frangelico

Topping:

4 oz. semisweet chocolate, chopped
1/2 cup dairy sour cream

1-1/2 cups Sugar-Fried Pecans,
  page 121, roughly chopped

To prepare Crust, in a food processor fitted with the steel blade, combine cracker crumbs and pralines. Process until pralines break into pieces the size of crumbs. Empty mixture into a 2-quart bowl; stir in butter or margarine until crumbs are coated. Thoroughly grease bottom and side of an 8'' x 3'' round cake pan. Cut a 9-inch parchment paper-circle. Line bottom and part of side with circle; grease paper. Pat 3/4 cup crumb mixture into bottom of pan, spreading evenly to cover. Refrigerate until ready to fill. Reserve remaining crumb mixture. Preheat oven to 350F (175C).

To prepare Filling, in a food processor fitted with the steel blade, process cream cheese and sugar until smooth, about 60 seconds. Add cornstarch; turn on and off 3 or 4 times to blend. Add eggs, 1 at a time, blending after each addition. Add remaining filling ingredients; process just until blended. Remove blade from processor.

To assemble and bake, pour batter into crust-lined pan. Set filled pan into a larger pan; pour in about 2 inches of boiling water. Bake in preheated oven until set, 1 hour. Turn oven off; leave cheesecake in closed oven 1 hour. Cool on a rack to room temperature. Cover and refrigerate 8 hours or until ready to serve.

To prepare Topping, in a heavy 1-quart saucepan over very low heat, melt chocolate, stirring. Remove from heat; fold in sour cream until blended. Fold in Sugar-Fried Pecans; set aside while unmolding cake.

To finish cake, run a thin knife around edges of pan to loosen cheesecake. Place a flat 10-inch plate over top of cake pan; invert cake onto plate. Carefully remove parchment paper and discard. The cake is now upside down. Carefully pat reserved crumb mixture into sides of cake. Place a serving plate over bottom of cake. Invert cake onto serving plate; spread topping over top using a metal spatula. Refrigerate until topping has set before serving. Makes 12 to 16 servings.

Cajun Country

Cajun food is good, hearty fare. It was created by people who work hard, play hard and love food. It has evolved over the years. The city motto of Lafayette, Louisiana, in the heart of Cajun country, is *"Laissez le bon temps rouller,"* or "Let the good times roll." Roll they do in the unique lifestyle of the Cajuns, and you can be certain that in the midst of every good time is FOOD.

What sort of food does a Cajun eat? The first time I asked that question many years ago, a larger-than-life Cajun mama told me: "Well, cher, me I tell you, we eat anything what can't get away from us." And they truly do eat every denizen of the wood and marshland, everything that swims in the water, and most creatures that fly.

To say that frogs proliferate in South Louisiana is like saying there are several people in Manhattan. There are frogs of every size and color—from the little bright green tree frogs that stick on your windows, to the granddaddy bullfrog, a huge, scary-looking creature whose nocturnal bellowings will keep you awake if you leave the windows open. It is not unheard of for South Louisiana frog legs to measure 12 inches in length. Now when you add a body, that is one fearsome frog!

Squirrel, rabbit, nutria and possum are no strangers to the Cajun family table, nor are alligators, terrapins or birds with names like coot, woodcock, jacksnipe or poule d'eau.

When cooking any type of wild game, take care to remove all traces of fat. A large measure of the "gamy" taste, which many people find objectionable, is found in the fat.

Cajun food is special, just like the people who created it. French in origin, the cuisine was broadened by Indian herbs and cooking methods, fiery Spanish spices and chilies and Black soul food. The result is spicy, down-home food with the subtle delicacy of haute cuisine lurking right under the surface.

Cajun cooking consists of many one-pot meals that, once started, can tend to themselves on the back burner for hours while

Cajun Buffet Supper

Duck & Artichoke Gumbo, page 40
Basil & Tomato Salad, page 45
Marinated Cole Slaw, page 46
Cajun Corn Salad, page 49
Crawfish Pie
Atchafalaya Jambalaya
Mixed Greens with Turnips & Tasso,
page 97
Cajun Corn Bread
Sweet Potato-Pecan Pie, page 111

mama tends to the chores of her usually large household. One-pot-meal cooking, as it evolved, fostered the practice of *cooking down*. Cooking down simply means cooking until the vegetables and perhaps

pieces of seasoning meat have totally disintegrated and become part of the sauce. The sauce is served over the main meat and the rice that is always served with traditional Cajun dishes. Some of the most delicious examples of Cajun home cooking are dishes which consist solely of cooked-down vegetables served with a piece of meat. These dishes are referred to as *smothered*. Ask a Cajun for a recipe and he will no doubt tell you something like, "Well, first you make a roux, then add your seasonings, vegetables, meat and stock. Then you cook it all down and add shallots—green onions in Cajun country—and parsley at the end."

Part of the cooking-down process involves another taste-building technique called *layering of flavors* that goes something like this:

First, the roux is prepared and developed to its own depth of flavor. Then the vegetables, usually onions, garlic, celery and bell peppers, are added and sautéed in the roux. This adds a "fried" taste and a subtle

sweetness if the onions are allowed to brown.

So far we have three layers of flavor—those of the roux, the fried vegetables and the onion sweetness. If tomatoes are used in the dish, they are added at this point to introduce an acid taste. Next come the herbs and spices for flavor and hotness, then the meat or seafood and a concentrated rich stock with its own dozens of tastes. Wine may be added and—I think we've lost the count! Then everything gets *cooked down* with each *layer* maintaining its own identity.

Oh, but good is never enough! After the dish has cooked down for a few hours or so, a second batch of vegetables is often added and gently poached 30 minutes or so, furnishing a second vegetable taste and a crunchy texture. Sometimes more meat or seafood is added here to further complicate the taste. The coup de grace is supplied about 10 minutes before serving with the addition of chopped green onions and minced flat-leaf parsley, both of which retain their crunch and most of their raw flavor.

To serve, the meat goes on the plate with steaming hot white rice cooked to perfection with moist, plump, nonsticky grains. The sauce goes on top. My friend, the taste is overwhelming.

There are several categories of traditional Cajun one-pot meals that are unique. Each deserves to have its story told.

Etouffée—(pronounced a-too-FAY), with the accent placed over the second "e," means a braised dish or a stew. When the Acadians first left France, their etouffée was probably quite different from the way it is prepared today. But underneath the mahogany roux and the cayenne, the dish is French. Cajun etouffées are dark-roux-based stews served over rice. The dish can be prepared from any meat, fish or shellfish. The liquid would, of course, be complementary to the meat. Tomatoes, tomato paste or tomato sauce may be included in etouffée depending upon personal opinion or what part of Cajun country you're from.

Jambalaya—(pronounced jahm-buh-LIE-ya) is generally believed to have been adapted from the classic Spanish dish,

(continued on next page)

paella. However, the name was derived from the French *jambon,* or ham, an ingredient often used in the dish.

Jambalaya, like etouffée, may be prepared from any combination of meats, fish or shellfish that are on hand, using a complementary stock. The dish is not a roux-based dish. In the authentic version, the raw rice is cooked in hot fat, usually lard, along with the vegetables and meats, until golden brown. Then the stock is added and the dish is cooked until the rice is tender. Jambalaya is generally known to be a very spicy dish.

Sauce Piquant—(pronounced pee-KAWNT) is fairly unknown outside of Louisiana, but it is certainly as delicious as the more well-known Cajun dishes. Sauce piquants are often made from local game such as squirrel, alligator or turtle, but may be prepared using any meat, fish or shellfish.

Sauce piquant is roux-based and generally includes tomatoes. A great many sauce piquant aficionados include red wine in the recipe. As the name implies, the dish is definitely spicy. Sauce piquant is similar to the famous "Creole sauce" of New Orleans.

Courtbouillon—(pronounced COO-bee-yon) is presumed to have been inspired by the memory of the great French bouillabaisse. The Cajuns added their beloved roux and substituted local fish such as red snapper or redfish. Even catfish and perch make delicious courtbouillons. Like most Cajun dishes, it is highly seasoned.

If there is a fisherman in your family who can provide whole small fish such as perch, or *sac-a-lait* as they are known in Cajun country, use them whole, minus heads, in the courtbouillon for an impressive presentation. You may also use fish fillets to prepare the dish.

When dealing with the subject of Cajun country food, I always feel it prudent to discuss spiciness. Cajun food is spicy, the spiciness being an inherent part of its complex taste. Tolerance to spicy seasonings varies among individuals. I like mine plenty hot, but there are some Cajuns who make their food so hot that the only explanation for the fact that they can eat it must be that they have no feeling left!

My personal philosophy is that the food should never be seasoned so highly that it detracts from the ability of the taste buds to distinguish the other elements of the dish.

The sinus need not be draining for food to be considered authentically Cajun—unless that's the way you like it! I feel that after the first three or four bites, a warm glow should begin to radiate at the back of the throat. It should not intensify, but should remain gently teasing throughout the meal. You should know that something refreshingly exciting is going on in your mouth—something that makes you want more!

Cajun food is not fussy fare. Most of the traditional dishes are so colorful that they require no garnishing. Picture a plate of Crawfish Etouffée. On the bottom of the plate is a mound of snow-white rice, covered with the deep mahogany-roux gravy flecked with the red crawfish and bright green of the barely cooked parsley and green onions. The dish is a study in rich natural tones that reflect its honest taste.

Hungry? Well, that's what this book is all about.

Smoked-Duck Etouffée

This could be called the ultimate etouffée. The dish is worth all the effort. To make preparation easier, smoke duck the day before completing the dish.

1 recipe Cajun Roux, page 12	1/2 teaspoon freshly ground black pepper
1 large onion, chopped	1-3/4 cups Louisiana Brown Poultry Stock,
1 medium, green bell pepper, chopped	page 14, or canned chicken broth
1 celery stalk, chopped	Salt to taste
2 large garlic cloves, minced	1 (14-oz.) can artichoke hearts,
1/2 recipe Mesquite-Smoked Duck, page 67	drained, quartered
1/4 teaspoon red (cayenne) pepper	6 green onions, chopped
1/2 teaspoon dried leaf thyme	1/4 cup minced parsley, preferably flat-leaf
1/4 teaspoon dried leaf marjoram	6 cups hot cooked brown rice
1/8 teaspoon rubbed sage	

Make roux in a 12-inch skillet or Dutch oven as directed on page 12 using duck fat or lard, cooking until mahogany-colored. Add onion, bell pepper, celery and garlic; cook, stirring often, until vegetables are wilted and transparent, 10 minutes. Discard skin from duck; chop meat into bite-sized pieces. Add cayenne, thyme, margoram, sage, black pepper and duck meat to pan; stir until blended. Slowly add stock or broth, stirring. Season with salt. Reduce heat; cover and simmer 45 minutes, stirring occasionally. Stir in artichoke hearts, green onions and parsley. Cook 10 minutes. To serve, place about 1 cup hot rice on each plate; spoon etouffée over top. Makes 4 to 6 servings.

Atchafalaya Jambalaya

Jambalaya is another of the wonderful Cajun dishes that can be prepared from whatever is on hand. Just follow the basic procedures and raid your refrigerator or freezer for ingredients to prepare a filling and economical supper. Serve with a tossed salad, French bread and wine. Or serve with cold beer as is traditional in Cajun Country.

1/4 cup olive oil
1 lb. peeled and deveined small shrimp
1 tablespoon all-purpose Cajun seasoning blend
1/3 cup vegetable oil
1/3 cup bacon drippings
2 medium onions, chopped
2 medium green bell peppers, chopped
3 celery stalks, chopped
4 large garlic cloves, minced
1 lb. smoked ham, such as Hormel Cure-81, cut into bite-size pieces

1 lb. andouille or Polish kielbasa, cut into bite-size rounds
2 cups uncooked long-grain white rice
2 large tomatoes, peeled and chopped
3 cups Brown Veal & Pork Stock, page 15, or canned beef broth
1/2 teaspoon freshly ground black pepper
1/4 teaspoon red (cayenne) pepper, or to taste
Salt to taste
6 green onions, chopped, including green tops
1/2 cup minced flat-leaf parsley

Heat olive oil in a heavy 12-inch skillet over medium-high heat. When oil is hot, add the shrimp and season liberally with the seasoning blend. Stir-fry just until shrimp are firm and have turned coral-pink, about 5 minutes. Drain well and set aside. In a heavy 8-quart Dutch oven, combine the vegetable oil and bacon drippings over medium heat. When fat is hot, add onions, bell pepper, celery and garlic; cook until vegetables are wilted and transparent, about 8 minutes. Add ham and sausage; cook, stirring occasionally, until sausage is lightly browned, about 8 minutes. Add the rice. Cook, stirring often, until rice is lightly browned, about 10 minutes. Do not allow rice to stick to bottom of pan. Add the tomatoes and stir until blended, scraping up any browned bits from bottom of pan. Stir in the stock or broth and reserved shrimp. Add seasonings, reduce heat. Cover pan and simmer until rice is tender and no liquid remains, about 30 to 45 minutes. Stir in the green onions and parsley. Cover and cook an additional 5 minutes. Serve hot. Makes 6 to 8 servings.

Red Beans & Rice with Sausage

Everyone in South Louisiana knows that Monday is red beans and rice with sausage day, and what a treat! The custom originated because Monday was wash day, and the lady of the house had little time to prepare a supper which required a lot of her attention. Traditionally red beans and rice with sausage were put into one pot on the back of the stove and left to cook virtually unattended.

2 lbs. chaurice, or any hot or smoked sausage	4 fresh bay leaves or 2 dried bay leaves
2 lbs. dried kidney beans	2 tablespoons sugar
1/4 cup vegetable oil	1 (12-oz.) can beer
2 large onions, chopped	Salt, freshly ground black pepper and red
1 large green bell pepper	(cayenne) pepper to taste
4 large garlic cloves, minced	Cooked white rice
1 meaty ham hock, about 1-1/2 lbs.	6 green onions, chopped
1 tablespoon minced fresh marjoram or	Minced flat-leaf parsley
1 teaspoon dried leaf marjoram	

Preheat oven to 350F (175C). Slice the sausage into bite-size pieces and spread in a single layer on heavy baking sheet. Bake sausage in preheated oven until it is cooked through and has rendered its fat. Drain sausage on paper towels and set aside. Sort through the beans, discarding any discolored ones or pebbles. Rinse the beans under running water. Heat vegetable oil in a heavy Dutch oven over medium heat. When oil is hot, add onions, bell pepper and garlic. Sauté until vegetables are wilted, about 8 minutes. Add the beans, ham hock, marjoram, bay leaves, sugar and beer. Stir to blend well and add enough water to cover beans by about 2 inches. Bring to a boil; reduce heat and add seasonings. Cover and simmer until beans are soft and juice has formed a thickened gravy, about 3 hours. Add additional water if necessary while cooking. When beans are tender, remove the ham hock and chop the meat into bite-size pieces, discarding skin and bones. Return the chopped meat to the beans and add the cooked sausage slices. Cook just to heat through. Serve over rice, garnished with chopped green onions and minced parsley. Makes 6 to 8 servings.

Cajun Corn Bread

The traditional pan for baking corn bread in the South is made of cast iron. The pans usually yield 8 to 10 large portions of bread. They are sometimes round, with pie-shaped divisions. Or they may be rectangular with divisions in the shape of an ear of corn. A standard-size muffin pan may be substituted.

1 cup all-purpose flour	1/4 cup lard or vegetable shortening,
1 tablespoon baking powder	melted
1/2 teaspoon salt	1/4 cup whipping cream
2 tablespoons sugar	3/4 cup milk
1 cup yellow cornmeal,	1/2 cup finely chopped onion
preferably stone ground	3 canned or fresh jalapeño peppers,
2 eggs, slightly beaten	seeds and veins removed, minced

Preheat oven to 425F (220C). Generously grease 2 corn-bread pans or 18 muffin cups. If using cast-iron pans, place greased pans in hot oven 20 minutes while preparing batter. For a crispy outside crust, batter should sizzle and hiss when spooned into pans. Sift flour, baking powder, salt and sugar into a large bowl. With a fork, blend in cornmeal. Add remaining ingredients to bowl; stir just until all dry ingredients are moist. Do not overbeat. Pour batter into each division in pan, filling each about 2/3 full. Bake in preheated oven until top springs back when pressed with fingertips, 20 minutes. Serve hot. Makes 16 to 20 pieces.

Top to bottom: Cajun Corn Bread, Red Beans & Rice with Sausage

Eggplant Steaks with Seafood Dressing

Every Cajun housewife has a variation of this dish. I have found that even those who claim to hate eggplant love this hearty dish.

2 medium eggplants
1/4 cup olive oil
1 lb. peeled and deveined small shrimp
All-purpose Cajun seasoning blend
1/3 cup vegetable oil
1 large onion, chopped
1 large green bell pepper, chopped
2 celery stalks, chopped
3 large garlic cloves, minced
2 teaspoons minced fresh thyme or
   1/2 teaspoon dried leaf thyme
1 tablespoon minced fresh basil or 1 teaspoon
   dried leaf basil
1/2 teaspoon dried leaf oregano
1/3 cup all-purpose flour

1-1/2 cups hot Seafood Stock, page 14,
   bottled clam juice or stock made from
   Knorr fish bouillon cubes
1/2 teaspoon red (cayenne) pepper, or to taste
Salt to taste
3/4 teaspoon freshly ground black pepper
1 lb. lump crabmeat
Vegetable oil for frying
2 cups all-purpose flour, seasoned with
   2 tablespoons Cajun seasoning blend
2 eggs, beaten with 1 cup milk
2 cups cornmeal, seasoned with 2 tablespoons
   Cajun seasoning blend
4 green onions, chopped
2 tablespoons minced flat-leaf parsley

Peel one of the eggplants and cut it into 1-inch cubes. Place in saucepan and add water to cover. Cook until eggplant is very tender, about 15 minutes. Drain and set aside. Slice the unpeeled eggplant into 1/2-inch-thick slices lengthwise; set aside. Heat the olive oil in a heavy 12-inch skillet over medium-high heat. When oil is hot, add the shrimp and season liberally with seasoning blend. Stir-fry just until shrimp are firm and coral-pink. Drain and set aside. Heat vegetable oil in a heavy, deep-sided 12-inch skillet over medium heat. Add onions, bell pepper, celery, garlic and herbs. Sauté until vegetables are wilted and onion is transparent, about 8 minutes. Add the flour all at once and stir to blend well. Cook, stirring constantly, 3 or 4 minutes. Add the hot stock and stir to blend. Stir in the reserved cooked eggplant and the shrimp. Add seasonings and stir. Cover and cook for 20 minutes. Pick through the crabmeat to remove any bits of shell or cartilage. Stir the crabmeat into the pan and cook to heat through. While dressing is cooking, fry the eggplant steaks. Heat 1 inch of vegetable oil in a heavy 12-inch skillet over medium heat to 365F (185C), or until a 1-inch bread cube turns golden brown in 65 seconds. Dip the eggplant slices in the seasoned flour, coating well and shaking off all excess flour. Next dip them into the egg wash, and finally into the seasoned cornmeal, coating well and shaking off all excess cornmeal. Fry slices in the hot oil until golden brown on both sides, turning once, 4 or 5 minutes. To serve, place an eggplant steak on each plate and top with a generous portion of the seafood dressing. Garnish with green onions and parsley. Makes 4 to 6 servings.

Fried Boudin Balls

Boudin is a popular Cajun sausage made from organ meats, green onions, lots of spice and rice. Every wonderful little grocery/meat shop and cafe in Cajun country makes their own version. Noted food writer Calvin Trillin once made a foray into Cajun country to seek out the best boudin. He found it in a drive-in grocery store in Lafayette, where he ate it in the parking lot wrapped in paper towels.

   This recipe, made from the rice stuffing, is similar to the little "munchies" brought to your table at many Cajun restaurants while you're waiting for your real food. They call it *lagniappe,* a little something extra.

**1 recipe Cajun Dirty Rice, page 106,
  well chilled
4 eggs beaten with 3 cups milk
4 cups unseasoned bread crumbs, seasoned**

**with 3 tablespoons all-purpose Cajun
  seasoning blend and 1 tablespoon
  granulated garlic
Vegetable oil for deep-frying**

Roll the dirty rice into balls about 2 inches in diameter. Dip the balls in the egg wash, coating well, then into the seasoned bread crumbs. Coat the balls thoroughly with the bread crumbs; shake off all excess crumbs. Refrigerate 1 hour. When ready to cook the boudin balls, heat oil for deep-frying to 365F (185C), or until a 1-inch bread cube turns golden brown in 65 seconds. Fry the balls 4 or 5 at a time, taking care not to crowd the pan. Cook until golden brown, about 4 minutes. Drain on paper towels. Serve hot. Makes about 24 boudin balls.

Cajun Duck with Mint

This easy recipe for wild duck came from a private recipe collection in Opelousas.

**4 to 6 green-winged teal ducks,
  drawn and plucked
Whole mint sprigs
Melted butter
Salt and pepper
Bacon slices**

**3 cups Louisiana Brown-Poultry Stock,
  page 14, or canned chicken broth
1/4 cup green creme de menthe
1/2 cup minced fresh mint
1/4 cup mint jelly**

Preheat oven to 350F (175C). Stuff the mint sprigs inside the ducks and brush them with melted butter. Salt and pepper the birds liberally. Lay bacon slices over the breasts and place ducks in a shallow, heat-proof baking pan. Roast in preheated oven for 45 to 60 minutes, or until juices run clear when bird is lightly punctured at thigh joint. Remove birds to a platter and set aside to keep warm. Pour off any fat from baking pan and place on burner over high heat. Add the stock and stir to scrape up any browned bits from bottom of pan. Reduce stock by half, about 7 minutes, then stir in remaining ingredients and cook until thickened, about 5 minutes. Strain sauce through a fine strainer. To serve, remove bacon strips from duck and discard. Serve duck hot. Pass sauce separately. Makes 4 to 6 servings.

Acadian Alligator Sauce Piquant

When alligators were taken off the endangered species list, enterprising Cajuns and restauranteurs developed ways to use the meat. There are now several plants in South Louisiana which process alligators under USDA inspection. There are three types of meat processed from the 'gator carcass, the choicest being tail meat. Tail meat is white and very much like veal in both taste and texture! The body meat is somewhat darker and has a stronger taste and slightly tougher texture. It is very similar to pork shoulder. The final grouping is leg meat, which is the strongest-flavored part of the carcass. The meat is very dark in color, resembling beef shank, and is very tough. Its use should be limited to braised dishes.

2-1/2 lbs. tail alligator meat or pork
  loin or shoulder,
  cut into cubes
Salt to taste
Finely ground black pepper
1 recipe Cajun Roux, page 12
2 medium onions, chopped
4 medium garlic cloves, minced
1 large green bell pepper, chopped
2 large celery stalks, chopped
3 medium tomatoes, peeled, chopped
2 tablespoons tomato paste
2 teaspoons Worcestershire sauce
1 teaspoon freshly ground black pepper
1-1/2 teaspoons chili powder

1 teaspoon dried leaf oregano or
  1 tablespoon chopped fresh oregano
1 teaspoon dried leaf basil or
  1 tablespoon chopped fresh basil
1 teaspoon dried leaf thyme or
  1 tablespoon chopped fresh thyme
1/2 teaspoon red (cayenne) pepper
Salt to taste
1/2 cup Burgundy wine
2 cups Brown Veal & Pork Stock, page 15,
  or canned beef broth
6 green onions, chopped
1/4 cup minced parsley, preferably flat-leaf
Hot cooked white rice

Season alligator meat or pork with salt and black pepper. In a heavy Dutch oven over medium heat, make roux as directed on page 12, cooking until mahogany-colored. Add seasoned meat; cook quickly, stirring until lightly browned. Add onions, garlic, bell pepper, celery and tomatoes. Stir until vegetables are slightly wilted and transparent, about 5 minutes. Add tomato paste, Worcestershire sauce, black pepper, chili powder, oregano, basil, thyme, cayenne and salt; cook 5 minutes, stirring to prevent sticking. Stir in wine and stock or broth. Reduce heat. Cover and simmer until meat is tender and liquid is thick and rich, 1-1/2 hours. Stir in green onions and parsley; remove from heat. Serve over rice. Makes 4 to 6 servings.

Smothered Cabbage with Sausage

This is one of the best of Cajun *cooked-down* dishes. If you wish to sample authentic Cajun home cooking, look no further.

2 quarts Louisiana Brown-Poultry Stock,
  page 14, or canned chicken broth
1 teaspoon salt
2 teaspoons freshly ground black pepper
1 medium head green cabbage
1/3 cup vegetable oil
12 oz. andouille sausage or Polish kielbasa,

  cut into bite-size pieces
1 lb. ham steak, trimmed of fat and cut into
  1-inch pieces
1 large onion, halved lengthwise, sliced
1/4 teaspoon red (cayenne) pepper, or to taste
1/2 teaspoon freshly ground black pepper
Salt to taste

Combine stock, salt and pepper in an 8- to 10-quart soup pot over medium heat. Cut cabbage into pieces about 1 inch wide and 2 or 3 inches long. Add the cabbage to the stock and cook until cabbage is tender, about 15 minutes. Drain cabbage and set aside, reserving about 1/2 cup of the cooking liquid. Heat the vegetable oil in a heavy Dutch oven over medium heat. When oil is hot, add the sausage, ham and onion. Cook, stirring often, until onion is thoroughly wilted, about 10 minutes. Stir in the cabbage and reserved cooking liquid; add seasonings. Cover and simmer for 25 minutes. Serve hot. Makes 4 to 6 servings.

Crawfish Pie

Crawfish pie is an institution in Cajun country, and the best to be had in a restaurant is found at the Crawfish Kitchen in Breaux Bridge, Louisiana, the Crawfish Capital of the World.

Double recipe Flaky Pie Pastry, page 110
3/4 recipe Cajun Roux, page 12
1 large onion, chopped
2 large garlic cloves, chopped
1 small green bell pepper, chopped
2 celery stalks, chopped
1/2 cup minced parsley, preferably flat-leaf
1/2 teaspoon dried leaf basil or
  1-1/2 teaspoons chopped fresh basil
1 bay leaf, minced
1/2 teaspoon dried leaf oregano or
  1-1/2 teaspoons chopped fresh oregano

1/2 teaspoon red (cayenne) pepper
1/4 teaspoon freshly ground black pepper
1 tablespoon fresh lemon juice
1 medium tomato, peeled, pureed
1-1/2 lbs. peeled crawfish tails
2 cups Seafood Stock, page 14, or
  2 (8-oz.) bottles clam juice
Salt to taste
6 green onions, chopped

Prepare pastry as directed on page 110. Divide into 2 equal pieces. Wrap with plastic wrap; refrigerate until chilled. Make roux in a heavy 12-inch skillet over medium heat, cooking until peanut-butter-colored. Add onion, garlic, bell pepper, celery, parsley, basil, bay leaf, oregano, cayenne and black pepper to hot roux. Cook, stirring, until vegetables are slightly wilted and transparent, about 5 minutes. Stir in lemon juice and tomato; cook 5 minutes. Add crawfish tails. Slowly add stock or clam juice, stirring. Season with salt; cook 20 minutes, stirring often. Stir in green onions; remove from heat. Cool to lukewarm. Preheat oven to 375F (190C). On a lightly floured surface. roll out 1 chilled pastry piece to a 1/16-inch-thick circle. Roll pastry loosely around rolling pin; unroll into a 9-inch, deep-dish pie pan. Gently lower pastry into bottom of pan; lightly press against side, taking care not to stretch pastry. Cut away excess pastry, leaving a 1/2-inch overhang at edge. Pour cooled crawfish filling into pastry-lined pan; set aside. Roll out second pastry piece same as first; place over filling. Cut off excess pastry, leaving about a 1-inch overhang at edges. Tuck edge of top pastry securely under edge of bottom pastry; flute edges, if desired. Or press pastry against edge of pan using tines of a fork. Cut 2 rows of steam vents in top of pastry. Bake in preheated oven until pastry is golden brown and flaky, 20 minutes. Serve hot. Makes 4 to 6 servings.

Variation
For an alternative presentation, divide pastry into 12 equal pieces. Roll out 6 pieces as directed above into circles to fit 1-cup au gratin dishes; fit pastry into 6 dishes. Spoon crawfish filling into pastry-lined dishes. Roll out remaining 6 pastry pieces into circles for tops; place over filled dishes. Bake 20 minutes.

How to Make Crawfish Etouffée

1/Add onions, garlic, bell pepper and celery to hot roux. Cook until slightly wilted.

2/Serve etouffée over rice.

Crawfish Etouffée

Etouffée is one of the most delicious foods to grace a table in Cajun country, or perhaps in the universe. The dish derives its sultry richness from a deep mahogany-brown roux, so don't be timid about the depth of color when you prepare the roux for this dish.

1 recipe Cajun Roux, page 12
2 medium onions, chopped
4 large garlic cloves, minced
1 large green bell pepper, chopped
1 large red bell pepper, chopped
3 celery stalks, chopped
1/3 cup minced fresh basil or 2 teaspoons
   dried leaf basil
1/4 cup tomato paste
2 lbs. peeled crawfish tails

1 cup Seafood Stock, page 14, bottled clam
   juice or stock made from Knorr fish
   bouillon cubes
1/2 teaspoon red (cayenne) pepper, or to taste
1/2 teaspoon freshly ground black pepper
Salt to taste
1/4 cup minced flat-leaf parsley
6 green onions, chopped
Cooked white rice

Place roux in heavy 12-inch Dutch oven over medium heat. Stir in onion, garlic, bell pepper, celery and basil. Cook, stirring often, until vegetables are wilted, about 5 minutes. Stir in tomato paste, blending well. Add crawfish tails and stock. Add cayenne, black pepper and salt to taste. Reduce heat and simmer about 30 minutes. Stir in parsley and green onions. Remove from heat. Serve hot over rice. Makes 4 to 6 servings.

Seafood Boudin with Green-Peppercorn Sauce

This is a delicious all-seafood version of the classic white Cajun sausage.

1/2 lb. sea scallops
1 lb. redfish fillets or other white-fleshed,
 non-oily fish
1 cup unsalted butter or margarine,
 cut into 1-inch cubes
3 eggs
1/2 lb. peeled uncooked shrimp, minced
1 lb. claw crabmeat
8 green onions, minced
1 medium, green bell pepper, minced

1/4 cup minced parsley, preferably flat-leaf
12 garlic cloves, minced
2 teaspoons salt
1 teaspoon red (cayenne) pepper
2 tablespoon fresh lime juice
About 36 inches of sausage casings,
 medium diameter
Green-Peppercorn Sauce, see below
6 cooked crawfish or shrimp
Curly-parsley sprigs

Green-Peppercorn Sauce:
1/4 cup white-wine vinegar
2 tablespoons green peppercorns
1-1/2 teaspoons fresh lime juice
1-1/2 cups whipping cream
1/2 teaspoon salt

1/4 teaspoon freshly ground pepper
4 egg yolks, slightly beaten
1 cup unsalted butter or margarine,
 cut into 1-inch cubes

In a food processor fitted with the steel blade, combine scallops, redfish, butter or margarine and eggs; process until pureed. Scrape mixture into a medium bowl; fold in shrimp, crabmeat, green onions, bell pepper, minced parsley, garlic, salt, cayenne and lime juice until combined. Tie a firm knot in 1 end of sausage casing. Using a sausage stuffer or 14-inch pastry bag fitted with a 1-inch plain tip, stuff sausage casings. Do not pack too tightly, or they will burst during cooking. Sausages should actually appear to be a little understuffed; sausages expand during cooking. Twist sausages into desired lengths. Tie a firm knot in other end of casing. Set sausage aside. Add 3 inches water to a heavy 12-inch skillet; bring to a simmer over medium heat. Add sausages; poach 15 minutes. While sausages are cooking, prepare Peppercorn Sauce. Remove sausages from water; drain well. To serve, spoon some peppercorn sauce into each plate; top with desired number of sausages. Garnish with a cooked shrimp or crawfish and parsley sprigs. Makes 4 to 6 servings.

To prepare Green-Peppercorn Sauce, in a heavy 2-quart saucepan, combine vinegar, peppercorns and lime juice. Using a wooden spoon or a flat potato masher, crush peppercorns in liquid. Cook over medium-high heat until reduced to 1 tablespoon, about 5 minutes. Add cream, salt and pepper; cook until thickened and reduced slightly, 7 to 8 minutes. Whisk often. Reduce heat; whisk in egg yolks. Cook, whisking constantly, until thickened, 3 to 4 minutes. Add butter or margarine cubes, a few at a time, whisking constantly, until all are added. Set aside. Makes about 1-3/4 cups.

Sac-a-Lait Courtbouillon

Courtbouillon (pronounced COO-be-yon) is one of the finest examples of country Cajun food. It holds a place of honor as a category of Cajun food. It is similar to other types of Cajun dishes, yet it has features that make it just a little bit different. It is one of the few Cajun dishes that is not served over rice. Courtbouillon may be prepared using any type of small, whole fish such as *sac-a-lait,* a tasty freshwater perch. You can substitute your favorite fish fillets or fish steaks. Serve with crisp French bread.

Broth, see below
6 (6- to 8-oz.) sac-a-lait or any small fish,
  fish fillets or fish steaks
About 2 cups all-purpose flour
2/3 cup lard or vegetable oil
3/4 recipe Cajun Roux, page 12

1 small onion, chopped
1 small green bell pepper, chopped
1 celery stalk, chopped
1 teaspoon Tabasco sauce
Minced parsley, preferably flat-leaf
Lemon wedges

Broth:
1/4 cup lard or vegetable oil
2 large tomatoes, peeled, chopped
1 large onion, chopped
3 large celery stalks, chopped
1 medium, green bell pepper, chopped
2 large garlic cloves, chopped
2 bay leaves, minced
1/2 teaspoon dried leaf oregano or
  1-1/2 teaspoons chopped fresh oregano
1/2 teaspoon dried leaf basil or
  1-1/2 teaspoons chopped fresh basil

1/2 teaspoon dried leaf thyme or
  1-1/2 teaspoons chopped fresh thyme
1 tablespoon sugar
1/2 teaspoon red (cayenne) pepper
1/4 teaspoon freshly ground black pepper
1 qt. Seafood Stock, page 14, or
  4 (8-oz.) bottles clam juice
1/2 cup Burgundy wine

Make broth. Meanwhile, in a heavy 12-inch skillet over medium-high heat, heat lard or oil. Dredge fish in flour, turning to coat well; shake off excess. When fat is hot, add fish; sear quickly on both sides just long enough to form a crispy crust. Drain on paper towels. Preheat oven to 375F (190C). Make roux in a heavy 10-inch skillet over medium heat as directed on page 12, cooking until mahogany-colored. Add onion, bell pepper and celery; cook 5 minutes, stirring. Remove from heat; stir in Tabasco sauce. Bring broth mixture to a rolling boil; stir in roux, a spoonful at a time. Reduce heat; cook 5 minutes. Remove pan from heat; add fried fish. Bake in preheated oven until fish turns from transparent to opaque, 15 minutes. To serve, place a whole fish or fillet in each soup plate; spoon some vegetables over top. Add a generous amount of broth to each serving. Garnish with parsley and lemon wedges. Serve hot. Makes 4 to 6 servings.

To prepare Broth, in an ovenproof Dutch oven, melt 1/4 cup lard over medium heat; add all ingredients except stock and wine. Cook until vegetables are slightly wilted and transparent, about 5 minutes. Stir in stock or clam juice and wine. Reduce heat; cover and simmer 25 minutes, stirring occasionally.

Fried Frog Legs with Roasted Garlic Sauce

Bullfrogs are particularly delightful denizens of the swampy south. In addition to providing resounding summer evening symphonies, their plump back legs are a favorite food for our tables. Often weighing as much as one half pound per pair, the legs have firm-textured, creamy white meat with a subtle musky undertone.

Roasted Garlic Sauce, see below
Vegetable oil for deep-frying
4 pairs (4- to 6-oz.) frog legs
3 cups all-purpose flour, seasoned with
  2 tablespoons all-purpose Cajun seasoning
  blend
3 eggs beaten with 2 cups milk
4 cups fresh bread crumbs from garlic bread,
  seasoned with 1-1/2 tablespoons all-purpose
  Cajun seasoning

Roasted Garlic Sauce:
8 large garlic cloves, unpeeled
3/4 cup Seafood Stock, page 14, bottled
  clam juice or stock made from Knorr
  fish bouillon cube
1 cup Brown Veal & Pork Stock, page 15,
  or canned beef broth
1 tablespoon fresh lemon juice
Dash red (cayenne) pepper
8 tablespoons (1/2 cup) unsalted butter,
  cut into chunks

Prepare garlic sauce through reduction of stock. Preheat oil for deep-frying to 365F (185C). Rinse frog legs and pat very dry using paper towels. Dredge frog legs first in the seasoned flour, shaking off all excess flour. Dredge next in the egg wash, then in the garlic bread crumbs, patting the crumbs firmly into the meat to coat well. Again, shake off all excess crumbs. Arrange on baking sheets and chill until ready to fry. Fry in batches until light golden brown, about 4 or 5 minutes for each batch. Do not crowd the pan. Drain on paper towels. Finish garlic sauce. Serve 2 pair per serving, with a small ramekin of Roasted Garlic Sauce.

To prepare Roasted Garlic Sauce, preheat toaster oven to 350F (175C). Combine garlic cloves and stocks in small baking pan. Roast in preheated oven 45 minutes, or until garlic has become very soft. Add additional stocks as necessary to maintain about 1-1/2 cups liquid. Remove garlic cloves from the stock, reserving stock. Mash the skin of the garlic to squeeze out the garlic pulp. Combine the reserved cooking stock, lemon juice and garlic pulp in work bowl of food processor fitted with steel blade and process until smooth. Transfer to medium saucepan and cook over medium heat until reduced by about 3/4. Add cayenne. Add butter all at once and whisk rapidly to form a smooth sauce. Remove from heat at once and serve immediately. Do not allow sauce to boil. This sauce *cannot* be reheated.

Cajun Oyster Pie

Both Oyster Pie and Crawfish Pie, page 131, have their devoted followers. Each group will argue to the death that one or the other is best. Try them both and then decide. But if you love oysters as intensely as I do, this recipe will have a slight edge. This recipe is another example of the Cajun's love of oysters combined with pork.

1 recipe Flaky Pie Pastry, page 110
1/2 recipe Cajun Roux, page 12
2/3 cup finely chopped smoked ham
1/2 lb. mushrooms, chopped
1 small green bell pepper, chopped
3 medium garlic cloves, minced
6 green onions, chopped
1/2 teaspoon red (cayenne) pepper
1/4 teaspoon dried leaf thyme or
   3/4 teaspoon fresh chopped thyme
1/2 teaspoon dried leaf basil or
   1-1/2 teaspoons chopped fresh basil

1/2 teaspoon dried leaf oregano or
   1-1/2 teaspoons chopped fresh oregano
1-1/2 teaspoons Worcestershire sauce
1 tablespoon fresh lemon juice
36 shucked oysters with their liquor,
   drained, liquor reserved
1/2 cup Seafood Stock, page 14,
   or bottled clam juice
Salt to taste
1/2 cup grated Parmesan cheese (1-1/2 oz.)

Prepare and chill pastry as directed on page 110. Make roux in a heavy 12-inch skillet over medium heat as directed on page 12, cooking until peanut-butter-colored. Add ham, mushrooms, bell pepper, garlic and green onions; cook, stirring, until vegetables are slightly wilted and transparent, 5 minutes. Add cayenne, thyme, basil and oregano; stir until blended. Stir in Worcestershire sauce, lemon juice and reserved oyster liquor. Slowly stir in stock or clam juice. Cook until thickened, about 15 minutes. Add oysters; stir into sauce. Season with salt. Cool to lukewarm. Preheat oven to 375F (190C). Spoon cooled filling into a 9-inch deep-dish pie pan; sprinkle with Parmesan cheese. Set aside. On a lightly floured surface, roll out chilled pastry to a 1/16-inch-thick circle. Roll pastry loosely around rolling pin; unroll over pie. Cut off and discard excess pastry; flute edges, if desired. Or press pastry onto edge of pan using tines of a fork. Cut 2 rows of steam vents in top of pastry. Bake in preheated oven until pastry is golden brown and flaky, 20 minutes. Serve hot. Makes 4 to 6 servings.

Variation
For an alternate presentation, spoon oyster filling into 6 (1-cup) au gratin dishes. Top each dish with 2 tablespoons Parmesan cheese; set aside. Divide pastry into 6 equal pieces; roll out as directed above into circles for tops. Top each dish with a pastry circle. Bake 20 minutes.

Creole-Italian

In the late 1800s, large numbers of immigrants from Sicily began to settle in South Louisiana. Many stayed in New Orleans to establish businesses. With the arrival of the Italians, a new dimension was added to Creole food. Like the many other earlier influences, Italian cuisine contributed many subtle nuances of taste. From the Italians, the Creoles cultivated a love of garlic. Its sensuous, sultry presence is encountered just barely beneath the surface in many classic Creole dishes. My personal theory is that it was from these hearty, vivacious and fun-loving Sicilians that the Creoles inherited much of their intense love affair with fine food.

Conversely, the Spanish roots of the Creole cuisine had a profound impact on Sicilian-American foods. An entire sub-cuisine evolved within the Creole cooking of New Orleans. Today, some of New Orleans' finest restaurants are owned by descendants of these Creole-Italians. They serve excitingly different food which started out many years ago as robust Sicilian fare but which, through the years of Creole influence, developed its present piquant patina—this due largely to the Spanish love of ground chilies. After you've eaten two or three bites and a titillatingly warm glow has developed at the back of your throat, you realize that this is no ordinary spaghetti sauce!

The best examples of Creole-Italian cooking, of course, are found in the homes. But if you don't know a New Orleanian with a last name like Bonnitelli, try one of the city's great Creole-Italian restaurants. Tortorici's, La Louisiane, Broussard's, Impastato's, Pascal's Manale, Mosca's, La Riviera and Tony Angelo's are all classic examples of this sub-cuisine. There are two outstanding Creole-Italian restaurants on the North Shore of New Orleans across the Lake Ponchartrain Causeway—The Shadows in Mandeville and Sal and Judy's in Lacombe.

The most unique feature of the cuisine is its tomato sauce, commonly referred to as *red gravy* or *tomato gravy*. This rich sauce used over meats and pasta has dozens of variations from family to family. Some red gravies are based on a brown roux. Some contain eggplant. Others contain anchovies, whole boiled eggs or meat. Two consistent threads in red gravy are the addition of sugar and the frying of the tomato paste!

When I learned the secret of frying tomato paste, everything I cooked for a week contained fried tomato paste! The procedure produces a specific taste without which you simply do not have authentic Creole-Italian tomato gravy. After the vegetables are sautéed in olive oil, tomato paste is added and, literally, fried before the liquids are added.

Creole-Italians incorporate local fish and shellfish in their cooking with delicious results in dishes, such as Crawfish Fettuccine, Crabmeat in Garlic-Cream Sauce and many more. Some dishes were borrowed from Creole kitchens and topped with red gravy, as is the case with Creole Daube.

Other dishes, among them some of the best, came directly from the heart of the Creole-Italian homemaker's domain. Spinach Bread is such a dish. This entire chapter could be filled with nothing but the many versions of this delicious and versatile bread. You can bake loaves of the bread, slice them into inch-thick slices and serve them in bread baskets as party food. Or, for your best pasta-and-tomato-gravy meal, nothing gives a better complement than a hot loaf of Spinach Bread. When your guests lift the napkin covering of the basket, the aroma that rises says "Italian!"

The Creole-Italians are very serious about their pasta. My favorite New Orleans pasta is made from semolina flour, eggs and a little dry white or red wine, depending on the sauce. The taste of the wine is neither pronounced nor discernable in the overall taste of the dish. Rather, its addition combines Italian and Creole with a *lagniappe*, a little something extra—flavor.

Creole-Italian Dinner Party

Olive Salad
Pepper Breads
Italian Baked Oysters
Green Salad with
Creole Roquefort Dressing, page 51
Brucholoni with Wine Pasta
Spinach Bread
Chocolate Marquis, page 121

Sweet & Sour Olives

This great relish is a must for the antipasta tray. Or use as a topping on your homemade pizza.

1/3 cup olive oil
2 medium onions, halved lengthwise, sliced

1 qt. pitted ripe olives
1/2 cup red-wine vinegar
2 tablespoons sugar

Heat olive oil in heavy 12-inch skillet over medium heat. Add onions; sauté until thoroughly wilted and transparent, about 10 minutes. Add olives; stir until combined. Add vinegar and sugar; bring mixture to a boil. Reduce heat; simmer until liquid has thickened slightly to form a thin syrup, 10 minutes. Cool completely. Spoon into a jar with a tight-fitting lid. Refrigerate until served or up to 1 week. Serve at room temperature. Makes about 6 cups.

Spinach Bread

Spinach Bread is the very essence of Creole-Italian cooking. The bread freezes well, so make several loaves. Serve with your favorite pasta dish for a satisfying meal. Or slice the loaves into 1-inch rounds; serve as party finger food.

1/4 cup warm water (110F, 45C)
1 cup milk, scalded, cooled to 110F, 45C
1 tablespoon sugar
1 (1/4-oz.) pkg. active dry yeast
  (about 1 tablespoon)
About 4 cups bread flour

1-1/2 teaspoons salt
2 tablespoons unsalted butter or margarine,
  room temperature
1 egg
Spinach Filling, see below
About 6 tablespoons olive oil

Spinach Filling:
2 (10-oz.) pkgs. frozen chopped spinach
3/4 cup grated Parmesan cheese (2-1/4 oz.)
4 large garlic cloves, minced
6 anchovy fillets, minced

2-1/2 teaspoons dried leaf oregano or
  2 tablespoons plus 1-1/2 teaspoons
  chopped fresh oregano
1/4 cup olive oil

In a 2-cup glass measuring cup, combine water, milk and sugar. Stir in yeast. Let stand until foamy, 5 to 10 minutes. In a food processor fitted with the steel blade, combine 4 cups flour, salt, butter or margarine and egg. Add yeast mixture. Process until dough forms a ball, 4 to 5 seconds. Stop machine; check consistency of dough. It should be smooth and satiny. If dough is too dry, add additional warm water, 1 tablespoon at a time; process just until blended. If dough is too sticky, add additional flour, 1 or 2 tablespoons at a time, process just until blended. Process 20 seconds to knead. Pour 2 tablespoons olive oil into a large bowl; swirl to coat bottom and sides. Place dough in oiled bowl; turn to coat all sides with oil. Cover bowl with plastic wrap. Let rise in a warm, draft-free place until doubled in bulk, 1-1/2 hours. Prepare filling. When doubled in bulk, punch down dough; divide into 2 equal pieces. Lightly oil work surface with olive oil; roll out each piece of dough into a 15'' x 12'' rectangle. Place 1/2 of filling lengthwise in a line down center of each dough rectangle, leaving a border of 1-1/2 inches at top and bottom. Fold top border down over filling and bottom border up over filling. Now fold sides of dough over filling to enclose, overlapping 1 side. Using your hands, rub all sides of loaves with olive oil. Place on an ungreased baking sheet, seam-side down, leaving 2 inches between loaves. Cover loosely with plastic wrap; let rise in a warm, draft-free place until almost doubled in bulk, 45 minutes. Place rack in center of oven. Preheat oven to 350F (175C). Remove plastic wrap. Bake in center of preheated oven until golden brown, 30 minutes. Carefully turn loaves; cook an additional 5 to 10 minutes to brown bottoms. Cool on wire racks until lukewarm before slicing. Refrigerate any leftovers. Makes 2 loaves.

To prepare Spinach Filling, thaw spinach completely; squeeze out all moisture. In a medium bowl, combine all filling ingredients. Divide into 2 equal portions; set aside.

How to Make Spinach Bread

1/Fold sides of dough over filling to enclose, overlapping 1 side.

2/Slice lukewarm loaves into slices. Arrange on a serving dish.

Pepper Breads

These garlicky little snack crackers laced with a sprinkling of pepper are very versatile munchies. Serve with salads or dips, top with Olive Salad, page 145, or eat them just as they are.

1/2 cup warm water (110F, 45C)	2 tablespoons freshly ground pepper
2 teaspoons sugar	2 teaspoons salt
1 (1/4-oz.) pkg. active dry yeast	About 1 cup olive oil
(about 1 tablespoon)	Salt
About 4 cups all-purpose flour	Garlic powder

In a 2-cup glass measuring cup, combine water and sugar. Stir in yeast. Let stand until foamy, 5 to 10 minutes. In a food processor fitted with steel blade, combine 4 cups flour, pepper and salt. Add yeast mixture; turn on and off 3 or 4 times to blend. With motor running, add 3/4 cup olive oil through feed tube in a slow, steady stream. When all oil has been added, stop machine; check consistency of dough. It should be smooth and satiny. If dough is too dry, add more warm water, 1 tablespoon at a time; process just until blended. If dough is too sticky, add more flour, 1 or 2 tablespoons at a time; process just until blended. Process 20 seconds to knead. Place 3 tablespoons olive oil in a large bowl; swirl to coat bottom and side of bowl. Place dough in oiled bowl; turn to coat all sides with olive oil. Cover bowl with plastic wrap. Let rise in a warm, draft-free place until doubled in bulk, 1-1/2 hours. Place rack in center of oven. Preheat oven to 400F (205C). Lightly oil work surface with olive oil. Punch down dough thoroughly; turn out onto oiled surface. Roll out dough to a 24-inch square. Using a sharp knife, cut dough into 16 (1-1/2-inch-wide) strips. Cut strips into 1-1/2-inch lengths. Place dough pieces on ungreased baking sheets. Using a pastry brush, lightly paint each square with olive oil; sprinkle with salt and garlic powder. Bake in center of preheated oven until light golden brown and crisp, 10 minutes. Cool on racks. Makes 256.

Sausage-Stuffed Zucchini

Creole-Italians produce some of the best Italian sausage this side of Italy. As with other "Creolized" Italian dishes, it has its own personality derived from the addition of chopped hot chilies and cayenne pepper. Italian sausage is usually sold in two varieties in New Orleans—hot and regular. It is used in all sorts of culinary concoctions, from the delicious Italian sausage po'boy, to stuffings, as in this recipe. The stuffed zucchini is a great do-ahead meal.

2 large zucchini (about 1 lb. each)
1/4 cup olive oil
3/4 lb. hot Italian sausage, casings removed
1 small onion, chopped
1 small green bell pepper, chopped
3 medium garlic cloves, minced
1 large tomato, peeled, chopped
1 tablespoon minced parsley,
    preferably flat-leaf
1 teaspoon dried leaf oregano or
    1 tablespoon chopped fresh oregano

1/2 teaspoon salt
1/2 teaspoon freshly ground black pepper
3/4 cup Italian-seasoned bread crumbs
4 green onions, chopped
1-1/2 cups shredded mozzarella cheese
    (6 oz.)
1 lb. fettuccine, cooked
2 cups hot Creole-Italian Tomato Gravy,
    page 145

Slice zucchini in half lengthwise; scoop out pulp, leaving a 1/4-inch shell. Chop pulp; set aside. Preheat oven to 350F (175C). Heat olive oil in a heavy 10-inch skillet over medium heat. Crumble sausage into hot oil; add onion, bell pepper and garlic. Cook, stirring, until sausage has browned and onions are slightly wilted and transparent, about 7 minutes. Add reserved zucchini pulp, tomato, parsley, oregano, salt and black pepper. Cook, stirring often, until tomato liquid evaporates, about 10 minutes. Remove pan from heat; stir in bread crumbs, green onions and cheese. Pack sausage mixture into zucchini shells, mounding tops firmly. Place stuffed squash in an ungreased 13'' x 9'' baking dish. Bake in preheated oven until cheese has melted and stuffing is bubbly, 20 minutes. To serve, place a mound of fettuccine on each plate; place a stuffed zucchini on fettuccine. Drizzle hot tomato gravy over top. Serve hot. Makes 4 servings.

Spinach Pie

This Creole-Italian version of quiche bears no resemblance to its delicate French counterpart. Robust in flavor and hearty in substance, this pie captures the essence of New Orleans Italian food. Unbaked Spinach Pie freezes well, ready to be popped into the oven on a busy night. Serve with a salad of fresh fruits.

1 recipe of Flaky Pie Pastry, page 110
1 large bunch fresh spinach
3 tablespoons extra-virgin olive oil
4 oz. prosciutto, finely chopped
6 anchovy fillets, minced
1 large red bell pepper, roasted, peeled
    and chopped
6 green onions, chopped
4 large garlic cloves, minced
1-1/2 teaspoons dried leaf oregano

2 tablespoons minced fresh basil or
    1-1/2 teaspoons dried leaf basil
1/4 teaspoon salt
1/4 teaspoon freshly ground black pepper
2/3 cup (about 3 oz.) shredded Provolone
    cheese, tossed with 1/2 cup grated
    Parmesan cheese
1/2 teaspoon Tabasco sauce
2 eggs beaten with 1/2 cup whipping cream

Prepare pastry according to recipe, page 110. On a lightly floured surface, roll out pastry to a 1/16-inch-thick circle. Roll pastry loosely around rolling pin; unroll over a 9-inch pie pan. Gently lower pastry into bottom and side of pan; do not stretch. Trim excess pastry, leaving a 1/2-inch overhang. Fold the overhang under the pastry, even with edge of the pie pan. Flute the edge, or press with the tines of a fork. Refrigerate pastry until ready to use. Wash the spinach, drain well and tear into bite-sized pieces, discarding fibrous stems; set aside. Heat the olive oil in a heavy 12-inch skillet over medium heat. Add the prosciutto, anchovies, red bell pepper, green onions, garlic, oregano, basil and salt and pepper. Sauté until onion is wilted, about 7 minutes. Add the spinach and cook, tossing, just until barely wilted, about 1 minute. Remove pan from heat and turn the mixture out into a large bowl to cool. Preheat oven to 375F (190C). When spinach mixture is cool to the touch, toss with the cheeses and turn out into the prepared pie shell. Whisk the Tabasco into the egg mixture and pour over the spinach. Bake in preheated oven 25 to 30 minutes, or until the pie is set and pastry is golden brown. To serve, slice in wedges and serve hot. Makes 6 to 8 servings.

Wine Pasta

Homemade pasta will spoil you. Once you have tasted those wonderful, egg-rich strands cooked to *al dente* perfection, it will be very hard to serve the store-bought variety again. It will seem somehow insulting to your homemade sauces. True to their reputation for uniqueness, Creole-Italians add a little *lagniappe* to the taste of their pasta. That something extra is wine. A little dry white or robust red wine added to the dough produces a rich pasta with a depth of taste that makes you want to simply add a bit of butter and eat the pasta otherwise unadorned.

1-3/4 cups semolina flour
2 eggs
1 teaspoon olive oil

About 1 tablespoon dry white or red wine
1 tablespoon salt
2 tablespoons olive oil

Combine flour, eggs, 1 teaspoon olive oil and 1 tablespoon wine in a food processor fitted with the steel blade. Process just long enough to form a smooth dough. Stop machine; check consistency of dough. If it is too dry, add more wine, 1 teaspoon at a time; process briefly after each addition. The dough should not be sticky, but must be moist enough to hold together in a smooth ball. If dough is too sticky, add more flour, 1 or 2 teaspoons at a time; process just until blended after each addition. Separate dough into 3 or 4 equal pieces. Cover with plastic wrap until ready to use. Using a pasta machine, knead pasta, 1 piece at a time. Start on number 1 setting; knead until smooth. Skip to middle setting; roll pasta through once. Skip to next to highest setting; roll pasta through once to final thickness. Using cutting head of pasta machine, cut pasta to desired size. Cook fresh, dry to store, or freeze, as desired. *To freeze pasta,* separate freshly made pasta, before it has begun to dry, into desired amounts. Freeze in plastic freezer bags up to 1 month. *To dry pasta,* spread strands on pasta drying racks, on wooden dowels or old broom handles. Separate strands as you spread them; dry several hours or overnight. Dry thoroughly to prevent spoiling. Each strand should be dry enough to snap when bent. Store in large, airtight containers. To cook fresh, frozen or fresh-dried pasta, fill a 6- to 8-quart pot 3/4 full of water, add 1 tablespoon salt and 2 tablespoons olive oil. Bring to a boil; add cut pasta. Cook until al dente, about 1 minute for fresh or frozen pasta, longer for dry pasta. Drain; serve hot with your favorite sauce. Makes about 13 ounces.

Muffuletta Bread

In order to enjoy a New Orleans Muffuletta Sandwich at its best, you must have authentic Muffuletta Bread. In New Orleans you can buy the crusty loaves in any bakery, but don't forego this treat just because you can't find the bread—make it yourself!

1 cup warm water (110F, 45C)
1 tablespoon sugar
1 (1/4-oz.) pkg. active dry yeast
  (about 1 tablespoon)

About 3 cups bread flour
1-1/2 teaspoons salt
2 tablespoons vegetable shortening
Sesame seeds

In a 2-cup glass measuring cup, combine water and sugar. Stir in yeast. Let stand until foamy, 5 to 10 minutes. In a food processor fitted with the steel blade, combine 3 cups flour, salt and shortening. Add yeast mixture. Process until dough forms a ball, about 5 seconds. Stop machine; check consistency of dough. It should be smooth and satiny. If dough is too dry, add more warm water, 1 tablespoon at a time, processing just until blended. If dough is too sticky, add more flour, 1 or 2 tablespoons at a time, processing just until blended. Process 20 seconds to knead. Lightly oil a large bowl, swirling to coat bottom and sides. Place dough in oiled bowl; turn to coat all sides. Cover bowl with plastic wrap. Let rise in a warm, draft-free place until doubled in bulk, about 1-1/2 hours. Lightly grease a baking sheet. When dough has doubled in bulk, punch down dough; turn out onto a lightly floured surface. Form dough into a round loaf about 10 inches in diameter; place on greased baking sheet. Sprinkle top of loaf with sesame seeds; press seeds gently into surface of loaf. Cover very loosely with plastic wrap; let rise until almost doubled in bulk, 1 hour. Place rack in center of oven. Preheat oven to 425F (220C). Remove plastic wrap. Bake loaf in center of preheated oven 10 minutes. Reduce heat to 375F (190C); bake 25 minutes. The loaf is done when it sounds hollow when tapped on bottom. Cool completely on a rack before slicing. Makes 1 loaf.

Muffuletta Sandwich

A visit to New Orleans without eating a Muffuletta would be like a trip to Ireland without kissing the Blarney Stone! A Muffuletta, one of life's great pleasures, is a 10-inch round sandwich stuffed with meats and cheese and topped with a concoction known as Olive Salad, page 145. In New Orleans the two best Muffulettas, bar none, can be had at Central Grocery or at Napoleon House on Chartres Street. At Central Grocery, you stand in line at the counter to shout your order. You can eat your sandwich while wandering through the tiny, crowded grocery. You'll find open barrels of flours and beans, wooden crates of dried salt cod, huge jars of olive salad and oil-cured olives, every brand of olive oil imaginable along with boxes of every size and shape of pasta made. The Napoleon House is a real cafe and bar located in one of the French Quarter's oldest buildings. Here you may dine unmolested by elbows and tromping feet.

1 (10-inch) Muffuletta Bread loaf, above
3 oz. honey ham, thinly sliced
3 oz. Mortadella with pistachios, thinly sliced

3 oz. Genoa salami, very thinly sliced
1 heaping cup Olive Salad, page 145
5 slices Provolone cheese

Preheat oven to 350F (175C). Cut bread in half crosswise to form a sandwich bun. Layer the honey ham on the bottom of the loaf. Next add the Mortadella, then the salami. Spread the Olive Salad over the meats evenly. Top with the slices of Provolone cheese and place the top on the sandwich. Press down to compress slightly. Wrap the sandwich in foil and bake in preheated oven 20 minutes, or until the cheese has begun to melt into the Olive Salad. Slice sandwich into 4 quarters. Use wooden picks to secure layers, if desired; remove picks before eating. Makes 1 to 4 servings, depending on appetite!

Top to bottom: Olive Salad, page 145; Muffuletta Sandwich

Veal & Pork Meatballs

It is truly hard to beat a plate of pasta cooked *al dente*, or "to the tooth," and topped with tomato gravy. Throw in these combination meatballs and you have a feast—Creole-Italian style.

3/4 lb. ground veal
3/4 lb. lean ground pork
1 medium onion, chopped
5 medium garlic cloves, minced
1/2 cup grated Parmesan cheese (1-1/2-oz.)
6 anchovy fillets, minced
1 teaspoon dried leaf oregano or
   1 tablespoon chopped fresh oregano
1-1/2 teaspoons salt
1 teaspoon freshly ground pepper

4 (1-inch-thick) French-bread slices,
   torn into tiny pieces
2 eggs, slightly beaten
2 tablespoons ketchup
1 tablespoon minced parsley,
   preferably flat-leaf
Olive oil
1 qt. Creole-Italian Tomato Gravy, opposite
   or favorite tomato sauce
1 lb. pasta, cooked

Combine all ingredients except olive oil, tomato gravy or tomato sauce and pasta in a large bowl. Divide mixture into 10 to 12 portions. Form round balls by rolling each portion between your hands. In a heavy 12-inch skillet, heat about 1/4-inch olive oil over medium heat. Add as many meatballs as will fit comfortably without touching. Sauté quickly until browned on all sides; remove with a slotted spoon. Brown remaining meatballs. Heat tomato gravy or tomato sauce in a Dutch oven over medium heat. Add meatballs; cook 30 minutes, stirring often to prevent sticking. Serve meatballs and sauce over your favorite pasta. Makes 5 to 6 servings.

Roux-Based Red Gravy

Roux-Based Red Gravy forms the very soul of Creole-Italian cuisine. The taste is rich and mysterious, and it says "More." One thing for sure, it was born in New Orleans. Serve gravy over meat dishes or pasta.

1/2 recipe Cajun Roux, page 12
1 large onion, finely chopped
4 medium garlic cloves, minced
1 (6-oz.) can tomato paste
1-1/2 teaspoons sugar
2 cups Brown Veal & Pork Stock, page 15,
   or canned beef broth

1 teaspoon salt
1/4 teaspoon red (cayenne) pepper
1 teaspoon freshly ground black pepper
1 teaspoon Worcestershire sauce
1/3 cup grated Parmesan cheese (1 oz.)

Make roux in a deep 12-inch skillet over medium heat, cooking until mahogany-colored. Add onion and garlic to hot roux; cook, stirring, until onion is completely wilted, about 10 minutes. Blend in tomato paste and sugar; cook, stirring, 5 minutes. Slowly stir in stock or broth. Stir in salt, cayenne, black pepper, Worcestershire sauce and cheese. Reduce heat. Cover and simmer 35 minutes, stirring often. Puree gravy, in batches, in a blender or food processor fitted with the steel blade; serve hot. Makes 4 cups.

Creole-Italian Tomato Gravy

This vegetable-and-tomato-laden sauce will delight even the most ardent connoisseur of Sicilian food. Tomato gravy freezes well. Make this large batch and have plenty on hand to serve over meat dishes or pasta.

1/2 cup olive oil
1/2 medium eggplant, peeled, finely chopped
6 anchovy fillets, minced
3 celery stalks, chopped
2 medium onions, chopped
6 large garlic cloves, minced
4 green onions, chopped
2 bay leaves, minced
2 teaspoons dried leaf oregano or
   2 tablespoons chopped fresh oregano
2 teaspoons dried leaf basil or
   2 tablespoons chopped fresh basil
2 teaspoons dried leaf savory or
   2 tablespoons chopped fresh savory
1/2 teaspoon dried leaf marjoram or
   2 tablespoons chopped fresh marjoram

1/2 teaspoon minced dried rosemary or
   1-1/2 teaspoons minced fresh rosemary
1-1/2 tablespoons sugar
1-1/4 cups tomato paste
3 (28-oz.) cans Italian plum tomatoes,
   drained, chopped
1-3/4 cups tomato sauce
1-1/2 teaspoons salt
1 teaspoon freshly ground black pepper
1 teaspoon red (cayenne) pepper
2 tablespoons minced parsley,
   preferably flat-leaf
1/2 cup grated Parmesan cheese (1-1/2 oz.)
3 qts. Brown Veal & Pork Stock, page 15,
   or canned beef broth

Heat olive oil in a heavy 8-quart Dutch oven. Add eggplant, anchovies, celery, onions, garlic, green onions, bay leaves, oregano, basil, savory, marjoram and rosemary. Cook, stirring often, until vegetables are thoroughly wilted, about 10 minutes. Add sugar and tomato paste; cook 5 minutes, stirring. Add remaining ingredients; stir until combined. Reduce heat. Barely simmer, uncovered, 1 hour. Puree in batches in blender or food processor; serve hot. Makes 5 quarts.

Olive Salad

No respectable Creole-Italian home would be without a container of Olive Salad in the refrigerator. The number-one use for the concoction in New Orleans is as a dressing for the famous Muffuletta Sandwich. It also makes a delicious addition to tossed green salads, pizzas, and is a great relish to spread on crackers! The recipe makes a lot, but it will disappear quickly when you discover all the things it's good for.

1 (32-oz.) jar pimento-stuffed green
   olives, chopped
2 cups pitted ripe olives, chopped
1-1/4 cups chopped pickled cocktail olives
2 celery stalks, finely chopped
2 cups blanched chopped cauliflower

1/4 cup minced garlic
2 medium carrots, peeled and minced
2 teaspoons dried leaf oregano
1 tablespoon minced flat-leaf parsley
2/3 cup red-wine vinegar
1/4 cup olive oil

Combine all ingredients in a large bowl and stir to blend well. Store in jars with tight-fitting lids in refrigerator. Makes about 3 quarts.

Fettucine with Oysters & Italian Sausage

1/4 cup extra-virgin olive oil
6 oz. bulk-style hot Italian sausage,
  or use mild, if preferred
6 green onions, chopped
4 large garlic cloves, minced
2 cups dry vermouth
1/2 cup minced fresh basil
1 tablespoon minced flat-leaf parsley
1 qt. whipping cream

1 qt. half and half
1/2 cup grated Parmesan cheese
2 dozen shucked oysters and their liquor
Salt and freshly ground pepper to taste
1 teaspoon Tabasco sauce
1 lb. fettucine, cooked al dente and
  well drained
Minced flat-leaf parsley

Heat olive oil in heavy, deep-sided 12-inch skillet over medium heat. When oil is hot, add the sausage, green onions and garlic. Cook, breaking up sausage with a large spoon, until sausage is done, about 10 minutes. Carefully pour off all fat from pan. Return pan to medium heat and stir in the vermouth, scraping up any browned bits from bottom of pan. Add the basil and parsley and stir to blend well. Cook to reduce vermouth by half. Stir in the whipping cream, half and half and cheese. Stir to blend well and cook until sauce is heated through and slightly thickened. Stir in the oysters and their liquor, salt, pepper and Tabasco sauce. Cook just until oysters begin to curl at the edges, about 10 minutes. Serve over fettucine, garnished with minced parsley. Makes 4 servings.

Italian Baked Oysters

Every oyster lover in the world should be able to have this dish. It is proof that often the simplest combination of fresh ingredients yields the finest taste. The finished product has a complex taste usually associated with dishes that have been "fussed with" for hours.

Seasoned Bread Crumbs, see below
1/2 cup unsalted butter or margarine
1 large onion, chopped
4 large garlic cloves, minced
1/2 teaspoon dried leaf thyme or
   1-1/2 teaspoons chopped fresh thyme
3/4 teaspoon dried leaf oregano or
   2-1/4 teaspoons chopped fresh oregano

2 tablespoons minced parsley,
   preferably flat-leaf
1/4 teaspoon red (cayenne) pepper
1/4 teaspoon freshly ground black pepper
1 teaspoon salt
48 shucked oysters with their liquor
1 cup grated Parmesan cheese (3 oz.)

Seasoned Bread Crumbs:
1-1/2 cups dry bread crumbs
2 teaspoons dried leaf basil or
   2 tablespoons chopped fresh basil
1 teaspoon dried leaf oregano or
   1 tablespoon chopped fresh oregano

1 teaspoon minced dried rosemary or
   1 tablespoon minced fresh rosemary

Prepare Seasoned Bread Crumbs; set aside. Grease a 3-quart casserole dish. Preheat oven to 375F (190C). In a heavy 10-inch skillet over medium heat, melt butter or margarine. Add onion, garlic, herbs, cayenne, black pepper and salt. Sauté until onion is wilted and transparent, about 5 minutes. Add oysters and their liquor, stirring gently to blend. Simmer mixture over medium heat just until oysters begin to curl at edges. Stir in Seasoned Bread Crumbs; spoon mixture into greased dish. Sprinkle top of casserole evenly with Parmesan cheese. Bake in preheated oven until bubbly and lightly browned on top, 15 minutes. Serve hot. Makes 6 to 8 servings.
To prepare Seasoned Bread Crumbs, in a medium bowl, combine all ingredients.

Brucholoni

There are as many ways to spell this New Orleans delight as there are recipes for making it! Brucholoni is a favorite family meal in Creole-Italian homes. However, you may share it with very good friends on less formal occasions. Serve with pasta of your choice.

2 beef or veal top round steaks, 1/4 inch thick	**1 medium, green bell pepper, thinly sliced**
1 cup Italian-seasoned bread crumbs	**2 hard-cooked eggs, thinly sliced**
2 eggs, slightly beaten	**Salt to taste**
4 large garlic cloves, minced	**Freshly ground black pepper**
1/2 cup grated Parmesan cheese (1-1/2 oz.)	**1/2 cup olive oil**
1 medium onion, halved lengthwise, thinly sliced	**1 recipe Roux-Based Red Gravy, page 144**

Place steaks on a cutting board; trim all fat from edges. Using a meat pounder, pound steaks to about 1/8-inch-thick, taking care not to tear. Preheat oven to 375F (190C). In a medium bowl, combine bread crumbs, eggs, garlic and cheese. Pat mixture evenly over pounded steaks, leaving a 1-inch border at long edges. Scatter onion and bell pepper over bread-crumb mixture; top with hard-cooked eggs. Beginning at long edges, roll tightly, jelly-roll fashion. Tie securely with kitchen string. Salt and pepper rolled steaks. Heat olive oil in a heavy 12-inch skillet over medium heat. Add steak rolls, 1 at a time; brown on all sides. Place browned rolls in a 13'' x 9'' baking dish; pour gravy over top. Bake in preheated oven until meat is fork tender, 45 minutes. To serve, remove string; slice Brucholoni into 1/2-inch-thick slices. Spoon gravy over each serving. Makes 4 to 6 servings.

How to Make Brucholoni

1/Beginning at long edge, roll filled steak tightly, jelly-roll fashion. Tie with kitchen string.

2/To serve, slice Brucholoni into 1/2-inch-thick slices. Serve with red gravy.

Veal Thomassina

This is a simple dish to prepare, but the taste is scrumptious. Serve with buttered pasta and a green vegetable for a very elegant meal.

Salt to taste
Freshly ground pepper
4 (4- to 5-oz.) veal cutlets
1-1/2 cups dairy sour cream
1 egg

2 tablespoons red-wine vinegar
2 tablespoons unsalted butter or margarine
3 tablespoons vegetable oil
3 cups Italian-seasoned bread crumbs
Mushroom Garnish, see below

Mushroom Garnish:
1/4 cup unsalted butter or margarine
1/2 lb. small button mushrooms
3 large garlic cloves, minced
Salt to taste

Freshly ground pepper
1 tablespoon minced parsley,
  preferably flat-leaf

Salt and pepper both sides of veal cutlets; place in a 13'' x 9'' baking dish. In a medium bowl, whisk together sour cream, egg and vinegar. Pour over cutlets; marinate 1 hour. In a heavy 12-inch skillet over medium heat, heat butter or margarine and oil. Remove cutlets from marinade; gently scrape off excess marinade. Dredge meat in bread crumbs; shake off all excess. Sauté meat in hot butter mixture about 3 minutes per side, turning once. Prepare garnish. To serve, place a sautéed cutlet on each plate; top with garnish. Serve hot. Makes 4 servings.
To prepare Mushroom Garnish, in a medium skillet, melt butter or margarine; add mushrooms and garlic. Cook, stirring, 5 minutes. Season with salt and pepper; stir in parsley.

Crabmeat in Garlic-Cream Sauce

A rich and sumptuous example of the Creole-Italian use of shellfish, this dish is a great do-ahead meal for company. Serve with a green salad.

1 lb. backfin lump crabmeat
2 tablespoons minced parsley,
  preferably flat-leaf
6 green onions, chopped
4 large garlic cloves, minced
2/3 cup dairy sour cream

3 tablespoons dry white wine
1/2 teaspoon salt
1 teaspoon freshly ground pepper
1 cup Italian-seasoned bread crumbs
1/2 cup grated Parmesan cheese (1-1/2 oz.)

Preheat oven to 350F (175C). Using your fingertips, carefully pick through crabmeat; remove and discard any bits of shell or cartilage. In a medium bowl, combine crabmeat, parsley, green onions and garlic; set aside. In a small bowl, combine sour cream, wine, salt and pepper. Gently fold cream mixture into crabmeat mixture; do not break up lumps of crabmeat. Divide crabmeat mixture among 4 (1-cup) au gratin dishes. In a small bowl, combine bread crumbs and cheese with a fork. Sprinkle bread-crumb mixture over top of each dish. Bake in preheated oven until golden and bubbly, 20 minutes. Makes 4 servings.

Creole Daube with Red Gravy

Creole Daube is one of the most classic beef dishes existing within this cuisine. Daube uses the beef rump roast, a cut which benefits from the Creole long-cooking methods. The vinegar marinade and the spices used in this dish suggest that its roots may have been in the soil of Cote des Allemands or "German Coast." This area, upriver from New Orleans, was settled by German immigrants in the early 1700s. The dish in itself provides a delicious and filling meal, but it becomes an exquisite buffet item when chilled in its own rich broth and served as Daube Glace. The Creole-Italians took it one step further by preparing the dish in its classic form, then serving it topped with Red Gravy and accompanied by pasta.

4 large garlic cloves, minced	1 large turnip, diced
1/4 lb. salt pork, diced into 1/2-inch cubes	1/2 cup Burgundy wine
1 teaspoon ground cloves	6 green onions, chopped
1 teaspoon ground allspice	3 bay leaves, minced
1 teaspoon dried leaf thyme or	2 tablespoons minced parsley,
1 tablespoon fresh chopped thyme	preferably flat-leaf
1 teaspoon red (cayenne) pepper	1-1/2 teaspoons freshly ground black pepper
1 (5-lb.) beef round rump roast boneless	1/2 teaspoon salt
1 cup red-wine vinegar	1/2 teaspoon red (cayenne) pepper
Salt to taste	2 qts. Brown Veal & Pork Stock, page 15,
Freshly ground black pepper	or canned beef broth
1/3 cup vegetable oil	1 lb. pasta, cooked
4 large carrots, thinly sliced	1 recipe hot Roux-Based Red Gravy, page 144
3 medium onions, halved lengthwise, sliced	

In a medium bowl, combine garlic, salt pork, cloves, allspice, thyme and 1 teaspoon cayenne with a fork. Toss until salt pork is coated with seasoning mixture. Using a small sharp knife, make slits in meat; insert seasoned salt-pork cubes into slits, leaving remaining seasoning mixture in bowl. Add vinegar to remaining seasoning mixture. Salt and pepper meat; place in a large bowl. Pour vinegar mixture over top. Cover with plastic wrap; refrigerate 3 days, turning occasionally. Remove meat from marinade; pat very dry with paper towels. Discard marinade. In a heavy 8-quart Dutch oven, heat oil over medium-high heat. When oil is very hot, add meat; sear quickly on all sides to form a crisp brown crust. Remove meat; set aside. Add carrots, onions and turnip to hot oil; cook quickly, tossing constantly, to lightly brown vegetables, about 7 minutes. Carefully pour off oil from pan. Return pan to heat; add wine, scraping up browned bits from bottom. Return meat to pan; add green onions, bay leaves, parsley, black pepper, salt, 1/2 teaspoon cayenne and stock or broth. Reduce heat. Cover and simmer until meat is fork tender, 3 hours. Place meat on a cutting board; cut, across grain, into serving slices. To serve, place meat slices and pasta on each plate. Spoon some sauce and cooked-down vegetables over meat; top with red gravy. Makes 6 to 8 servings.

Brunch

Special-Occasion Brunch

Brandy Milk Punch, page 167
Ramos Gin Fizzes, page 169
Peaches in Soft Brandy Cream
Eggs Nouvelle Orleans
South-Louisiana Buttermilk Biscuits
Pecan Crescents
Bayou-Country Beignets
Cafe au Lait, page 172

Even today, amidst the hustle and bustle of everyday life, the Deep South has managed to hold onto a few precious relics of quiet times gone by. South Louisianians live life at a slower "internal" pace, with great emphasis placed on enjoying each moment to its fullest.

The Cajuns and Creoles work hard, often six days a week, but you can bet your red beans that they have arranged their lives to make the absolute best of the one day of the week on which they may do exactly as they please. Since the early days of settlement in Louisiana, Sunday brunch has remained a pleasant tradition. Sunday is known as a day for morning worship at church, after which a full day looms ahead for relaxing, visiting with family and friends and, best of all, enjoying good food.

The tradition of the full-meal breakfast in New Orleans began in the late 1800s in fine restaurants such as Madame Begue's. The French Quarter merchants started their workday long before dawn and by "breakfast time" were hungry for a full meal.

With the 1884 Cotton Exposition, the fame of such dishes as Eggs Benedict and fancy stuffed and sauced omelettes spread. French Market coffeehouses opened, serving New Orleans famed Cafe au Lait with beignets or *rice calas*—tasty deep-fried rice fritters made from a yeast starter.

Brunch or breakfast in South Louisiana includes some of the most unique dishes in

the cuisine. Virtually the same dishes would be served on a French Quarter balcony rich with "iron lace" railings and on the houseboat where a Cajun trapper and his family live, moored to a rickety dock. The difference is that one meal would be served from antique china and crystal on cut-work linens adorning a 17th-century French table. The other would be eaten from graniteware and mismatched canning jars and mugs placed securely in one's lap to avoid accidental spilling from the gentle rocking of the boat.

A hearty Cajun-Creole brunch may be served on any occasion and on any day. It is a great celebration of the bounties of life—and a wonderful excuse for overeating.

A simple weekend brunch would consist of one or two breads, a seasonal fruit in heavy cream laced with a complimentary liqueur, a meat dish and an egg dish. Cafe au Lait is a must. Brandy Milk Punch, though certainly optional, is ethereal and reminiscent of lazy afternoons on the deck of a slow-moving paddle-wheeler headed upriver to Natchez.

If you serve a Cajun-Creole brunch on New Year's Day, tradition dictates that you add a pot of purple hull or black-eyed peas for good luck and smothered cabbage for wealth during the coming year.

Many of the classic New Orleans brunch dishes are structured around egg-based sauces—hollandaise and béarnaise and their variations. Once you master these sauces, you can serve Eggs Benedict to rival "breakfast at Brennan's."

Crawfish Folklore

Within their fascinating "lore" the Cajuns have a delightful story about the origin of the crawfish. The story, of course, centers around the Cajuns, and it goes like this. It seems that when the Acadians were exiled from Nova Scotia in the mid-1700s, they packed up and started walking all the way to Louisiana. Now, they had grown especially fond of the delicious lobsters indigenous to the region. Therefore, they decided to bring lots of lobsters to Louisiana so that they could continue to enjoy them. They tied strings on all the lobsters and off they went, Cajuns and lobsters, heading for Louisiana and a new life.

Well, you know, my friend, it was a long trip from Nova Scotia to Louisiana. By the time they got here, those poor lobsters had lost so much weight that they were just pitiful little things only a fraction of their original size. Why, they looked just like bugs! But, like the Cajuns, they had found a new home, and they were happy. They just made themselves at home in the muddy bayous and marshlands. That's where they've been ever since, but they never grew big again.

Pain Perdu

Pain Perdu, or *lost bread,* is a sinfully rich and delicious dish concocted by frugal Cajuns to make use of the household's leftover French bread. If only all leftovers tasted this good!

1/3 cup vegetable oil
6 eggs
3 tablespoons Grand Marnier or
    other orange-flavored liqueur
2 tablespoons milk
1/3 cup sugar

Grated zest of 1 large lemon
8 to 12 slices leftover French bread,
    cut 3/4-inch-thick
Powdered sugar
Butter
Syrup

In a heavy 12-inch skillet over medium heat, heat oil. In a medium bowl, combine eggs, liqueur, milk, sugar and lemon zest. Whisk until eggs are frothy and sugar is dissolved. When oil is hot, dip bread slices into batter, turning to coat well. Place coated bread in hot oil in batches. Fry until golden brown on both sides, turning once, 5 to 6 minutes. Drain on paper towels; sprinkle with powdered sugar. Keep warm while frying remaining slices. Serve hot with butter and your favorite syrup. Or, use real cane syrup. Makes 4 to 6 servings.

Cajun Coush-Coush

Coush-Coush is a thick breakfast cereal made from cornmeal. The name, derived from the Moroccan grain dish, couscous, was given by African slaves. It is hearty and delicious Cajun fare when served with butter, milk and sugar or—to be authentic—real cane syrup.

2 cups yellow cornmeal
1-1/2 teaspoons salt
1 teaspoon freshly ground pepper
2 teaspoons baking powder
1/2 cup bacon drippings or lard

1-1/2 cups boiling water
Butter
Sugar or cane syrup
Milk or half and half

In a medium bowl, combine cornmeal, salt, pepper and baking powder with a fork. In a heavy 10-inch skillet over medium heat, heat bacon drippings or lard. Pour boiling water into cornmeal mixture; stir to form a smooth paste. Spoon mixture into hot fat; fry until a light crust forms on bottom, about 10 minutes. Stir mixture, breaking up crust and distributing browned bits throughout. Cook 10 minutes, without stirring. To serve, scoop Coush-Coush into individual bowls. Add your choice of butter, sugar or cane syrup and milk or half and half. Serve hot. Makes 4 servings.

Quail in Sherry Sauce over Fluffy Eggs

Quail was a favorite among the plantation owners, who presented lavish and sumptuous Sunday brunches for neighbors and friends. Neighbors often lived several miles away and were ready for hearty food after the long trip. Dishes such as these are still found on the brunch menus of some of New Orleans finer restaurants and hotels. Serve with biscuits or French Bread.

6 quail
About 2 cups all-purpose flour
2 teaspoons salt
2 teaspoons freshly ground black pepper
2 teaspoons red (cayenne) pepper
2 tablespoons unsalted butter or margarine
1/2 cup bacon drippings
1/2 lb. mushrooms, sliced

2-1/2 cups Louisiana Brown-Poultry Stock, page 14, or canned chicken broth
1/2 cup dry sherry
1/2 teaspoon freshly ground pepper
Salt to taste
Fluffy Eggs, see below
6 green onions, chopped
Minced parsley, preferably flat-leaf

Fluffy Eggs:
8 eggs
1/2 cup warm water
1 teaspoon salt

1/2 teaspoon freshly ground pepper
1 teaspoon Tabasco sauce
2 tablespoons unsalted butter or margarine

Pat quail dry with paper towels; set aside. In a medium bowl, combine flour, 2 teaspoons salt, 2 teaspoons black pepper and cayenne with a fork. In a heavy 12-inch skillet over medium heat, heat butter or margarine and bacon drippings. When fat is hot, dredge quail in seasoned flour, turning to coat well; shake to remove excess flour. Reserve 3 tablespoons seasoned flour. Add floured quail to hot fat in batches. Cook quail until browned on all sides, 6 to 7 minutes. Remove from skillet; set aside. Add mushrooms to skillet; sauté until wilted, about 5 minutes. Add reserved 3 tablespoons flour all at once; stir until combined. Cook, stirring constantly, 3 to 4 minutes. Slowly stir in stock or broth. Add sherry, 1/2 teaspoon black pepper and salt. Bring to a boil. Return browned quail to skillet. Reduce heat. Cover and barely simmer quail until tender, 20 minutes, stirring often. Meanwhile prepare eggs. Remove quail from heat; stir in green onions. Cover; let stand 2 to 3 minutes. To serve, place a mound of eggs in center of each plate; nest 1 quail in middle of eggs. Drizzle sauce over top; sprinkle with minced parsley. Serve hot. Makes 6 servings.

To prepare Fluffy Eggs, in a medium bowl, combine eggs, water, salt, pepper and Tabasco sauce. Whisk until eggs are very frothy. In a heavy 12-inch skillet over medium heat, melt butter or margarine. Add egg mixture; cook, stirring constantly, until eggs are cooked, dry and fluffy.

Marchand de Vin Sauce

Marchand de Vin is but one of the rich and flavorful sauces born of High-Creole cuisine. The sauce originated at Antoine's Restaurant, a New Orleans institution with a reputation for fine cuisine. This is a time-consuming sauce, but, alas, excellence cannot be rushed. Canned stock simply will not do in this recipe. Before tackling the sauce, have a supply of Brown Veal & Pork Stock, page 15, for the Espagnole Sauce from which you then prepare Marchand de Vin Sauce!

For those students of the classic French way of doing things, let me state up front, that through the years, Creole chefs have taken a few liberties with classic dishes. These subtle changes were made to adapt to local ingredients and taste. Forgive us, Monsieur Escoffier, but then, if you could have dined on fine Creole cuisine, you would know why we took these liberties. Marchand de Vin is one of two sauces used in the classic brunch dish, Eggs Hussarde, page 157. But this wonderful sauce is not limited in use to one egg dish. The sauce, served over beef tournedos at Antoine's, is one of the restaurant's most popular dishes. This sauce freezes well, a fact that helps compensate for the time involved in its preparation.

Espagnole Sauce, see below
6 tablespoons unsalted butter
2 medium onions, finely chopped
1 lb. mushrooms, finely chopped
6 large garlic cloves, finely minced

1/4 lb. ham, finely chopped
6 tablespoons all-purpose flour
2-1/2 cups red wine
Salt to taste
Freshly ground pepper

Espagnole Sauce:
1-1/4 recipes Cajun Roux, page 12
4 qts. Brown Veal & Pork Stock, page 15
2 medium onions, finely chopped
2 carrots, finely chopped
2 celery stalks, finely chopped

1 teaspoon dried leaf thyme or
  1 tablespoon chopped fresh thyme
1 bay leaf, minced
4 large tomatoes, peeled, seeded and chopped

Prepare Espagnole Sauce; set aside. In a 4-quart Dutch oven over medium heat, melt butter. Add onions, mushrooms, garlic and ham. Cook, stirring often, until onions are thoroughly wilted and lightly browned, about 12 minutes. Add flour all at once; stir until blended. Cook 3 to 4 minutes, stirring constantly. Stirring, add wine in a slow, steady stream. Bring to a boil. Puree sauce mixture in blender or food processor fitted with the steel blade. Return pureed sauce to pan over medium heat. Add Espagnole Sauce; season with salt and pepper. Simmer 30 minutes. Serve hot. Makes about 2 quarts.

To prepare Espagnole Sauce, make roux in a heavy 4-quart Dutch oven as directed on page 12, cooking until mahogany-colored. Meanwhile, heat 3 quarts stock in a heavy 6- to 8-quart saucepan over medium-high heat. Add onions, carrots, celery, thyme and bay leaf to roux. Cook, stirring, until onions are wilted and transparent, about 10 minutes. When stock comes to a simmer, rapidly whisk about 2 cups hot stock into roux mixture. When blended, pour mixture into remaining hot stock; whisk until combined. Bring to a boil. Reduce heat. Barely simmer, uncovered, 1 hour, skimming surface often to remove grey foam. Strain sauce through a fine strainer, pressing down hard on vegetables to remove all moisture. Discard vegetables. Return strained stock to a clean pot over medium-high heat. Add remaining 1 quart stock; bring to a boil. Reduce heat. Barely simmer, uncovered, 1 hour. Skim grey foam from surface often. Add tomatoes. Simmer, uncovered, 1 hour, skimming surface frequently. Line a strainer with cheesecloth or clean kitchen towel; strain sauce into a clean 5-quart saucepan. Cook over medium-high heat until sauce is reduced to 6 cups. Makes 6 cups.

Hollandaise Sauce

This regal and delicious sauce has an important role in Cajun-Creole brunches. It is easy to make a perfect hollandaise that is as smooth as silk if you are mindful of two things: First, relax! If you fret yourself into a state of disarray over making the sauce, you can't concentrate and are doomed to failure. Second, and most important, do not think of hollandaise as a HOT sauce. Keep in mind that egg yolks coagulate—or curdle—at about 180F (80C)—considerably below the boiling point 212F (100C). The temperature of the finished ready-to-serve sauce should be tepid. If you try to serve it hot, it will curdle, plain and simple.

3 egg yolks
1 tablespoon fresh lemon juice
3/4 teaspoon salt

1/4 teaspoon red (cayenne) pepper
1-1/2 cups melted unsalted butter,
  heated until hot

Place egg yolks in top of a double boiler over hot water. Whisk until thickened and light lemon in color. Remove from heat. Combine egg yolks, lemon juice, salt and cayenne in a food processor fitted with steel blade. Process 2 minutes, or until mixture is thickened. With the machine running, add the hot melted butter in a slow, steady stream through the feed tube. When all has been added, process 10 seconds to form a smooth emulsion. Transfer to bowl and cover with plastic wrap to keep warm until ready to serve. Makes about 2 cups.

Béarnaise Sauce

Béarnaise sauce, like hollandaise sauce, must be cooked in a double boiler. A whisk is important for making these egg-based sauces. Select a whisk made of stainless wire, making sure that wires are flexible. Now all you need are eggs, butter and some energy for whisking.

3 egg yolks
Herb Mixture, see below
2 teaspoons tepid water
1 teaspoon Creole mustard, or substitute
  other whole-grain mustard

3/4 teaspoon salt
1/4 teaspoon red (cayenne) pepper
1-1/2 cups melted unsalted butter,
  heated until hot

Herb Mixture:
4 green onions, finely minced
2 medium garlic cloves, finely minced
1 tablespoon dried leaf tarragon
1 tablespoon dried leaf chervil

1/4 cup fresh lemon juice
1/4 cup dry white wine
1 teaspoon Tabasco sauce
3/4 teaspoon freshly ground black pepper

Place egg yolks in top of a double boiler over hot water. Whisk until thickened and light lemon in color. Remove from heat. Prepare Herb Mixture. In work bowl of food processor fitted with steel blade, combine Herb Mixture, egg yolks, tepid water, mustard, salt and cayenne. Process 2 minutes, or until mixture is thickened. With machine running, add the hot butter in a slow, steady stream through the feed tube. When all has been added, process an additional 10 seconds to form a strong emulsion. Strain the sauce through a fine strainer, stirring; discard solids. Cover tightly with plastic wrap and set aside to keep warm until ready to serve. Makes about 2 cups.
To prepare Herb Mixture, combine all ingredients in a heavy 1-quart saucepan over medium-high heat. Cook until liquid is reduced to about 1 tablespoon, about 10 minutes.

Poached Eggs

To be a successful New Orleans brunch cook, you must master the art of poaching eggs. Most of the classic brunch dishes are built around poached eggs. Fortunately, egg poaching is a task that is simple to master.

1/4 cup white vinegar or lemon juice   **3 to 6 eggs**

In a heavy, deep 12-inch skillet, combine 1-1/2 quarts water and vinegar or lemon juice. Bring liquid to a simmer. Break 1 egg into a saucer, taking care not to break yolk; slide egg into simmering water. Repeat with remaining eggs. *To serve at once,* cook eggs 3 minutes; remove with a slotted spoon. Use as directed in recipe. *To make ahead,* before you begin cooking eggs, prepare a large bowl of water and ice cubes. Cook eggs as directed above 2 minutes only. Remove at once with a slotted spoon; place in iced water. Set aside up to 2 hours, adding ice cubes as necessary. To serve, heat fresh water to a simmer in deep skillet. Remove eggs from iced water with a slotted spoon; place in simmering water. Cook 1 minute; remove with slotted spoon. Serve at once. Makes 3 to 6 servings.

Eggs Sardou

This now-famous dish was created by Antoine Alciatore, proprietor of Antoine's Restaurant, for a dinner he hosted for French playwright Victorien Sardou in 1908. It has remained a popular dish throughout the years.

Creamed Spinach, see below
1/4 cup unsalted butter or margarine
4 large artichoke bottoms
8 anchovy fillets

1/4 cup minced baked ham (about 2 oz.)
4 Poached Eggs, above
2 recipes warm Hollandaise Sauce, page 155
Orange slices

Creamed Spinach:
1 (10-oz.) pkg. frozen chopped spinach
3 tablespoons unsalted butter or margarine
4 green onions, chopped
2 tablespoons all-purpose flour
2/3 cup whipping cream

2 teaspoons Herbsaint
1/2 teaspoon sugar
1/2 teaspoon salt
1/4 teaspoon freshly ground pepper
1/4 teaspoon freshly grated nutmeg

Prepare spinach; keep warm. In a 10-inch skillet, melt butter or margarine over medium heat. Add artichoke bottoms; sauté just until heated through. Remove from skillet. Set aside. Add anchovy fillets to skillet; cook 3 minutes; set aside with artichoke bottoms. Add ham to skillet; toss to coat with butter or margarine. To assemble, place a mound of spinach in center on each of 4 serving plates. Nest an artichoke bottom into each mound; crisscross 2 anchovies across each artichoke bottom. Place a poached egg in each artichoke bottom over anchovies; top each egg with 1/2 cup Hollandaise Sauce. Sprinkle with ham. Garnish plates with orange slices; serve at once. Makes 4 servings.
To prepare Creamed Spinach, cook frozen spinach according to package directions; drain and press out as much moisture as possible. Set aside. Melt butter or margarine in a 10-inch skillet over medium heat. Add green onions; sauté 4 minutes, stirring. Add flour all at once; stir until blended. Cook 3 minutes, stirring. Add cream, stirring; cook until thickened. Stir in Herbsaint, sugar, salt, pepper and nutmeg. Stir in cooked spinach; remove from heat.

How to Make Poached Eggs

1/Break 1 egg into a saucer; slide egg into simmering water.

2/Remove eggs with a slotted spoon.

Eggs Hussarde

A New Orleans original, this variation of Eggs Benedict adds a second sauce to the traditional hollandaise, rich and flavorful Marchand de Vin.

2 tablespoons unsalted butter or margarine
4 baked-ham slices, trimmed to fit rusks or
   bread rounds
4 (3/8-inch-thick) tomato slices
Salt to taste
Freshly ground black pepper

4 Holland Rusks or 4 (3-inch) rounds cut
   from white bread slices, toasted
1 cup Marchand de Vin Sauce, page 154
4 Poached Eggs, opposite
2 recipes warm Hollandaise Sauce, page 155
Minced parsley, preferably flat-leaf
Orange slices

In a 10-inch skillet over medium heat, melt butter or margarine. Add ham slices; sauté on both sides until lightly browned, about 5 minutes. Remove from skillet; keep warm. In same skillet, sauté tomato slices just until heated through, about 30 seconds per side, turning once. Salt and pepper tomato slices. To assemble dish, place a toasted rusk or bread round on each plate; top with a browned ham slice. Spoon 1/4 cup Marchand de Vin Sauce over each; add a hot tomato slice and a poached egg. Top each egg with 1/2 cup Hollandaise Sauce; sprinkle with minced parsley. Garnish plates with orange slices. Serve at once. Makes 4 servings.

Eggs Benedict

Eggs Benedict is the number one brunch dish across the country. Although this dish probably originated at New York's famed Delmonico's, it is most often associated with breakfast at Brennan's.

2 English muffins	**4 Poached Eggs, page 156**
2 tablespoons unsalted butter or margarine	**2 recipes warm Hollandaise Sauce, page 155**
4 baked-ham slices, trimmed to	**Paprika**
fit English muffins	**Orange slices**
2 tablespoons Madeira	**Curly-parsley sprigs**

Halve English muffins. Toast and butter halves; keep warm. In a 10-inch skillet over medium heat, melt butter or margarine. Add ham slices; sauté on both sides until lightly browned, about 5 minutes. Pour Madeira over ham; cook until liquid evaporates. To assemble dish, place a toasted English-muffin half on each plate; top with a browned ham slice. Place a poached egg on top of ham; pour 1/2 cup Hollandaise Sauce on each egg. Sprinkle with paprika; garnish plates with orange slices and parsley. Serve at once. Makes 4 servings.

Cajun Skillet-Baked Eggs

Here's a delicious, no-fuss breakfast dish for those times when you need a hearty family breakfast in a hurry. Slice into pie-shaped wedges; serve with biscuits or toast.

6 eggs	**1/4 cup unsalted butter or margarine**
1/2 cup water	**7 green onions, chopped**
1/2 pint whipping cream (1 cup)	**1-1/2 cups sliced mushrooms**
1 teaspoon salt	**1 medium, green bell pepper, chopped**
2 teaspoons Creole mustard or	**3 medium garlic cloves, minced**
other stone-ground mustard	**6 crisp-cooked bacon slices, crumbled**
1/2 teaspoon freshly ground black pepper	**1 cup shredded Cheddar cheese (4 oz.)**
1 teaspoon Tabasco sauce	**2 teaspoons paprika**

Preheat oven to 300F (150C). In a medium bowl, combine eggs, water, cream, salt, mustard, black pepper and Tabasco sauce. Whisk until eggs are very frothy; set aside. In a 12-inch ovenproof skillet, melt butter or margarine. Add green onions, mushrooms, bell pepper and garlic. Cook, stirring often, until onions are slightly wilted and transparent, about 5 minutes. Stir in beaten egg mixture and bacon; blend well. Remove pan from heat; sprinkle cheese over eggs. Garnish with paprika. Bake in preheated oven until eggs are set and a knife inserted off center comes out clean, 35 minutes. Serve hot. Makes 4 to 6 servings.

Eggs Nouvelle Orleans

Shirred eggs have declined in popularity in recent years, but they are still found on the menu at a few of New Orleans' finer hotels. This dish is one of my favorites for a casual brunch. The sauce may be completed ahead of time, and the eggs assembled, ready to bake.

Creole Sauce, see below
2 tablespoons unsalted butter or margarine
1/3 cup finely chopped tasso, page 16, or smoked ham (about 3 oz.)
2/3 cup whipping cream
1 teaspoon dry mustard

2 teaspoons Worcestershire sauce
4 eggs
Salt to taste
Freshly ground pepper
Minced parsley, preferably flat-leaf

Creole Sauce:
1/4 cup vegetable oil
4 green onions, chopped
1 medium onion, chopped
1 medium, green bell pepper, chopped
1 large celery stalk, chopped
2 medium garlic cloves, chopped
2 large tomatoes, peeled, chopped
1/2 teaspoon dried leaf thyme or 1-1/2 teaspoons chopped fresh thyme

1 bay leaf, minced
1/2 teaspoon salt
1/4 teaspoon freshly ground black pepper
1/4 teaspoon red (cayenne) pepper
1 cup Louisiana Brown-Poultry Stock, page 14, or canned chicken broth
2/3 cup Burgundy wine
2 teaspoons fresh lemon juice

Prepare Creole Sauce; keep warm. Preheat oven to 375F (190C). In a small skillet, melt butter or margarine. Add tasso or ham; sauté until heated through, 3 to 4 minutes. Set aside. In a small bowl, combine cream, mustard and Worcestershire sauce. Pour equal amounts of mixture into 4 individual au gratin dishes. Break 1 egg into each dish, taking care not to break yolks. Top each dish with a sprinkling of tasso or ham. Salt and pepper. Bake in preheated oven just until eggs are set, about 7 minutes. To serve, spoon a generous amount of hot Creole Sauce over each egg, sprinkle with minced parsley. Serve hot. Makes 4 servings.

To prepare Creole Sauce, in a heavy 12-inch skillet over medium heat, heat oil until hot. Add green onion, onion, bell pepper, celery and garlic. Cook, stirring often, until vegetables are slightly wilted and transparent, about 5 minutes. Add tomatoes, thyme, bay leaf, salt, black pepper and cayenne. Stir to blend well. Add stock or broth; cook until reduced by 1/2, about 15 minutes, stirring often. Add Burgundy and lemon juice; cook until reduced by 1/2 again, about 20 minutes.

Grillades & Grits

Grillades (pronounced GREE-odds) & Grits is just about the best breakfast South Louisiana has to offer. Grillades are pounded pieces of round steak which are seasoned, seared quickly in hot fat, then cooked slowly in a rich, roux-based gravy with vegetables and tomatoes. The grillades and thick, rich gravy are served with old-fashioned slow-cooking grits.

2 teaspoons salt
1-1/2 teaspoons freshly ground black pepper
1-1/2 teaspoons red (cayenne) pepper
About 2 cups all-purpose flour
1-1/2 lbs. beef round steak, trimmed, cut into 2-inch squares
1/3 cup lard or bacon drippings
1 recipe Cajun Roux, page 12
2 medium onions, chopped

1 large green bell pepper, chopped
4 large garlic cloves, minced
1 large celery stalk, chopped
3 tomatoes, peeled, chopped
2 cups Brown Veal & Pork Stock, page 15, or canned beef broth
1 tablespoon cider vinegar
Old-Fashioned Grits, see below
6 green onions, chopped

Old-Fashioned Grits:
5 cups water
1 teaspoon salt
1 cup slow-cooking grits

1/4 cup unsalted butter or margarine, room temperature
1 egg, slightly beaten

In a medium bowl, combine salt, black pepper, cayenne and flour with a fork. Sprinkle seasoning mixture over both sides of meat squares. Using a meat pounder, pound meat until doubled in size, taking care not to tear meat; set aside. In a heavy 12-inch skillet over medium-high heat, heat lard or bacon drippings. When fat is hot, add pounded meat in batches; brown quickly on both sides. Remove from heat; set aside. Make roux in a heavy 12-inch skillet as directed on page 12, cooking until mahogany-colored. Add onions, bell pepper, garlic and celery to hot roux; cook, stirring, until vegetables are slightly wilted and transparent, about 5 minutes. Stir in tomatoes. Slowly stir in stock or broth and vinegar. Add browned meat. Reduce heat. Cover and simmer until meat is tender, 1 hour, stirring occasionally. Meanwhile, prepare grits. To serve, remove grillades from gravy with a slotted spoon; place on individual plates. Stir green onions into gravy; remove from heat. Spoon grits on each plate; top grillades and grits with gravy. Serve hot. Makes 4 to 6 servings.
To prepare Old-Fashioned Grits, combine water and salt in a heavy 3-quart saucepan over medium-high heat; bring to a boil. Stir in grits; reduce heat to low. Cover; cook until thickened, 30 to 35 minutes, stirring occasionally. Remove from heat; quickly stir in butter or margarine and egg until blended.

Clockwise from top left: Pecan Crescents, page 162; Peaches in Soft Brandy Cream, page 162; Grillades & Grits

Pecan Crescents *Photo on page 161.*

These easy-to-make little rolls are one of my favorite things to eat for breakfast—or for any occasion.

2 cups sifted all-purpose flour
1/4 teaspoon salt
1 cup frozen unsalted butter or margarine,
** cut into 1-inch pieces**

1 egg yolk, slightly beaten
3/4 cup dairy sour cream
Pecan Filling, see below

Pecan Filling:
3/4 cup sugar
1-1/2 teaspoons ground cinnamon

3/4 cup coarsely chopped pecans

In a food processor fitted with the steel blade, combine flour and salt. Add butter or margarine. Turn on and off to break butter or margarine into chunks the size of peas. In a small bowl, combine egg yolk and sour cream; add to flour mixture. Process just until combined. Place dough on a lightly floured surface; gather into a ball. Divide dough into 4 pieces; pat into small circles. Wrap each circle in plastic wrap; refrigerate overnight. Prepare filling; set aside. Preheat oven to 375F (190C). Remove 1 circle of dough, at a time, from refrigerator. On a lightly floured surface, roll out dough into a 12-inch circle. Cut circle into 8 wedges. Sprinkle filling evenly over surface of dough. Roll up each wedge, starting at outside edge. Place on ungreased baking sheet; bend into crescent shapes, curving ends in toward each other. Repeat with remaining circles. Bake in preheated oven until golden brown and crispy, 20 to 25 minutes. Cool on a rack. Makes 32 crescents.
To prepare Pecan Filling, in a medium bowl, combine sugar, cinnamon and pecans.

Peaches in Soft Brandy Cream *Photo on page 161.*

Starting in late June, sweet and scrumptious Ruston, Louisiana peaches are available at roadside stands. We all do our best to get our fill of them fresh. We put a bushel or so by in the freezer, and we put up dozens of jars of peach preserves to remind us of summer throughout the year. They are especially pleasing on a wet and cold winter's day. Of all the ways to eat peaches, however, this is my favorite. It is a great eye-opener for a weekend brunch.

6 large peaches, peeled, sliced
1 cup powdered sugar, sifted
1 pint whipping cream (2 cups)

1/2 cup peach brandy
1 teaspoon vanilla extract
Mint sprigs

Place peaches in a medium bowl; sprinkle with 1/2 cup powdered sugar. Stir gently to coat all slices. Set aside. In a medium bowl, beat cream with an electric mixer on medium-high speed until peaks just begin to form, about 3 minutes. Beat in remaining 1/2 cup powdered sugar, peach brandy and vanilla. Beat just until soft peaks form, about 2 minutes. Fold whipped-cream mixture into peaches; serve in glass bowls. Garnish with mint sprigs. Makes 4 to 6 servings.

Creole Rice Calas

At the turn of the century, Rice Calas sellers made their way through the marketplace in the French Quarter with their baskets of delightful rice fritters calling "Belles calas! Belles calas tout chauds." The name *calas* came from an African word for rice. Sadly, calas vendors are gone. The secret for preparing rice calas was kept alive in Creole homes where the dish originated as a means of using leftover rice. If you are serving a New Orleans-style brunch, add calas for a delicious note of authenticity.

1/2 cup warm water (110F, 45C)
2 tablespoons granulated sugar
1 (1/4-oz.) pkg. active dry yeast
  (about 1 tablespoon)
1-1/2 cups leftover cooked white rice
3 eggs, slightly beaten

1-1/2 cups sifted all-purpose flour
1/2 teaspoon salt
1/2 teaspoon vanilla extract
1/4 teaspoon freshly grated nutmeg
Vegetable oil
Powdered sugar

The night before you wish to serve calas, combine water and granulated sugar in a 2-cup glass measuring cup. Stir in yeast. Let stand until foamy, 5 to 10 minutes. In a medium bowl, combine yeast mixture and rice. Cover bowl with plastic wrap; set aside in a warm, draft-free place overnight. This step forms a **soured-rice starter** for calas. Do not be alarmed by its less than enticing aroma the next morning! Next morning, stir rice mixture thoroughly. Add eggs, flour, salt, vanilla and nutmeg. Beat mixture with a wooden spoon until combined. Cover with plastic wrap. Let rise in a warm, draft-free place place 1 hour. Heat 3 inches oil in a large saucepan over medium heat to 365F (180C) or until a 1-inch bread cube turns golden brown in 60 seconds. Drop rice mixture by rounded tablespoons into hot oil. Do not crowd pan. Fry until golden brown, 5 to 6 minutes, turning once. Drain calas on paper towels; sift powdered sugar over hot calas. Serve hot. Makes about 24.

South-Louisiana Buttermilk Biscuits

The very mention of southern biscuits makes my mouth water and sends visions of biscuits with heavenly soft, fluffy layers floating through my mind. Biscuits are so much a part of the southern way of living that we even have several different kinds! Biscuits freeze beautifully, uncooked, so make lots.

4 cups soft, southern wheat flour, page 164,
  or all-purpose flour
2 tablespoons plus 2 teaspoons baking powder

2 teaspoons salt
1/4 cup lard or vegetable shortening
1 cup buttermilk

Lightly grease 2 baking sheets. Preheat oven to 400F (205C). Sift flour, baking and salt into a large bowl. Work in lard or shortening with your fingertips until mixture resembles coarse cornmeal. Add buttermilk slowly, stirring with a fork until blended. When dough is smooth, turn out onto a floured surface. The dough will be sticky, so flour work surface and surface of dough fairly heavily; do not work more flour into dough itself. Roll out to 1/2 inch thickness. Using a 2-inch biscuit cutter, cut dough into rounds. Place on greased baking sheets. Gather scraps of dough together. Repeat rolling and cutting until all dough has been used. Bake in preheated oven until light golden brown, 15 to 18 minutes. *To freeze,* freeze unbaked biscuits, unwrapped, on baking sheets just until firmly frozen; place in freezer bags to store up to 1 month. To bake, preheat oven as directed in recipe; place frozen biscuits on a baking sheet. Bake in preheated oven, allowing 3 to 5 minutes longer. Serve hot. Makes 24 biscuits.

Bayou-Country Beignets

One of the most enjoyable aspects of living in New Orleans is being able to sit under the softly whirring ceiling fans at Cafe du Monde in the French Market eating beignets and sipping Cafe au Lait. The whole experience has a way of removing your mind from the realities of the day. It allows you to peacefully contemplate the passing world as powdered sugar filters silently into your lap. I have never met anyone who didn't like beignets. Children are positively transformed into models of good behavior with the mere promise of beignets for breakfast. No Cajun-Creole brunch is complete without them.

3/4 cup water	1/3 cup sugar
2 teaspoons sugar	1 egg
1/2 cup evaporated milk	2 tablespoons lard or vegetable shortening
1 (1/4-oz.) pkg. active dry yeast	1 teaspoon salt
(about 1 tablespoon)	1/2 teaspoon freshly grated nutmeg
3 to 3-1/2 cups soft, southern wheat flour,	Vegetable oil
below, or all-purpose flour	Powdered sugar

In a medium saucepan over low heat, combine water, 2 teaspoons sugar and evaporated milk; heat to 110F (45C). Pour into a 2-cup glass measuring cup. Stir in yeast. Let stand until foamy, 5 to 10 minutes. In a food processor fitted with the steel blade, combine 3 cups of flour and all remaining ingredients except oil and powdered sugar. Turn on and off 3 or 4 times to blend ingredients. Add yeast mixture. Turn on and off 4 or 5 times to bring dough together. Check consistency of dough. It should be fairly smooth and nonsticky. If additional flour is needed, add 1 to 2 tablespoons at a time; process just until blended. Process 15 seconds to knead dough. Turn out dough on a lightly floured surface; form into a smooth ball. Lightly oil a large bowl. Place dough in oiled bowl, turning to coat all sides. Cover with plastic wrap. Let rise in a warm, draft-free place until doubled in bulk, about 1-1/2 hours. Punch down dough. Turn out onto a lightly floured surface. Roll out dough into a rectangle about 1/2 inch thick. Working at a diagonal to rectangle, with a sharp knife, cut dough into 2-inch-wide strips, moving from left to right. Starting at top left and moving toward bottom of rectangle, cut dough diagonally into 2-inch-wide strips to form diamond shapes. See photos for Crawfish Beignets, page 27. Carefully place all completed diamonds 1/2 inch apart on ungreased baking sheets. Cover loosely with plastic wrap. Gather up remaining dough scraps; knead together. Cover loosely with plastic wrap; let rest 15 minutes to relax dough. Roll out and cut as before. Repeat until all dough has been used. Cover beignets loosely with plastic wrap; let rise in warm, draft-free place until almost doubled in bulk, 45 minutes. In a large saucepan, heat 3 inches oil to 365F (185C) or until a 1-inch bread cube turns golden brown in 60 seconds. Carefully slide beignets into hot oil, 3 or 4 at a time; do not crowd. Fry until puffy and golden brown on both sides, turning once with tongs. Cooking time is about 2 to 3 minutes per side. Remove with a slotted spoon; drain on paper towels. Sift powdered sugar over hot beignets; serve hot. Makes about 36.

In the South, flour from soft wheat is often used for biscuits and other baked goods. This soft, southern wheat flour has a gluten content of about 8 percent. All-purpose flour is an acceptable substitute, or mail order, page 176.

Beverages

South Louisianians have long been noted for their love of strong drink even if the "drink" happens to be coffee! Chicory adds a rich color to coffee and an indescribably sweet and pungent flavor. Coffee with chicory is available by mail order, page 176.

The chicory that is added to coffee is the roasted and ground chicory root. The root resembles parsnips and is an off-white color. It was the Dutch who first added chicory to coffee when the beverage was introduced to Europe in the 1600s. The combination soon became popular all over Europe and was brought to the New World, and eventually, to South Louisiana by the Acadians

Cafe au Lait, the famous coffee-and-milk drink sipped with French Quarter beignets, is a New Orleans favorite among residents and tourists alike. The elegant Cafe Brulot is an after-dinner flambéed coffee drink that is still served in grand style at some of New Orleans finest restaurants. It is quite a rewarding experience.

As early as the first part of the 18th century, when New Orleans was no more than a walled city of mud streets in a cypress swamp, its residents enjoyed their fine French wines and brandies. Indeed, the early order of Ursuline nuns had already classified the area as being possessed by the demon spirits of alcohol.

As New Orleans grew and prospered, the social custom of imbibing also grew. The *cocktail* was born in the city. In 1793, a French refugee from Santo Domingo arrived in New Orleans with a secret formula for a tonic which he called *bitters*. Antoine Amdee Peychaud opened an apothecary shop in the Vieux Carre where he served his concoction with cognac. The potion

---

Sandwich Buffet Football Party

Cajun Party Punch
Home-Smoked Sausage with
Horseradish Sauce, page 24
Cajun Party Spareriblets, page 20
New Orleans Oyster Loaves, page 82
Muffuletta Sandwiches, page 142
Marinated Cole Slaw, page 46
Cajun Deviled Eggs, page 47
Satsuma Cake, page 113

---

was served in an egg cup, or "coquetier." The Americans gradually mispronounced the word into its present form, cocktail.

In the heyday of the plantation era, fine

cognacs, brandies and heady Jamaica rum were popular drinks, while the French Quarter boasted world-famous bars serving the most popular European liqueurs. No social affair was complete without a huge sterling silver punch bowl filled with gigantic portions of alcohol, fruit and spices. After the Civil War, New Orleans became more Americanized and bourbon whiskey became increasingly popular.

Pairing South Louisiana foods with beverages can be a complex matter. For the refined foods of New Orleans restaurants follow traditional guidelines for wine service. With fish, veal and poultry, serve a dry white wine, such as chardonnay. With beef, pork and game dishes, serve a red wine, such as Bourdeaux or cabernet sauvignon. For a delightful luncheon or light supper, serve rosé wine with chilled dishes and salads. Champagne (extra-dry rather than brut) may be served with any food, including desserts, but for a specific dessert-course wine, select a Sauterne, cream sherry or malmsey Madeira. You may also serve a Spatlese or Auslese Rhine wine with desserts. Port should not be served with the dessert, but rather with nuts after dessert.

Now we seem to have beverage service taken care of—or do we? When the country Cajun dishes enter the picture, the standard rules of beverage etiquette do not apply. These robust and spicy dishes totally overwhelm delicate wines

Beer is often the beverage chosen by locals to accompany gumbo, barbecue and other roux-based dishes. If you wish to serve wine, select a full-bodied red wine, such as cabernet sauvignon or zinfandel. The French wines of the Rhone Valley, such as Chateauneuf du Pape, are also good choices.

If you are serving fish, shellfish, poultry or veal dishes that are moderately spicy, try serving a dry California gewurztraminer, chardonnay, a French vouvray or one of the Sancerre wines.

For those who do not partake of alcoholic beverages, the fog vanishes. Iced tea is wonderful with everything, and nothing sets off dessert better than coffee—of whatever strength you prefer.

Planter's Rum Punch   *Photo on page 168.*

Rum Punch was the gentleman's drink during the plantation era. Untold numbers of dollars, acres, crops and what-have-you changed hands over this potent drink in the owner's private study. It is still popular in many parts of the Deep South, but it is delicious anywhere.

1 teaspoon light-brown sugar	2 tablespoons rosé wine (1 oz.)
2 teaspoons water	Mint sprig
1/4 cup dark Jamaican rum (2 oz.)	Maraschino cherry
Juice of 1 lemon	Orange-slice half
2/3 cup cracked ice	

In a small bowl, dissolve brown sugar in water; pour into a cocktail shaker or jar with a tight-fitting lid. Add rum, lemon juice and ice; shake until well chilled. Pour in a glass. Float wine on top by pouring over the back of a spoon. Decorate with mint sprig, cherry and orange slice. Serve cold. Makes 1 drink.

Cajun Party Punch

This old Louisiana recipe will be a hit the next time you serve punch.

1 qt. strong tea	1 cup fresh lime juice
1-1/2 cups sugar	2 (1-qt.) bottles club soda
10 mint sprigs	Ice ring or large block of ice
4 (3-inch) cinnamon sticks	1 lemon, sliced
1 teaspoon whole cloves	1 lime, sliced
1 qt. dark rum	1 orange, sliced
2 cups unsweetened pineapple juice	

Place tea in a heavy 3-quart saucepan over medium heat. Add sugar, mint, cinnamon and cloves. Cook, stirring, until sugar dissolves. Cool slightly; refrigerate until chilled. To serve, strain tea into a punch bowl; discard spices. Add rum, pineapple juice, lime juice and club soda. Stir until blended. Add ice and fruit slices. Ladle into punch cups. Makes about 5 quarts.

The Ultimate Egg-Nog Punch

Egg Nog is a traditional American punch served during the Christmas holiday season. Not to be outdone, New Orleanians also serve this rich and highly spirited version at their gala holiday parties.

12 eggs, separated	1 qt. milk (4 cups)
2 cups sugar	1 teaspoon vanilla extract
2 cups bourbon whiskey	Cracked ice
1/2 pint whipping cream (1 cup)	Freshly grated nutmeg

In a large bowl, beat egg yolks with an electric mixer on medium-high speed until thick and lemon-colored, about 5 minutes. Slowly beat in sugar; beat 5 minutes. Slowly beat in bourbon in a slow, steady stream. Beat in cream and milk; add vanilla. In a medium bowl, beat egg whites until medium-stiff peaks form. Fold beaten egg whites into yolk mixture. To serve, add 1/4 cup ice to punch cups. Add punch; top with nutmeg. Makes about 5 quarts.

Brandy Milk Punch

No matter how many times I make the trip, I never tire of the tourist-oriented Mississippi River excursions on the steamboat Natchez. The river is fascinating, and each time I am reminded of how exciting it is to live in such a unique area. But just perhaps my favorite part of the trip is sitting at the fine old bar sipping Brandy Milk Punch, the southern "nectar of the gods."

2 cups brandy
3/4 cup white creme de cocoa
1 teaspoon vanilla extract
1-3/4 cups Simple Bar Syrup, page 169

1/2 gallon milk
1 qt. whipping cream (4 cups)
Freshly grated nutmeg
3 cups cracked ice

In a large bowl, combine all ingredients except cream, nutmeg and ice. Cover and refrigerate until ready to serve. Just before serving, in a medium bowl, beat cream with an electric mixer on medium speed until medium-stiff peaks form. Fold whipped cream into brandy mixture; pour into a punch bowl. To serve, add ice to punch cups. Add punch; top with nutmeg. Makes 12 (8-oz.) servings.

Cajun Mimosas   *Photo on pages 4-5.*

If you want to immortalize your next social affair, serve this delightfully spicy and different drink. The citrus juice moderates some of the fire from the chilies so that you can actually taste their flavor! It's a must for a Cajun-style cookout.

1 qt. orange juice
6 pickled jalapeño peppers, brine packed, drained

1 magnum Champagne, well chilled
Cracked ice

Place orange juice in a 1-quart, non-metallic container with tight-fitting lid. Slice well-drained peppers into rounds; add to juice. Do not remove seeds. Place lid on container; shake well. Refrigerate 3 days. When ready to serve, strain juice; discard peppers. Fill glasses half full of ice. Fill halfway with orange juice; add enough Champagne to fill glass. Stir and serve. Makes 8 servings.

Minted Brandy Ice

Fresh mint and mint-flavored liqueurs play a big role in the beverage selection of South Louisiana. Mint is very refreshing, and combined with ice cream in this recipe, it makes a drink so delicious it makes you feel wonderful all over.

1 qt. rich vanilla ice cream
3/4 cup brandy
1/2 cup white creme de cocoa

1/4 cup white creme de menthe
10 ice cubes
6 to 8 mint sprigs

Combine all ingredients except mint in a blender; process until smooth. Serve in brandy snifters or Old Fashioned glasses; garnish with mint. Makes 6 to 8 servings.

Sazerac

This potent cocktail was invented in New Orleans and named for the bar in which it made its debut. The drink was originally prepared using brandy. But American tastes eventually won out, and the drink is now prepared with either bourbon or rye whiskey. At the Sazerac Bar in the Fairmont Hotel, Sazeracs are still prepared in the grand style of the past. The Herbsaint is added to the glass, which is then twirled into the air to coat with the liqueur. Try it only if you happen to be a very good catcher!

1 teaspoon sugar	**1 cup cracked ice**
2 drops Peychaud Bitters	**1/4 cup bourbon or rye whiskey (2 oz.)**
1 teaspoon water	**1 teaspoon Herbsaint**
2 drops Angostura Bitters	**Lemon twist**

In a cocktail shaker or jar with a tight-fitting lid, muddle sugar with Peychaud Bitters and water. Add Angostura Bitters, ice and whiskey; shake until well chilled. Pour Herbsaint into an Old Fashioned glass; swirl to coat bottom and sides. Strain drink mixture into glass; add lemon twist. Makes 1 drink.

Ramos Gin Fizz

This light-as-a-cloud and deceivingly non-alcoholic-tasting drink was born in New Orleans in the late 1800s. The drink, now world-famous, has often been a frustration to those who try to duplicate it at home. The secret to its taste is the addition of a few drops of an obscure ingredient, orange-flower water. It is available at large liquor stores throughout the country. The egg white must be beaten until very frothy. Then the entire drink must be shaken madly until thickened and creamy. Use a container with a screw-top lid to prevent the drink from spilling over.

1 egg white, beaten until very frothy	**2 tablespoons whipping cream**
1 teaspoon powdered sugar	**1/4 cup gin (2 oz.)**
3 drops orange-flower water	**2 tablespoons club soda**
Juice of 1/2 lime	**1 cup cracked ice**
1 drop vanilla extract	**1 orange slice**

Combine all ingredients except orange slice in a cocktail shaker or jar with a tight-fitting lid. Shake until thickened and creamy, about 3 minutes. Pour into a tall glass. Decorate with orange slice. Serve immediately. Makes 1 drink.

Simple Bar Syrup

Keep this simple syrup on hand to sweeten all your drinks.

2 cups sugar	**1 cup water**

Combine sugar and water in a 3-quart saucepan. Bring to a boil, stirring. Boil 5 minutes. Cool before using. To store, pour into a jar with a tight-fitting lid. Refrigerate until needed. Makes 3 cups.

Left to right: Sazerac; Ramos Gin Fizz; Planter's Rum Punch, page 166

Absinthe Drip

Absinthe is a liqueur which originated in Switzerland but became very popular in the bars of New Orleans in the mid-1800s. The original Brennan's restaurant was called The Old Absinthe House in the 1860s. The city became known as the absinthe capital of the world.

The original absinthe was made of wormwood, anise seed, fennel, star anise, coriander seeds, hyssop and 190-proof alcohol! After large numbers of absinthe devotees succumbed to madness or death, it was determined that wormwood was a narcotic with devastatingly addictive properties. The substance was subsequently banned in most areas of Europe, and in the United States, in 1912.

Several anise-flavored liqueurs, made without wormwood, are produced today, including Pernod, anisette, Ojen and Herbsaint. The latter was created by a New Orleans pharmacist, J. Marion Legendre. It is marketed today by his heirs. The Absinthe Drip was the fashionable drink of the day when absinthe was in its heyday.

Cracked ice
1 sugar cube

2 tablespoons Herbsaint (1 oz.)
2 tablespoons club soda

Fill a brandy snifter with cracked ice; set a small strainer over mouth of snifter. Place sugar cube in strainer; drip Herbsaint over it onto ice. Then drip club soda through. Remove strainer; stir drink. Discard any remaining sugar. Serve immediately. Makes 1 drink.

How to Make Absinthe Drip

1/Place sugar cube in strainer; drip Herbsaint over it onto ice.

2/Discard any remaining sugar. Serve immediately.

Absinthe Suissesse

This is another of the famous absinthe cocktails created in the 1800s. Though not as fashionable as it once was, it is still a delightful drink.

2 egg whites, beaten until very frothy
2 tablespoons Herbsaint (1 oz.)
1/2 teaspoon orgeat syrup
2 tablespoons whipping cream

2 drops orange-flower water
2 tablespoons club soda
Cracked ice

Combine all ingredients except ice in a cocktail shaker or jar with a tight-fitting lid. Shake until frothy. Fill glass with cracked ice. Serve immediately. Makes 1 drink.

New Orleans Rye Old Fashioned

Leave it to the mixologists of New Orleans, the city that invented the cocktail and spread the fame of bitters, to add its unique touch to this old standby drink.

1 sugar cube
3 dashes Angostura Bitters
1 whole clove
1 (3-inch) orange-peel strip
3 tablespoons rye whiskey (1-1/2 oz.)

Cracked ice
1 tablespoon club soda
Maraschino cherry
Orange-slice half

In an Old Fashioned glass, combine sugar, bitters, clove and orange peel. Muddle together with a wooden spoon, crushing sugar cube and bruising clove and orange peel. Add whiskey; stir until blended. Fill glass with ice; add club soda and enough water to fill glass. Stir until blended; add cherry and orange-slice half. Serve immediately. Makes 1 drink.

Cafe Noir

At any time of the day or night, dark roasted coffee with chicory is the universal drink in South Louisiana. Both Cajuns and Creoles like it strong. Tourists can't abide it, and natives can't live without it. But one thing can be said for sure—it WILL wake you up in the morning. To make the best quality coffee, use either a traditional French drip pot, called a *biggin,* or one of the modern electric coffee makers which drip hot water slowly over the grounds.

Pinch of salt
3/4 cup drip-grind dark-roast coffee
with chicory

2-1/2 quarts boiling water

Place salt and coffee in top of drip pot. Pour 1/2 cup water over coffee; let drip through completely. Add remaining water, 1/2 cup at a time, letting each addition drip through completely before adding more. Serve hot. Makes 12 cups.

Cafe au Lait

Cafe au Lait is an integral part of New Orleans society. Beignets are just not the same without it. No visit to the French Quarter is complete without a stop at the Cafe du Monde, New Orleans' famous bastion of coffeedom, for a cup or two. The secret to real New Orleans Cafe au Lait is the caramel milk! The extra large pot for preparation of the caramel is very important. When the boiling milk is added to the caramel, it boils, froths, spits and sputters ferociously. It would overflow a smaller pan and could result in serious burns.

3 tablespoons sugar
2 cups boiling milk

2 cups hot dark-roast coffee with chicory

Place sugar in a heavy 8-quart pan over medium heat. Cook until sugar caramelizes, stirring once or twice after sugar begins to dissolve. When caramel is a deep hazelnut color, about 7 minutes, remove pan from heat; slowly add boiling milk. When all milk has been added, wait for foam to subside; stir until blended. Add coffee; stir. Serve hot. Or for a truly authentic presentation, place caramel-milk in 1 coffeepot and hot coffee in a second coffeepot. Pour equal amounts of each into cups at the same time. Special cafe au lait pots are available. Makes 4 cups.

Cafe Brulot

For a very special occasion, this spectacular after-dinner coffee drink may be prepared at the table with great fanfare. The Creoles have special *brulot bowls* in which to prepare the drink, but you may use a round chafing dish. Serve in demitasse cups.

Finely grated zest of 2 oranges
Finely grated zest of 1 lemon
2 (3-inch) cinnamon sticks,
 broken into small pieces
2 teaspoons whole coriander seeds
1 large bay leaf
6 whole cloves

1/2 cup pecan halves
12 sugar cubes
3/4 cup cognac or other brandy
1/4 cup Grand Marnier or
 other orange-flavored liqueur
8 cups hot dark-roast coffee with chicory

Using a mortar and pestle or grinder, mash together orange and lemon zest, cinnamon, coriander, bay leaf, cloves, pecans and sugar. Transfer mashed spices, zest and sugar to brulot bowl or chafing dish. Place bowl or dish over a heat source; add cognac and liqueur. Just as liquid starts to simmer; ignite. Using a long handled spoon, stir mixture. As flame begins to subside, stir in coffee. Ladle into demitasse cups; serve hot. Makes 8 servings.

Index

A

Abinthe Suissesse, 171
Absinthe Drip, 170
Acadian Alligator Sauce Piquant, 130
Alligator Sauce Piquant, Acadian, 130
Andouille & Green Onion Bisque, 36
Andouille & Mushrooms, Baked Cheese
    with, 23
Appetizers, 17-27
Artichoke Bisque, Oyster-, 36, 37
Artichoke Gumbo, Duck &, 40
Artichoke Hearts, Trout with Crabmeat
    &, 80

B

Baked Cajun Meat Pies, 4-5, 21
Baked Cheese with Andouille &
    Mushrooms, 23
Bananas Foster, 115
Basil & Tomato Salad, 45
Beans & Rice with Sausage, Red, 126
Béarnaise Sauce, 155
Beef
    Boiled Beef with Parsnips, 57
    Creole Daube with Red Gravy, 150
    Oyster-Stuffed Beef Fillet, 61
    Rib-Eye Steak with Merlot-Mushroom
        Sauce, 56
Beignets, Bayou-Country, 164
Beverages, 165-172
Biscuits, New Orleans Luncheon, 41
Biscuits, South-Louisiana Buttermilk, 163
Bisque, Andouille & Green Onion, 36
Bisque, Crawfish, 32-33
Bisque, Oyster-Artichoke, 36, 37
Bisque, Shrimp, 34
Bisque, Yellow-Squash, 34, 37
Bittersweet Chocolate Cake, 118
Blueberry-Cream Dressing, 52
Brandy Milk Punch, 167
Bread Pudding with Rum Sauce &
    Chantilly Cream, Cajun-Country, 109
Breads
    Bayou Country Beignets, 164
    Cajun Corn Bread, 126
    Hearty Country Bread, 41
    Muffuletta Bread, 142
    New Orleans French Loaves, 42-43
    New Orleans Luncheon Biscuits, 41
    Pecan Crescents, 161, 162
    Pepper Breads, 139
    South-Louisiana Buttermilk Biscuits,
        163
    Spinach Bread, 138, 139
    Sweet & Spicy Hush Puppies, 87
Broccoli & Rice Casserole with Cress
    Sauce, 103

Brown Veal & Pork Stock, 15
Brunch, 151-164

C

Cabbage with Sausage, Smothered, 130
Cafe Brulot, 172
Cafe Noir, 171
Cafe au Lait, 172
Cajun Caesar Dressing, 53
Cajun Corn-Bread Dressing, 63
Cajun Corn Salad, 48, 49
Cajun Country, 123-136
Cajun-Country Bread Pudding with Rum
    Sauce & Chantilly Cream, 109
Cajun Coush-Coush, 152
Cajun Deviled Eggs, 47
Cajun "Dirty" Rice, 106
Cajun Glazed Mushrooms, 4-5, 22
Cajun Maque-Chou, 99
Cajun Mimosas, 167
Cajun Party Punch, 166
Cajun Roux, 12
Cajun Skillet-Baked Eggs, 158
Cake, Bittersweet Chocolate, 118
Cake, Satsuma, 113
Calas, Creole Rice, 163
Caribbean Cheese & Vegetable Salad, 47
Carrot Salad, Marinated, 48, 49
Cayenne Toasts, 4-5, 20
Caesar Dressing, Cajun, 53
Cheese & Vegetable Salad, Caribbean, 47
Cheese with Andouille & Mushrooms,
    Baked, 23
Cheesecake, Praline, 122
Chicken, Boned & Stuffed, 64, 65
Chicken Fricassee, 65
Chili-Cheese Grits Piquant, 102
Chocolate & Bourbon Pie, Creamy, 116
Chocolate Cake, Bittersweet, 118
Chocolate Marquis with Custard Sauce,
    121
Chocolate-Sherry Sauce, 116
Cole Slaw, Marinated, 46, 48
Corn-Bread Dressing, Cajun, 63
Corn Pudding, Creole, 100
Corn Salad, Cajun, 48, 49
Corn Soup, Crab-, 37, 38
Courtbouillon, Sac-a-Lait, 134
Coush-Coush, Cajun, 152
Crab
    Acadian Crabmeat Tarts with
        Creole, 74
    Baked Crab Cakes with Roasted Bell
        Pepper & Pineapple Salsa, 80
    Blue-Crab-Stuffed Mushrooms, 18
    Boiled Blue Crabs, 71, 73
    Crab-Corn Soup, 37, 38
    Crabmeat & Vegetable Salad, 50, 51
    Crabmeat au Gratin, 75
    Crabmeat in Garlic-Cream Sauce, 149

    Crabmeat-Stuffed Baked Flounder, 94,
        95
    Stuffed Crabs Lafitte, 76, 77
    Veal Cutlets with Crabmeat & Creolaise
        Sauce, 62
Crawfish
    Boiled Crawfish, 72, 73
    Crawfish or Shrimp Savory Beignets,
        27, 28
    Crawfish Bisque, 32-33
    Crawfish Dauphine, 74
    Crawfish Etouffée, 132
    Crawfish Pie, 131
    Flounder Rockefeller with Crawfish-
        Buttercream Sauce, 90
    Fried Crawfish Tails, 86
Cream Cheese, Homemade Creole, 114
Creole Corn Pudding, 100
Creole Cream Cheese, Frozen, 114
Creole-Italian, 137-150
Creole-Italian Tomato Gravy, 145
Creole-Onion Soup, 38, 39
Creole Oyster Dressing, 63
Creole Rice Calas, 163
Creole Roquefort Dressing, 51
Creole Spinach Mousse, 102, 105
Creole Stewed Okra & Tomatoes, 97
Creole Sweet-Potato Pone, 100
Crepe Soufflé with Custard Sauce, 108
Crepes, Praline, 120
Crepes, Sweet, 120
Croutons, Garlic, 50
Cucumber Soup, Cold, 39

D

Desserts, 108-122
Deviled Eggs, Cajun, 47
Dip, Paula's Dill, 4-5, 26
Duck
    Boned Stuffed Duck with Wine
        Sauce, 66
    Cajun Duck with Mint, 129
    Duck & Artichoke Gumbo, 40
    Lee Hebert's Braised Wild Duck, 69
    Mesquite-Smoked Duck, 67
    Smoked-Duck Etouffée, 124

E

Easy Strawberry Sauce, 117
Egg-Nog Punch, The Ultimate, 166
Eggplant Steaks with Seafood Dressing,
    128
Eggs Benedict, 158
Eggs, Cajun Deviled, 47
Eggs, Cajun Skillet-Baked, 158
Eggs Hussarde, 157
Eggs Nouvelle Orleans, 159
Eggs, Poached, 156, 157
Eggs, Quail in Sherry Sauce over Fluffy, 153
Eggs Sardou, 156

F
Fish & Shellfish, 70-95
Fish
  Baked Flounder & Tomatoes, 88, 89
  Barbecued Red Snapper, 80
  Blackened Redfish, 92, 93
  Crabmeat-Stuffed Flounder, 94, 95
  Flounder Rockefeller with Crawfish-
    Buttercream Sauce, 90
  Fried Fish Tails, 19
  Grilled Red Snapper with Mango Salsa,
    80
  Mustard-Fried Catfish, 88, 89
  Pompano en Papillote with
    Champagne Sauce, 91
  Red Snapper a la Creole, 81
  Sac-a-Lait Courtbouillon, 134
  Trout Marguery, 78
  Trout with Roasted Pecans, 79
Flaky Pie Pastry, 110
French Loaves, New Orleans, 42-43
Fried Boudin Balls, 129
Frog Legs with Roasted Garlic Sauce,
    Fried, 135
Frozen Creole Cream Cheese, 114
Frying, about, 15

G
Garlic-Cream Dressing, 53
Garlic Croutons, 50
Garlic Dressing, Pecan-, 53
Green-Peppercorn Sauce, Seafood Boudin
    with, 133
Greens with Turnips & Tasso, Mixed, 97
Grillades & Grits, 160, 161
Grits Piquant, Chili-Cheese, 102
Grits, Grillades &, 160, 161
Gumbo
  Chicken & Andouille-Sausage
    Gumbo, 29
  Duck & Artichoke Gumbo, 40
  Gumbo Z'Herbes, 30
  New Orleans Seafood Filé Gumbo, 31

H
Hearty Country Bread, 41
Hollandaise Sauce, 155
Home-Smoked Sausage, 24
Homemade Creole Cream Cheese, 114

I
Introduction, 6-16

J
Jambalaya, Atchafalaya, 125
  Vegetable, 99
Jezebel Sauce, 4-5, 22

L
Lemon Chess Pie, Louisiana, 112

Louisiana Brown-Poultry Stock, 14

M
Magic Steak Dip, 56
Marchand de Vin Sauce, 154
Marinated Carrot Salad, 48, 49
Marinated Cole Slaw, 46, 48
Meatballs, Veal & Pork, 144
Meat Pies, Baked Cajun, 4-5, 21
Mimosas, Cajun, 167
Minted Brandy Ice, 167
Muffuletta Sandwich, 142
Mushroom-Cream-Filled Patty Shells, 25
Mushrooms, Blue-Crab-Stuffed, 18
Mushrooms, Cajun Glazed, 4-5, 22
Mustard Sauce, 72, 73

N
New Orleans Butter Pralines, 111
New Orleans French Loaves, 42-43
New Orleans Rye Old Fashioned, 171
New Orleans Seafood Filé Gumbo, 31

O
Okra & Tomatoes, Creole Stewed, 97
Olive Salad, 145
Olives, Sweet & Sour, 137
Onion & Almond Casserole, Scalloped,
    104, 105
Oysters
  Cajun Oyster Pie, 136
  Fettucine with Oysters & Italian
    Sausage, 146
  Italian Baked Oysters, 147
  Italian Sausage Oysters, 146
  New Orleans Oyster Loaf, 82
  Oyster-Artichoke Bisque, 36, 37
  Oyster Dressing, Creole, 63
  Oyster-Filled Patty Shells, 4-5, 25
  Oysters Bienville, 84, 85
  Oysters in Brochette, 82
  Oysters Rockefeller, 84, 85
  Oysters Rousseau, 85, 86

P
Pain Perdu, 152
Parsnips, Boiled Beef with, 57
Pasta, Wine, 141
Patty Shells, 24
Paula's Dill Dip, 4-5, 26
Peach Pie, Fresh, 110
Peaches in Soft Brandy Cream, 161, 162
Pecan Crescents, 161, 162
Pecan-Garlic Dressing, 53
Pecan Pie, Sweet-Potato-, 111
Pecans, Sugar-Fried, 121
Pecans, Trout with Roasted, 79
Pie
  Creamy Chocolate & Bourbon Pie, 116
  Fresh Peach Pie, 110

Louisiana Lemon-Cornmeal Pie, 112
  Sweet-Potato-Pecan Pie, 111
Planter's Rum Punch, 166, 168
Poached Eggs, 156, 157
Ponchatoula Strawberry Shortcake, 117
Poppy-Seed Dressing, Spinach, Orange &
    Onion Salad with, 46
Pork
  Barbecued Pork Spareribs, 68
  Cajun Party Spareriblets, 20
  Orange-Glazed Pork Roast, 58, 59
  Veal & Pork Meatballs, 144
Potatoes, Rosemary, 98
Poultry & Meat, 55-69
Poultry Stock, Louisiana Brown-, 14
Praline Cheesecake, 122
Praline Crepes, 120
Pralines, New Orleans Butter, 111
Punch, Brandy Milk, 167
Punch, Cajun Party, 166
Punch, The Ultimate Egg-Nog, 166

Q
Quail in Sherry Sauce over Fluffy
    Eggs, 153

R
Ramos Gin Fizz, 169
Red Beans & Rice with Sausage, 126
Red Cocktail Sauce, 72
Red Gravy, Roux-Based, 144
Rice, Cajun "Dirty", 106
Rice Casserole with Cress Sauce,
    Broccoli &, 103
Rice, Spinach, 106
Rice with Sausage, Red Beans &, 126
Roquefort Dressing, Creole, 51
Rosemary Potatoes, 98
Roux, about, 13
Roux, Cajun, 12
Roux-Based Red Gravy, 144
Rum Sauce & Chantilly Cream, Cajun-
    Country Bread Pudding with, 109
Rutabagas, Sweet-Sour, 103
Rye Old Fashioned, New Orleans, 171

S
Salads & Salad Dressings, 44-54
Satsuma Cake, 113
Sauce, Béarnaise, 155
Sauce, Chocolate-Sherry, 116
Sauce, Easy Strawberry, 117
Sauce, Hollandaise, 155
Sauce, Marchand de Vin, 154
Sauce, Mustard, 72, 73
Sauce, Red Cocktail, 72
Sauce, Rib-Eye Steak with
    Garlic-Mushroom, 56
Sauce, Veal, Crabmeat & Artichoke
    Hearts with Mustard Hollandaise, 62

Sausage, Home-Smoked, 24
Sausage Oysters, Italian, 146
Sausage, Red Beans & Rice with, 126
Sausage, Smothered Cabbage with, 130
Sausage-Stuffed Zucchini, 140
Sazerac, 169
Scalloped Onion & Almond Casserole, 104, 105
Seafood Boudin with Green-Peppercorn Sauce, 133
Seafood Dressing, Eggplant Steaks with, 128
Seafood Filé Gumbo, New Orleans, 31
Seafood Stock, 14
Sherry Sauce, Chocolate-, 116
Shortcake, Ponchatoula Strawberry, 117
Shrimp
    Acadian Peppered Shrimp, 77
    Boiled Shrimp, 71, 73
    Garlic-Broiled Shrimp, 76
    Grilled Bacon-Wrapped Shrimp, 87
    Shrimp Bisque, 34
    Shrimp Creole, 75
    Shrimp in Mustard Sauce, 4-5, 18
    Shrimp Savory Beignets, Crawfish or, 27, 28
Simple Bar Syrup, 169
Smothered Cabbage with Sausage, 130
Soup, Cold Cucumber, 39
Soup, Crab-Corn, 37, 38
Soup with Madeira, Turtle, 35
Soups, Gumbos, Bisques & Breads, 28-43

Spareriblets, Cajun Party, 20
Spareribs, Barbecued Pork, 68
Spinach & Artichoke Stuffed Tomatoes, 104, 105
Spinach Bread, 138, 139
Spinach Mousse, Creole, 102, 105
Spinach, Orange & Onion Salad with Poppy-Seed Dressing, 46
Spinach Pie, 140
Spinach Rice, 106
Spinach Salad Vermillion, 45
Spinach with Squash & Pine Nuts, Stir-fried, 107
Squash Bisque, Yellow-, 34, 37
Steak Dip, Magic, 56
Stock, about, 13
Stock, Brown Veal & Pork, 15
Stock, Louisiana Brown-Poultry, 14
Stock, Seafood, 14
Strawberry Sauce, Easy, 117
Strawberry Shortcake, Ponchatoula, 117
Strawberry-Cream Dressing, 54
Stuffing, Creole Oyster, 63
Stuffing, Hearty Poultry, 63
Sugar-Fried Pecans, 121
Sun-Dried Tomato Pesto, 22
Sweet & Sour Olives, 137
Sweet-Potato-Pecan Pie, 111
Sweet-Potato Pone, Creole, 100
Sweet-Potato Puffs, 101
Sweet-Sour Rutabagas, 103
Sweetbread Sauce, Veal Scallops with, 60

Syrup, Simple Bar, 169

T
The Ultimate Egg-Nog Punch, 166
Three-Layer Vegetable Casserole, 98
Tomato Aspic with Cheese Centers, 52
Tomato Gravy, Creole-Italian, 145
Tomato Salad, Basil &, 45
Tomatoes, Spinach & Artichoke Stuffed, 104, 105
Turtle Soup with Madeira, 35

V
Veal
    Brown Veal & Pork Stock, 15
    Breaded Veal Panné, 60
    Brucholoni, 148
    Veal Cutlets with Crabmeat & Creolaise Sauce, 62
    Veal & Pork Meatballs, 144
    Veal Scallops with Sweetbread Sauce, 60
    Veal Thomassina, 149
Vegetable Jambalaya, 99
Vegetable Salad, Caribbean Cheese &, 47
Vegetable Salad, Crabmeat &, 50
Vegetables & Rice, 96-107

W
Wine Pasta, 141

Z
Zucchini, Sausage-Stuffed, 140

Metric Chart

Comparison to Metric Measure

When You Know	Symbol	Multiply By	To Find	Symbol
teaspoons	tsp	5.0	milliliters	ml
tablespoons	tbsp	15.0	milliliters	ml
fluid ounces	fl. oz.	30.0	milliliters	ml
cups	c	0.24	liters	l
pints	pt.	0.47	liters	l

When You Know	Symbol	Multiply By	To Find	Symbol
quarts	qt.	0.95	liters	l
ounces	oz.	28.0	grams	g
pounds	lb.	0.45	kilograms	kg
Fahrenheit	F	5/9 (after subtracting 32)	Celsius	C

Liquid Measure to Milliliters

1/4 teaspoon	=	1.25 milliliters
1/2 teaspoon	=	2.5 milliliters
3/4 teaspoon	=	3.75 milliliters
1 teaspoon	=	5.0 milliliters
1-1/4 teaspoons	=	6.25 milliliters
1-1/2 teaspoons	=	7.5 milliliters
1-3/4 teaspoons	=	8.75 milliliters
2 teaspoons	=	10.0 milliliters
1 tablespoon	=	15.0 milliliters
2 tablespoons	=	30.0 milliliters

Liquid Measure to Liters

1/4 cup	=	0.06 liters
1/2 cup	=	0.12 liters
3/4 cup	=	0.18 liters
1 cup	=	0.24 liters
1-1/4 cups	=	0.3 liters
1-1/2 cups	=	0.36 liters
2 cups	=	0.48 liters
2-1/2 cups	=	0.6 liters
3 cups	=	0.72 liters
3-1/2 cups	=	0.84 liters
4 cups	=	0.96 liters
4-1/2 cups	=	1.08 liters
5 cups	=	1.2 liters
5-1/2 cups	=	1.32 liters

Fahrenheit to Celsius

F	C
200—205	95
220—225	105
245—250	120
275	135
300—305	150
325—330	165
345—350	175
370—375	190
400—405	205
425—430	220
445—450	230
470—475	245
500	260

Mail-Order Sources

Cajun Sausages & Seasoning Meats

K-Paul's Louisiana Kitchen
406 Chartres, Apartment 2
New Orleans, LA 70130
1-800-654-6017
Tasso and andouille sausage. 48-hour delivery.

Poché's Meat Market
Rt. 2, Box 415
Breaux Bridge, LA 90517
(318) 332-2108
Tasso, pickled marinated pork, andouille, smoked Cajun sausage, pure pork sausage, boudin. Chaurice in winter only. Will ship fastest and best way for area.

Coffee

Neighbors Coffee Company
P.O. Box 46
Covington, LA 70434
(504) 892-2741
Dark Roast Coffee with Chicory, Special Blend Dark Roast, Dark Roast Decaffeinated. Uniquely packaged in amounts to make 8 and 12 cups. Eliminates the guesswork!

Community Kitchen
Box 3778
Baton Rouge, LA 70821-3778
(504) 381-3900
Community Dark Roast Coffee, New Orleans Blend with Chicory. Write or call for catalog.

Luzianne-Blue Plate Foods
P.O. Box 60296
New Orleans, LA 70160
1-800-692-7895
Luzianne Dark Roast Coffee with Chicory, CDM Dark Roast Coffee with Chicory. Call or write for brochure.

Merchant Coffee Company
P.O. Box 50654
New Orleans, LA 70150
(504) 581-7515
Union Coffee and Chicory, French Market Dark Roast Coffee and Chicory. Call or write for brochure.

Corn Flour (Unseasoned fish fry)

Louisiana Fish Fry Product
5267 Plank Rd.
Baton Rouge, LA 70805
(504) 356-2905
Corn flour. Write or call for prices.

Flour

White Lily Flour Company
Box 871
Knoxville, TN 37901
Soft, southern wheat flour. Write for prices.

War Eagle Mill
Route 6, Box 127
Rogers, AR 72756
Stone-ground flours and cornmeals. Write for catalog and price list.

Pecan Rice

Konriko Company Store
301 Ann St.
New Iberia, LA 70560
1-800-551-3245
Pecan rice available in 7-oz. boxes, 2-lb. and 10-lb. bags. Write for catalog and prices.

Seafood

Harlon's Old New Orleans Seafood
126 Airline Highway
Metairie, LA 70001
(504) 831-4592
All types of Gulf Coast fish and shellfish, including turtle meat, frog legs, alligator meat and shark meat. Will air freight and arrange for delivery to your door. Accepts all major credit cards.